OFFBEAT TRACKS IN MAHARASHTRA

Milind Gunaji

Popular Prakashan
www.popularprakashan.com

Published by
Harsha Bhatkal for
POPULAR PRAKASHAN PVT. LTD.
301, Mahalaxmi Chambers
22, Bhulabhai Desai Road
Mumbai 400026
www.popularprakashan.com

First Reprint 2006
Second Reprint 2007
Second Edition 2010
First Reprint 2010
Second Reprint 2016

(4326)
ISBN 978-81-7991-578-3

2003 Edition: Book & Cover Design by Subhash Awchat
2010 Edition: Cover Design by Namita Jadhav
Photo of the author on the back cover by Uddhav Thackerey
Cover photograph by Shekhar Godbole
Inside Photographs by Milind Gunaji

Processing by
Supressa Graphics Pvt. Ltd.
G. Kadam Marg, Mumbai 400013

Typesetting by
Vans Information Pvt. Ltd.

Printed in India
by Saurabh Printers (P) Ltd.
Plot No. 67 A-68, Ecotech, Ext. I
Kasna, Greater Noida-201306 (U.P)

C O N T E N T S

FORTS 10-87

The Unknown Fort of Kohoj/Harishchandragad/Karnala Fort and its Surroundings/Avchitagad/Ghosalgad/Talgad/Murud-Janjira/Korlai/Kathingad or Tung/Koraigad/Tikona/Panhala/The Peaks of Gorakh and Machhindragad/Gambhirgad/Rajgad/Torna/Sinhgad/Rajmachi/Sudhagad/Raigad/Pratapgad/Lohagad-Visapur/Sajjangad/Naldurg/Dhakoba/Prabalgad/Dhodap/Mahuli/Chandan-Vandan/Jeevdhan/Pandavgad/Hadsar/Purandar/Ajinkyatara/Shivneri/Devgiri/Kothligad/Chanderi/Manikgad/Bhairavgad/Alibag/Sindhudurg/Vasota/Vishalgad

TEMPLES 88-119

Kankeshwar/Pateshwar/Saptashrungi/Tungareshwar/Kundal : A religious place of Jains/Shri Gondeshwar Temple at Sinnar/Shegaon/Theur/Trimbakeshwar/The Temples of Chaul/Ranjangaon/Pali/Ozar/Siddhtek/Mrutyunjeshwar/Morgaon/Marleshwar/Mahad/Lenyadri/Kukdeshwar/Jyotiba/The Shiva temple of Ambarnath/Amruteshwar of Bhor/Amruteshwar of Ratanwadi/Ganapatipule

HILL STATIONS 120-151

Chikhaldara/Mandhardevi/Varandha Ghat/Meera Hill/Igatpuri/Ajoba Mountain and its Surroundings/Aahupe Ghat/Mahabaleshwar/Matheran/Khandala/Lonavala/Tadgaon, Uddhar, Unhere/Khodala, Jawhar, Mokhada, Devbandh, Suryamal/Bhimashankar

JUNGLES, SANCTUARIES & NATURE PARKS 152-189

Dajipur Sanctuary/Sagreshwar/The man-made forest of Sagareshwar/Nandur Madhyameshwar/Vikramgad/Bilya Mountain/Pal-Yaval Sanctuary/Tansa Sanctuary/Khanwel/Nagzira/Tadoba Sanctuary/Melghat (Semadoh and Kolkas)/Navegaon/The Murud Forests/Pench-The Pandit Jawaharlal Nehru National

Park/Ambakhori/Nannaj Bird Sanctuary/The Borivali National Park/The Gautala Forest Reserve/Chandoli/Koyna Forest Reserve/ Rehkuri Kalveet Wildlife Park/Melghat Tiger Project/Navegaon National Park

LAKES, RESERVOIRS, HOT SPRINGS, WATERFALLS, CAVES 190-231

Tapola Lake : A Mini Kashmir/Gadeshwar Lake/Kalote Lake/Kaas Lake/Kakuli Lake/Bhandardara/Uppar Vaitarna/Manikdoh/Bhoj Lake and Kukdeshwar Lake/Panshet/Shivsagar Lake, Bamnoli and its Periphery/The Pelher Lake/Vandri Lake and the Hot Springs at Sativali/Hot Springs at Sav/Nadhal Lake/Mulshi Lake/Bhilawale Lake/Devkop Lake/The Surya River Area/Savne Lake at the Foothills of Manikgad/Sakhre Lake/Dabhosa Waterfall/Waterfall near Vihigaon Village/Pallu Waterfall/Pandavgad/Thoseghar/Kuna Caves/Ajanta Caves/Ellora Caves/Pitalkhora Caves/Lonad Caves/ Karla, Bhaje, Bedse Caves/Other Caves/Tilsa/Phalatan/Potholes of Nighoj

MUSEUMS AND UNUSUAL PLACES OF INTEREST 232-256

The Lokmanya Tilak Museum/The Satara Museum/The Karmarkar Museum/The Wood Exhibits of Kolad/The Raja Dinkar Kelkar museum/Kapuskar/Joshi Miniature Railway Museum/The Dr. Ambedkar Museum and Memorial/Naney Ghat/Darya Ghat/ Mastani Lake/Doorshet/Manikdoha/Thebaw Palace/Aurangabad/ Tara Paanwala/Bibi Ka Maqbara/Mhaismal/Vathar Nimbalkar/ Sitabai hill/Shivtharghal/The Rock Bridge of Gulanchwadi/The Salt Pillar of Vadgaon Darya/Ramtek and Khindsay Lake/Parvati/ Manas Resorts

INDEX (in alphabetical order) 257-260

MAPS (with page references).......... 261-292

PREFACE

For me travelling puts me in touch with my essential self. Away from the world of glamour and arc lights, I feel one with nature. Alone in a cave under a starlit sky you are small and insignificant, confronting the mysterious universal force.

My romance with nature started early. I travelled all over India as a child with my father and later, alone as a teenager. Maharashtra holds a very special place in my heart. I have traversed the length and breadth of the state (armed with my many cameras, six to date) by motorcycle, State Transport buses, by jeep. I want to share my discoveries, my sense of wonder and joy my travels have brought me with a wider audience.

Many people have helped me bring this book to the reader. My dear friends, Uddhav Thackeray, Subhash Awchat and Jagdish Maali. Also Anusha Srinivasan, Santosh Kolhe, Shubha Gadkari and Dr. Ravi Rupawate, the camera and crew of my travel shows, my colleagues from Bhatkanti, Nitin Vaidya of Alpha Television, Uma Prabhu, Dilip Majgaokar and the publisher of this English book Harsha Bhatkal plus other friends who have helped me in this endeavour. I thank them all.

Om Kripa Sindhu Sai Nathaya Namah

I dedicate this book to Bapu, my parents, Rani, Abhishek, my family and friends whose loving support accompanies me on all my journeys.

F O R T S

F O R T S

The Sahyadri mountain range dominates the landscape of Maharashtra. Perched atop several peaks in this range are massive stone forts that have played a decisive role in the history of Maharashtra. The rugged environment helped shape the courageous and daring spirit that characterizes the people of this region. Several temples with ornate rock-cut sculptures adorn these mountain tops - the result is a dramatic juxtaposition of the contrasting architectural features of forts and temples.

There are around 225 forts spread over ten districts of Maharashtra. While many are hill forts on mountain tops, there are naval forts on the sea coast and land forts on flat land, telling us a great deal of the character of the rulers of those times. Most of the forts were ruled by ancient dynasties like the Satavhanas, the Rashtrakutas, the Chalukyas, the Yadavs, the Mughals, the Bahamanis, the Kadambas, Adil Shah, the Shivshai and the Peshwas and all were finally taken over by the British. While some dynasties built new forts, others just took over the old forts for their use.

The construction of the forts reflects the foresight of the rulers who built them. The choice of the site itself made each fort virtually impregnable, the garrison being so located that it was well-protected against attack and controlled a strategic region. Most of these forts are today in a state of dilapidation. While some are well-preserved, others lie in virtual ruins, but even these speak to us of the grandeur of these places in times gone by.

Stony Sentinels

District-wise break up of the forts

District	Number of forts
Pune	28
Raigad	51

Satara	26
Kolhapur	11
Thane	53
Ratnagiri	24
Nashik	48
Sangli	06
Aurangabad	01

Among the well-known forts in Pune district are Shivneri, Sinhgad, Purandar, Rajgad, Lohgad, Tikona and Rajmachi. Raigad and Karnala are famous in Raigad district. The Pratapgad and Sajjangad forts in Satara district attract large crowds during the summer season. Panhala in Kolhapur district is very popular with tourists. There are some well-known naval forts on the Konkan coast, such as Alibag, Sindhudurg and Murud-Janjira. The land fort (known as Bhumikot) at Daulatabad in Devgiri, Aurangabad is also popular. The other forts are relatively unknown, except to enterprising trekkers.

The Unknown Fort of Kohoj

> **Fact File**
>
> *Best time- Monsoon months between June to September; also December to March*
>
> *Location - Waghote village on the Mumbai-Ahmedabad Highway*
>
> *Getting there - Manor is a one and a half hour drive from Mumbai. By train get down at Palghar and take the Manor-Wada ST bus to Waghote village that is at the foot of the mountain*
>
> *Time taken- A day's trek.*
>
> *Where to stay-Manor, Wada or Vikramgad*
>
> *Where to eat - Food and drinking water will have to be carried to the fort.*

A traveller journeying on the Mumbai-Ahmedabad highway will notice an imposing mountain to the right, just short of Manor. At the top of this mountain is the 2,000 ft- high Kohoj fort. To get there you have to take the Manor-Wada road. The Manor-Wada S.T. bus will take you to Waghote village at the foothill of the mountain. A path from the village leads you to a small lake from where you can make the two-hour climb up to the ruined walls of the fort. This fort has two adjoining peaks which look like a human figure and are easily recognizable from a distance. However, it is not easy to get to these peaks. The outer wall lies in ruins, while inside, some temples as well as a cannon can be seen. There are water tanks on the mountain with plenty of water. From the northern side of this fort, you can see the Deheraja River valley and the Vikramgad area; while to the south the Pinjal and Vaitarna river valleys provide a picturesque view. Beyond the river Vaitarna is Vandri Lake, while in the distance the outline of the top of the Takmak fort can be spotted. To the west is the Tandulwadi in the Asavgad range of mountains.

This is a wonderful trek during the monsoon season. An overnight stay at Manor, Wada or Vikramgad would enable you to undertake this trek in one day. The distance between Waghote and Vikramgad is 20 kilometres. Food and drinking water must be carried along on this trip.

Harishchandragad

Travelling on the Mumbai-Kalyan road via Murbad you have to cross the Malshej ghat. To the left of the road is an imposing mountain wall with three distinctive peaks. The slightly shorter one visible to the left as soon as you enter the Malshej ghat is Rohidas. In the centre, and the tallest, is Taramati, while the one to the right is Harishachandragad. Although little remains of the actual fort, once upon a time, Harishchandragad was probably the largest in the Deccan region.

Fact File

Best time- Monsoon months between June to September; also November to February, but it is very cold in December

Location - Malshej Ghat near Murbad on the Mumbai-Kalyan road; a three and a half hour drive from Mumbai.

Getting there - Can be approached from Thane, Pune and Nagar

Time taken- A day's trek can be exhausting so it is better to do a two day trek.

Where to stay- Guest house at Malshej or living with villagers of Rajur near the Malegaon junction. There are caves at the top where one can spend the night provided one has necessary equipment like sleeping bags etc.

Where to eat - Food and drinking water has to be carried to the top. Some trekking groups even carry portable stoves and cook inside the caves. Approaching from Rajur, you can hire a villager from village Pachnaj to cook for you.

The view of the sheer rock wall of Harishchandragad from the Malshej ghat is awe-inspiring. Standing at a height of 4,671 feet from mean sea level, the edge of the hill plunges straight down into the Konkan. In fact, the unique feature of this entire mountain range which includes the mountains of Nakta, Ghodishep, Aajoba and Ratangad, right up to Kulangad, is that the western slopes plunge directly into the Konkan. The edge of Harishchandragad is like a deep pan. Because of its distinctive shape and height, Harishchandragad is a popular trekking spot.

A first-time visitor looking down from the edge will be taken aback at the sheer drop. There is always a strong wind here and if you toss a light object down, you will see it thrown back to the top some times by the sheer force of the wind. During the rains, a thick cloud cover accompanies the wind. In 1853, Col. Sykes, an Englishman who was conducting the first-ever geological survey of the Deccan hills, recorded a curious phenomenon. In the midst of the fog and mist, he observed a circular rainbow with his own shadow in the centre. Only some lucky observers have since witnessed this phenomenon.

Among the ruins of the Harishchandra fort are visible a portion of the boundary wall and the Junnar gateway. There are nine caves on the Taramati hill, and though there is not much sculpted work here, the caves are a good place to spend the night. Slightly further down from the caves is the Harishchandra temple with a water tank called Saptatirth facing it. This tank has 14 compartments, each of which contains an idol of Vishnu.

This temple is probably the most astonishing part of the Harishchanadra fort. Before you enter it you have to cross a stone bridge under which flows the Mangalganga river. Adorned with rock- cut sculptures, there are several inscriptions on the temple walls. Well-known historian and author, the late G. N. Dandekar says that the main inscription mentions the sage Changdeo who lived here with his disciples and completed his book of philosophy. Changdeo was a contemporary of Maharashtra's great saint-poet, Sant Dnhyaneshwar.

Inside the temple is an idol of Nandi the bull, and a *shivling*. If you stand in front of the temple to the right, you can see another cave within which are four inscription-covered pillars and a huge *shivling*. This cave is full of ice-cold water, and just dipping your hand into it needs much will power, let alone entering the cave. However some sadhus who are residents of Harishachandragad can be seen going inside and performing rituals around the *shivling*.

It is possible to climb to the Konkan edge of this fort but to get there you will have to walk through dense forest cover. A large variety of trees like umbar (ficus family), beheda, jamoon, amla and even teak trees can be seen. Hares, foxes, boars, porcupines and leopards are known to frequent the forests here, which also provide a home to a large variety of reptiles. Innumerable varieties of birds including the warbler, the crow pheasant, the skylark, bulbuls, the Indian bee-eater, koels, swallows and hornbills are a delight to watch. Migrating flamingos also pay a visit. A large number of birdwatchers gather here in and around the month of September to watch the arrival of these migratory birds.

Getting There:

Harishchandragad is situated on the borders of three districts, Thane, Pune and Nagar and therefore can be approached from all three places. The visitor travelling from Mumbai, will reach the village of Khubi after Malshej ghat. A *kuccha* road leads from Khubi to Khireshwar at the foothills; just before Khireshwar a path goes to the Nageshwar temple. From here another path leads up to the fort, through the Junnar gateway. This is a difficult route; an easier alternative is the path from Khirshwar village through Tolarkhind. A tiger has been sculpted at the commencement of the path which leads you up to the top. Once on the peak you have to walk through about four kilometres of forest before reaching the Harishchandra temple.

Another approach to Harishchandragad is via the Ghoti-Bari-Sangmaner road off the Mumbai-Nashik highway. A right turn on this road after Rajur village takes you to the other side of Harishchandragad where the villages of Pachnai, Lavhale and Kotula are situated. Harishchandragad can easily be climbed from any of these three places. The distance between Mumbai and Ghoti is 145 kilometres and from Ghoti to Rajur about 45 kilometres. This circuitous route is actually a treat for nature lovers, with its tall mountains, dense forest, deep valleys, and the river Mula cutting across the road several times. While the road is difficult to drive on during the monsoon, at all other times travelling by jeep or motorcycle is quite a thrilling experience. This road reaches Pachnai, the village at the foothills of Harishchandragad. This is the easiest and most pleasant route to climb Harishchandragad. Villagers claim that the medicinal ingredient called shilajeet can be found here. Stopping over at the Malshej guesthouse is a good idea for those wishing to visit Harishchandragad. If you carry your personal requirements along with you, spending the night in one of the caves on top of the hill could be a lot of fun. If you take the approach from Igatpuri, it is possible to make arrangements for an overnight stay at Rajur village near the Malegaon junction. Harishchandragad is a good destination for all trekkers.

Karnala Fort and its Surroundings

Just before the town of Pen on the Mumbai-Goa highway is Karnala.You will see the distinct shape of a peak which stands out, literally like a sore thumb. Lying about 55 kilometres from Mumbai and 13 kilometres from Panvel this hill fort is often confused with the naval fort of Arnala near Virar. People tend to be similarly confused between the Raigad fort in the Konkan district and Rajgad fort on the Deccan plateau.

The entire area of Karnala is now a protected wild-life sanctuary and this refreshing green cover only serves to enhance its natural beauty. Just off the Mumbai-Goa highway, it tempts many tourists to stop for a cup of tea at the roadside dhaba, but few actually venture further to see the fort.

Fact File

Best time- All year round

Location - 55 kms. from Mumbai and 13 kms. from Panvel on the Mumbai-Goa highway

Getting there - By road.

Time taken- A day.

Where to stay- There is a rest house located close to the highway near the village Shirdhon that is ideal for a two-day break. There is a forest rest house on the edge of the park that can be booked through the forest department in Thane.

Where to eat - The place has eateries at the base. Ekvira Hotel serves gavran *(rural) Marathi food*

The 4 square kilometres of sanctuary is home to monkeys and other animals and to a variety of plants. Neem, karvanda, jamoon, mango, fig and crocodile bark tree are among the several trees you can see here. Monkeys, hares, foxes, mongoose, monitor lizards and boars have made their home here along with birds of various types.

While the usual Drongo, the crow pheasant, koels and robins are aplenty, rare birds like the Shaheen Falcon and the Small Minivet have also been spotted by birdwatchers in this forest.

Since the path to the fort goes through the forest, you do not immediately become aware of its height. The fort is nearly 1,500 feet from mean sea level and takes about 45 minutes to climb up. As you reach the top you cross a broken gate, while near the peak are a water tank, a granary and ruins of some buildings. The central peak is quite difficult to climb, rendered even more dangerous because of the beehives on it. A few years ago, a brave traveller attempted to climb the peak but died after the vicious bees attacked him. So, this is best avoided.

From the top of Karnala, you can see a vast area below. To the north-east you will find Haji Malang, and just before that, Prabalgad and Matheran. To the east, in the distance, is a hazy view of Bhimashanker. To the south is Rajmachi and the Duke's Nose, to the southwest is the Mahal Mira hill range while to the west is the metropolis of Mumbai.

Near the foothills is another place worth visiting, the village of Shirdhon, birthplace of freedom fighter Vasudev Balwant Phadke. The rest house here is very conveniently located close to the highway and is an ideal place to enjoy a two-day break. The forest rest house located on the edge of the park is excellent .

For booking contact the Forest Department in Thane.

Avchitgad

Sitting among the hills of the southern Konkan, near the town of Roha are some little-known or more correctly, forgotten forts. Among these are Avchitgad, Talgad and Ghosalgad. The village of Medha at the foothill of Avchitgad is just 7.5 kilometres from Roha, while another village, Pingalsai, also at the foot of the hill is just 5 kilometres from Roha. After the bridge over the River Kundalika at Roha, you will find a turning to the right, 6 kilometres down on the Roha-Wakan road, leading to Medha. The Roha-Nagothane State Transport bus will set you down here. 5 kilometres further down is

Medha. Near the Vithoba temple here a dusty path takes you to the top. Somewhere at mid-point this path joins the other path coming from Pinghalsai village. It is an hour's climb up to Avchitgad. Experienced trekkers can take the shortcut via Wagh Dhondi, from where it is only a 30-minute climb to the top.

Fact File

Best time- Monsoon months

Location - The village of Medha, 7.5 kms. from Roha or village Pingalsai about five kms. from Roha.

Getting there - Roha is a two and a half hour drive from Mumbai. There are regular ST buses to Roha from Mumbai. The Roha-Nagothane ST bus goes to Medha.

Time taken- Two days

Where to stay- Government guest house at Roha and small hotels.

Where to eat - Eateries at Roha. Carry food to the top of the fort.

Avchitgad has two main bastions. The one to the south side has inscriptions on it. There are 4 gateways to the fort. The main entrance is situated next to a rock-cut carving of a horse. At the entrance there is a large water tank, with steps leading into the water. To the left is a small roofless temple, enclosing a miraculously intact idol of Shiva. At the western-most edge of the fort, there are a number of water tanks, one small and seven large ones next to one another. One tank still contains potable water. You can see a small idol of Bhavani Devi near here as well as a small one of Pingalsai Devi. Two cannons sit atop the fort. From the southeastern side of the fort there is a view of the river Kundalika and the Rohaghat area. To the west you get a view of the creek at Salav. On a clear day, it is possible to see southern Murud and its surroundings, characterised by dense vegetation. The entire path to the fort is through lush green trees. The trees found here are the Australian Acacia, the teak, mango, and jamoon. From the top, you also get a splendid view of the green cover below. Several varieties of birds and animals such as boar, monkeys, foxes, hares and even the occasional leopard, can be found here.

Every *Sankrant*, villagers from the surrounding 7 or 8 villages gather enthusiastically on top of the hill for their annual fair.

Avchitgad is 1,000 feet from mean sea level, offering a lovely view from the top, and with so many trees, provides the opportunity to see a lot of birds. This is an easy climb and even the very young or very old will not find it difficult. The small Ganpati temple in the village of Pingalsai near the foot of the hill and the waterfall at Medha village are worth seeing. To see this place you have to stay at Roha which has a government guesthouse, as well as several small hotels. The distance between Mumbai and Roha is 115 kilometres. There is a regular State Transport bus service from Mumbai to Roha. It is also possible to reach here by rail.

Ghosalgad

Approximately 9 kilometres south of Roha and 32 kilometres east of Murud is a mountain which rises majestically to the sky. The fort on top of this hill has been named Ghosalgad after the village Ghosal below. Located between the Salwe creek and the Rev Danda creek, this fort was used as a look-out post for those ruling over the Murud Janjira area. Historical notes say that this fort was held by Shivaji Maharaj for some time.

Ghosalgad stands 1200 feet above sea level. Since the village Ghosal is also at a considerable height, the climb from the village to the top does not seem all that steep. There is an easy path up to the top of the fort from the Ganpati temple in the village. This Ganpati temple holds a special place in the hearts of all villagers in this locality; wishes made here are believed to be granted.

Fact File

Best time- Monsoon months

Location - The village Ghosal, nine kms. south of Roha and 32 kms. east of Murud.

Getting there - There are regular ST buses to Roha from Mumbai. ST bus to Ghosal.

Time taken- Two days

Where to stay- Government guest house and small hotels at Roha. There is no place to stay on top of the fort.

Where to eat - Eateries at Roha. Carry food and water to the top of the fort. None of the water tanks on the fort have potable water.

According to folklore the idol in this temple was not man-made; its size is believed to have grown steadily over the years. The path up to the fort has well-planted Australian acacia trees on either side and within 20 minutes, you reach the steps near the ramparts of the fort. Most of the fort is now in ruins and it is hard to guess where the gateway must have actually stood. Just as you enter the fort near the steps is a tank of water called the Wajta Haud. This water is not fit for consumption. There are rock carvings of horses on the walls of the tank.

From here, there is a wonderful view of Ghosal village below and of the approach road. There is a path (a difficult one) to the peak of the mountain from this point. At the southern edge, you can spot an ancient gun. Straight ahead is the view of Murud and its creek and to the left is Talgad. Below is a forest known in local parlance as *Khoryanche jungle.* Villagers here say that the forest today is not as dense as it was formerly, yet wild animals including the occasional leopard can still be spotted. The approach from the southern side is quite difficult, not only because of the steep slope but also because of the dried grass. There are a couple of water tanks near the temples on the peak, but none of the tanks have potable water.

It takes about two hours to see the entire fort and return to Ghosal village. There is no lodging or boarding facility in the village, so you have to stay at Roha and then return the same evening.

Talgad

About 135 kilometres down the Mumbai-Goa highway, about 15 kilometres from the town of Indapur, is the small fort of Talgad. At a height of about 88 to 100 feet from mean sea level, the village of Tal is located in the foothills. Since the village is at a considerable height the climb to the actual top is only about 500 feet and takes only about 30 to 40 minutes. If you take the *kuccha* road beyond the Tal village, you reach Pusatiwadi. Jeeps and motorcycles can make it to this point. The distance between Pusatiwadi and Talgad is probably 250 feet, so from here you can be in the fort within 10 to 15 minutes.

There is dense forest near Pusatiwadi, and a simple path through this forest takes you to the outer area of the fort. You can see mango, jamoon, teak and kokum trees in this forest. In some places you can see bamboo growing. Near the outer wall you can see an underground tunnel that villagers claim goes straight down to the village. Also visible are the remains of a large gateway and a water tank which has now been filled up. The innermost bastion is relatively intact giving you an idea of the excellent quality of construction during those times.The ruins of the Chandika temple can also be seen. In all there are eleven water tanks here, three in the central part of the fort and eight on the other side; none of them have potable water. There is a small Shiva *mandir*. Ruins of another building and some guns can be seen lying near the approach from Pusatiwadi.

Fact File

Best time- Monsoon months

Location - Village Tal, 135 kms. down the Mumbai-Goa highway and 15 kms. from the town of Idnapur.

Getting there - There are regular ST buses to Roha from Mumbai.

Time taken- Three days

Where to stay- Government guest house and small hotels at Roha. There is no place to stay on top of the fort. There are facilities for staying at Indapur too.

Where to eat - Food is available from villagers at Tal. There is no food at the top and one has to carry both food and water.

It is possible to get food in the village of Tal but there is no facility for staying overnight. The best place to stay is either at Indapur or Roha. There is a direct road via Tambdi Khurd on the Roha-Ghosalgad road. The distance between Tambdi Khurd and Tal is 13 kilometres. If you stay in Roha, you can cover the forest of Ghosalgad, Talgad and Kuda caves in a matter of two days.

Murud-Janjira

The taluka of Murud is 48 kilometres south of Alibag. This palm lined coastal town is not only picturesque but is historically important and has several spots for tourists to visit. To get to Murud from Mumbai there are two roads, one via Alibag (148 kilometres) and the other via Roha (156 kilometres). If you travel

Chandoli Sanctuary

Mulshi to Lonavla

Walking Tree of Sanjan

Fact File

Best time- All seasons

Location - Murud, 48 kms. south of Alibag.

Getting there - ST bus to Murud via Alibag or Roha, or turn off 9 kms. before Murud on the Mumbai-Goa highway

Time taken- Three days.

Where to stay- Hotels in Murud, MTDC holiday camp.Also great seaside hotels at Kashid.

Where to eat - Eateries in Murud. Carry food and water to the fort.

via Alibag, on your way you can visit Korlai fort, see the Kashid sea beach and the Siddhivinayak temple at Nadgaon.

To the right as you enter Murud, is the grand old mansion of the Nawab of Murud. To the left, hidden behind the trees, you can see red-tiled roofs, and to the right, the sea.

The major attraction in Murud is the large naval Janjira fort about two kilometres off the main coast in the seawaters, to reach which you have to take a small boat from Rajpur village.

The fort is surrounded by water. At high tide, you have to take the boat to get there. The boat will deposit you right at the entrance of the fort.

The main archway has inscriptions in Arabic, and on entering, to the right you will notice a carving of a tiger standing upon an elephant. Near the main entrance door of the fort is a *Peer Panchayatan,* where every November devotees gather for a fair. Some old graves and relics from ships have been found near here. At the centre of the fort are the ruins of a building known as the *Surulkhan wada*. The building must have been magnificent in its days, now much of it has been overrun by creepers and trees. The ramparts of the fort are very strong and still intact. All along the wall are 19 bastions, each 30 to 40 feet high. Each bastion has a cannon pointing towards the sea. Three huge cannons, historically famous, still stand near the main door. The cannon with handles on both sides is called the *Kalak Bangdi*, the middle gun *Chawri* and the third *Landa Kasam*. The cannons once had a good range and enemy soldiers feared the range of these guns. The Janjira fort is built upon an island which belonged to the Koli (fisherfolk) community in the fifteenth century. At that time, the ramparts of the fort were wooden. Later the island fell into the hands of Peeramkhan, an officer of the Nizamshah. It was Burhan Khan, the next ruler, who strengthened the ramparts, making them virtually impregnable. During Shivaji's reign, he attacked this fort, but failed. This fort has gone down in history as one of the most difficult to capture because of its tight security, the long range cannons and the open sea.

Shivaji built the Padmagad fort to counter the Janjira fort. Here too the ramparts were very strong. Inside the fort is a sweet water lake and some cannons. It is possible to see both Janjira and Padmagad forts in just one boat trip. Other places of tourist interest near Murud include the dense forest of Kesoli-Phansad and the caves near Kuda. The MIDC has holiday camps at Murud, which can be booked from Mumbai. There are regular State Transport bus services between Mumbai and Murud and Alibag and Murud.

Korlai

About 10 kilometres south of Alibag near Rev Danda village is the naval fort of Korlai. Located just 3 kilometres down the Rev Danda-Murud road near Korlai village, it can be reached via a road leading to the fort from the village, which is just 2 kilometres away. The fort is on a small hill (about 250 to 300 feet high) in the sea. The main door of the fort faces the east, but if you go up from the village, you can enter the fort from the western side. It is possible to drive right up to the steps of the fort. There is a naval lighthouse near the fort from which cement steps lead to the fort. If you enter from this side you will see the ruins of a gateway to

Fact File

Best time- All seasons

Location - Village Rev Danda, ten kms. south of Alibag.

Getting there - Three hour drive from Mumbai; ST bus to Murud via Alibag or Roha.

Time taken- Three days.

Where to stay- Hotels in Murud, MTDC holiday camp.

Where to eat - Eateries in Rev Danda. Carry food and water to the fort.

the left. A little further down is the fortified plain called Pachuchi Dhar that goes straight into the sea and affords a wonderful view of the boats in the creek. Inside the fort you come to the stronghold wherein you can see the remains of a Portuguese church and water tanks. A few cannon remain on the bastion. At different points of time, the fort has been ruled over by the Nizam, the Portuguese, the Marathas and finally the British.

It is not only history buffs who will find this fort fascinating but naturalists as well. To the south and west is the view of the entire stretch of Korlai beach. The sunset here is a breathtaking sight. To the east you get the view of Rev Danda and its surroundings, the fishermen and their colourful boats.

While there is no place to stay in Korlai, you can stay at Alibag and then visit this fort. This can be combined along with a visit to the Kashid beach. The distance between Alibag and Korlai is 21 kilometres while the distance between Murud and Korlai is 28 kilometres. So one can also stay at Murud, visit Korlai and Kashid and return there for the night. There are regular State Transport bus services between Murud and Korlai and Alibag and Korlai.

Kathingad or Tung

Most people are familiar with the hill stations of Lonavala and Khandala due to their proximity and easy accessibility to the metropolis of Mumbai. While there are several spots within 2 to 3 kilometres of these two hill stations, frequented very often by tourists, few people venture any further. The more resourceful will find that there are some beautiful spots, a little off the beaten track, but well worth visiting.

One such place is the Tung Fort or what is popularly known as Kathingad. *Kathin* in Marathi means difficult and when you see the vertical slope to the fort it is easy to understand how the fort got its name.

To get to Kathingad you have to take the road from Lonavala town towards the naval base of INS Shivaji. This is about 7 kilometres from the main town. Continue down this road till you get to Ambawane village. This road runs more or less parallel to the Sahyadris, to the left lie the mountain ranges, while to the right deep in the valleys you can see the Konkan region, the Duke's Nose, the lake near INS Shivaji and Umbarkhind. About 15 kilometres from Lonavala, down this same road is the small village of Ghusalkhamb. Only about 12 kilometres of this road is tarred, the rest is a *kuchcha* road, which is traversable by jeep or motorcycle. At Ghusalkhamb village you turn left off the main road and proceed to Tungi village. This road takes a circuitous route around Jambhuli hill and by the Morvi and Tungi hills, before it reaches the village of Tungi. Or both sides of the road is thick forest and to the left you can see the blue waters of the Pauna Lake. About 8 kilometres from Ghusalkhamb you see a signpost directing you to the path leading to Tung fort.

Fact File

Best time- All seasons

Location - Tungi village near Ghusalkhamb on the INS Shivaji Road, about 25 kms. from Lonavala.

Getting there - Lonavala is a one and a half hour drive from Mumbai by the Expressway, two hours by train. ST bus to Tungi village via Lonavala.

Time taken- Two days.

Where to stay- Hotels in Lonavala.

Where to eat - Carry food and water from Lonavala where there are hotels and eateries.

The height of Tung fort from mean sea level is 3,500 feet and from the foot of the hill to the top is about 1,200 feet. As you climb you first come across a Hanuman temple and then some steps carved into the hillside. Further ahead is a Tulzai Devi temple and water tanks. Right at the top is the Tungi Devi temple from where you get a view of the semi circular Pauna Lake which encircles three sides of this hill, Lohagad and Visapur to the north and Tikona to the east. To the south west, you can spot the fort of Koraigad on the Jambhuli mountain range.

To get here you travel by rail on the Mumbai-Pune line and alight at Kamshet. There is a State Transport bus service from Kamshet to the Kale colony, near Phagane dam. From the dam there are launches which in 30 to 45 minutes take you to the village of Pansoli or Kevre. From here, you begin climbing the hill just after the Hanuman temple. The road via Lonavala, is, howeve,r an easier route, and there is a State Transport bus service from Lonavala. If you carry a picnic lunch you can spend a day at Kathingad and return to Lonavala in the evening.

Koraigad

South of Lonavala in the Maval region is the Koraigad fort which offers a panoramic view of the Deccan plateau as well as the Konkan region. To get here you have to take the INS Shivaji road from Lonavala to Ghusalkhamb, Peth-Shahpur and Ambawane, the village at the foothill. From here is a slightly arduous path leading to the fort. An easier route is to take the path from the earlier village of Peth Shahpur. The distance between Lonavala and Peth Shahpur is just 20 kilometres. The first 12 kilometres of road is tarred, while the rest of the road is *kuchcha*.

Fact File

Best time- All seasons

Location - Peth-Shahpur and Ambavane village near Lonavala.

Getting there - ST bus to Peth-Shahpur and Ambavane from Lonavala.

Time taken- Two days.

Where to stay- Hotels in Lonavala.

Where to eat - Carry food and water from Lonavala where there are hotels and eateries.

From the village of Peth-Shahpur you can see the Koraigad hill rising like a steep wall. Its height is 3,000 feet from mean sea level, but the height from Peth-Shahpur to the top of the hill is about 800-1,000 feet. The path to the fort goes along a flat plain for quite a while before entering the forest just below the fort. From here to the main doorway is a steep climb, through dense vegetation. Among the various trees which can be found here are the fig, mango, bamboo, hirda, kokum, nirgudi, karti, raanwangi, ghasodi. Barking deer, boars, peacocks and peahens and doves are among the animals and birds who live here. Half-way along the path to the left, you can see a carved Ganpati idol in a rock, while to the right is large storeroom for storing grain. Further ahead, just short of the main doorway, is a water tank, containing cool and fresh water. On entering the main door, you find a cannon lying to one side. To the left is the main gateway, the Ganesh Gate. From here far to the left, you can see the Duke's Nose and the INS Shivaji area, while straight ahead is the Jambhuli mountain range beyond which is Tung hill. The southern side of the fort has a temple dedicated to Koraidevi. The roof of this temple had been blown away some time ago, but now some enthusiasts have got together and had a new roof fixed. Outside the temple are two stone lamps. Inside is a four feet tall idol of the goddess. Behind the temple, adjacent to the ramparts of the fort, is a large cannon. Of the five or six cannons on the fort, this is by far the largest. To the south is the well-fortified Ambavane gateway. There are two lakes on the hill where groups of vultures often hover. Visible from here are the Mulshi lake, the Bhamburda mountain and the Durga hill. The western part of the fort contains some caves and an idol of Vishnu. From the northern bastion of the fort, there is a panoramic view of the Konkan area.

There is a regular State Transport bus service from Lonavala to Peth-Shahpur and Ambavane. It is possible to spend the day at the fort and return to Lonavala in the evening. You must remember to carry your own food and water.

Tikona

While travelling from Mumbai to Pune by rail, you pass through the stations of Lonavala, Khandala, Malavali and Kamshet. Near Malavali station to the right, you can easily spot the Lohagad and Visapur forts. Just beyond these forts are the Pauna River and the Phagane Dam, to one side of which is the Tung fort and on the other, the Tikona fort, Of the four forts in this area – Lohagad, Visapur, Tung and Tikona – the latter is most easily recognizable because of its distinct shape. With its triangular peak, this hill resembles a pyramid from a distance.

To get here you disembark at Kamshet on the Mumbai-Pune rail line. From Kamshet there is a bus service to Paud Kale Colony near the Phagane dam. After walking across the wall of the dam, you reach the village of Tikona Peth. The distance between Kale colony and Tikona peth is about 6 kilometres. A short, easy climb and you reach the fort. Inside is an ancient temple and a water tank. To reach this, however, is a steep climb and really leaves you perspiring! On top are some caves and a large water tank.

Fact File

Best time- All seasons

Location - Kale Colony near the Phagane dam near Lonavala.

Getting there - Kamshet by Mumbai-Pune rail, bus service from Kamshet to Kale colony.

Time taken- Two days.

Where to stay- Hotels in Lonavala.

Where to eat - Carry food and water from Lonavala where there are hotels and eateries.

From the top towards the west, you can see the Tung fort ringed by the Pauna Lake. To the north, are the forts of Lohagad and Visapur. Tikona is nearly the same height as Tung, around 3,500 feet. One of the best views of Tikona is from the villages of Pansoli or Kevre, which can be reached by launch from Kale colony. From here, the reflection of Tikona in the blue waters of the Pauna Lake is a magnificent sight. This is a day's trip from Lonavala.

Panhala

Shivaji's exploits are well-known in Maharashtra and even young children will tell you tales about his victory at Sinhgad, his escape from Agra, his attack on Torna and his flight from Panhala. It was in 1660 that Shivaji was surrounded by the troops of Siddhi Johar while he was in Panhala fort. Today Panhala is a well-developed taluka town, with schools, hospitals and hotels. The Panhala fort covers an expansive area and is probably the best developed of all forts in Maharashtra. Its height from mean sea level is 3,100 feet, while from Kolhapur it is only about 1,000 feet high. From the actual foot of the hill, the fort is only 300-400 feet high. Panhala is just 25 kilometres from Kolhapur. There is a State Transport bus terminal at the top, and regular services from Kolhapur. In addition to government rest houses there are also some good hotels like the Meghdoot and The Hilltop Hotel

Mahalaxmi (MTDC). Panhala has a pleasant climate all the year round which makes it popular as a hill station. Among the places of interest are:-

> **Fact File**
>
> *Best time- All seasons except during the July to September rains*
>
> *Location - 25 kms. from Kolhapur.*
>
> *Getting there - Kolhapur is an 80 km drive from Mumbai; ST buses to the top of the fort from Kolhapur.*
>
> *Where to stay- Government rest houses, hotels like Meghdoot and Hilltop Hotel Mahalaxmi, MTDC resort.*
>
> *Where to eat - Hotels and eateries in Panhala.*

1. The birthplace of Moropant, a well-known poet from Maharashtra. This is close to the State Transport terminal at Panhala. Nearby is a small lake called Kapurbav.
2. Palace of Tararani: Formerly a palace, today this building houses the Panhala municipality offices, the Panhala High School and a boys hostel.
3. Nehru Park: A small park in the centre of town.
4. Sajikothi: Shivaji had installed his son Sambhaji Raje to administer this area. This place was used as a conference room. It is at one end of the fort and therefore from its windows you get a wonderful view of the region below.
5. Tiger Doorway and Tabak Baug: Further ahead from the Sajikothi and slightly to the east is the Tiger Doorway. A few steps below this is a small garden called the Tabak Baug. From here, you can see the entire Warna valley.
6. Rajdindi: If you continue walking from the left of Tabak Baug you come to various bastions, namely Dutondi, and Daulati. Beyond these is the historical Rajdindi from where Shivaji escaped from Siddhi Johar.
7. Pusati Buruj: A short walk beyond the Rajdindi and you come to the other end of the fort. From here, you can see the plateau of Mhasai.
8. Teen Darwaja: When you turn back from Pusati Darwaja you first come to Khokad Lake. On the right bank of the

lake is the western doorway of the fort. This is a three-storeyed doorway. Sixty of Shivaji's men under the command of Kondaji entered the fort from here.

9. Ambarkhana: Behind the Teen Darwaja, to the east, you come to the main *balekilla*. This is at the centre of the fort and inside are three storerooms – Ganga, Yamuna and Saraswati – where rice, *nachni* and *warai* were once stored.
10. Andharbav: A three-storeyed building south of the Teen Darwaja with water at the bottom and a small path running through the middle.
11. Parashar Cave and Kali Burj: South of the post office is the Parashar Cave. There are five rooms inside. It is here that the poet Moropant wrote his poems. The bastion at the end is called the Kaliburuj. From here, a tunnel leads to the Rede Ghat garden

The old fort on the Pavandgad hill is visible from here. There are several other places likely to interest history buffs such as the Sadoba Dargah, Rede Mahal, Kalavantinicha Sajja and the Someshwar Lake. The well-known historian. M. G. Gulawani has written a book on Panhala and this along with a map is easily available at the ST Stand (the State Transport bus terminus). It is a must-buy for tourists.

The Peaks of Gorakh and Machhindragad

These two peaks along with Siddhgad lie slightly apart from the main mountain range near Murbad, standing out because of their peculiar shape. Siddhgad is almost square in shape and close to this are the slimmer twin peaks of Machhindragad and Gorakh gad.

To get to these peaks you have to go to Murbad via Narivali. The road to these peaks is through dense forest and will take you to the cave at the foothills of Gorakhgad. The other route is via Murbad to Dehri or Khopivali, the villages at the foothills of the Aahupe ghat. From here, an easy path takes you to Gorakhgad. The Gorakhgad fort faces north-south. The path from the southern side enters the fort through a doorway cut into the rocks. To the east of the fort are several large caves and water tanks. Gravel steps from the northern end lead up to this 2,137-foot-high fort. The neighbouring Machhindragad, the Kulang, Kalsubai and Siddhgad forts are easily recognizable, as are the mountains of Matheran and Mahuli. There is a perilous path of about 1500 feet between the Khind of Gorkhagad and Machhindragad which only experienced climbers should attempt.

Fact File

Best time- Monsoon months

Location - Villages of Khopivali or Dehri near Murbad.

Getting there - Murbad is 80 kms. from Mumbai, a 2 hour drive. ST buses from Mumbai and Kalyan go to Murbad via Narivali, from there is a road through dense forest. Another approach is via Murbad to Dehri or Khopivali.

Where to stay- There is a cave atop Gorakhgad.

Where to eat - Although water is available in the cave it is better to carry both food and water.

Trekkers can spend the night in the cave at Gorakhgad. If you have two to three days at your disposal, then you can climb Gorakh-Machhindragad, Khopivali via Ahupe ghat. Though water is available you must carry your own food.

Gambhirgad

On the border of Maharashtra and Dadra-Nagar Haveli, quite close to Mumbai yet relatively unknown, is the Gambhirgad fort. Any naturalist would love this place. Gambhirgad standing at a height of 2,250 feet is the tallest mountain in this area. The top of the mountain resembles a turban and can be spotted from a distance. The Gambhirgad mountain can be seen while driving from Vikramgad to Kosala, at the far end of Kavdas Lake. While travelling from Kasa to Sayvan, Gambhirgad appears very close. If you are travelling from Sayvan to Udhav, you have to go around the Gambhirgad mountain thus getting the chance to view it from different angles.

The usual route to Gambhirgad is via Sayvan. Two kilometres ahead of Sayvan is the village of Ashona, from where a *kuchcha* road takes you to the village of Vehali at the foothills of Gambhirgad. The 2-kilometre distance takes about an hour to cover. You then get a rewarding glimpse of the water tanks at the edge of the fort. Some ramparts of the fort still remain. The view from the top is out of this world. The forests below, the valleys, the mountain ranges, the plateau of Maltalaseri straight up to the Surya project and the Kavdas and Dhamni lakes suddenly appear, filling you with joy.

Fact File

Best time- June to February

Location - The border of Maharashtra and Dadra Nagar Haveli.

Getting there - Mumbai to Charoti is a three hour drive.ST buses from Mumbai to Charoti then to Kasa, and from there to Sayvan. There are regular ST buses between Sayvan and Girthad from where the fort is easily accessible.

Where to stay- Charoti

Where to eat - Carry your own food and water to the top and while traveling in this region.

Gambhirgad can also be climbed from the opposite side. To do this, you have to take the Sayvan Kinavali road from Sayvan village. After 4 kilometres you reach Girthad. From here, you take a path climbing for about an hour and a half to reach the top. The forest here is extremely thick and is home to lots of animals. Partridges, peacocks and the crow pheasant can be heard. Leopards abound in this forest. Villagers residing in these parts say that sometimes you can hear the leopards calling out to each other during the day, sounding very much like dogs barking. The tiger, which is almost extinct in Maharashtra, has been spotted here. The local tribals and shepherds claim that they see tigers very regularly; in fact some people showed me a tiger's cave. Barking deer, boars, hares, hyena and the jungle cat can also be seen here.

There are regular State Transport buses plying from Sayvan to Gambhirgad. The distance from Mumbai to Charoti is 110 kilometres, another 2 kilometres ahead is Kasa and 15 kilometres after that is Sayvan. State Transport buses are available between Sayvan and Girthad. You must carry food and water while travelling in this area.

Rajgad

Fact File

Best time- June to March

Location - 40 kms. south west of Pune

Getting there - ST buses from Pune to Bhor from where you have to take a launch to Bhutonde. Or take the Pune-Velha bus to Margasani village and from there via Sakhargaon to Gunjavane village. The easiest route is via Vinzar village from Vazeghar or from Velha to Pali. A favourite route is to take the Velhe bus to Vinzar village, cross the Kanandi river and climb up via Sakhargaon.

Where to stay- On top of the fort is the Padmavati temple where one can stay.

Where to eat - Carry your own food and water to the top.

The name of this fort is itself an indication of why it is known as the king of all forts! Of course, the main reason probably lies in the fact that this fort was Shivaji's home for the major part of his life. Before he became Chhatrapati, he used Rajgad as his base and is said to have spent nearly 25 years here. Although his capital was Raigad after his coronation, a lot of administrative work was controlled from Rajgad.

Rajgad is 40 kilometres south-west of Pune, and is 4,514 feet high. The fort is situated at the end of a spur, surrounded on three sides by fortified machees (plains)– the Padmavati Machee, the Sanjivani Machee and the Suvela Machee. The main summit is about 500 feet high. The Padmavati Machee is the largest of the three plains; perhaps this was where most people stayed at that time. Three main doorways of the fort open onto this plain: the Chor darwaja, the Pali darwaja and the Gunjawane darwaja. The ruins of the Padmavati temple, the Padmavati lake, the Maharaja's residential palace, the havaldar's *wada* (constable's residence) can all be seen here. The only place which can be used by trekkers for an overnight stay here is the Padmavati temple. Of the three plains, the narrowest is the Suvela Machee. Stone steps, ramparts and a bastion can be seen here. On this plain is a 15 foot-diameter opening called Waghacha Dola (tiger's eye). Several of Shivaji's officers including Tanaji, Yesaji and Shemkar built houses here. The view of the sunrise from this point is really beautiful. The third plain, Sanjivani Machee is about two kilometres in length. Double fortification and a bastion can be seen here. There is a direct route from this point, through the Alu Darwaja, to the Budhala Machee on Torna.

The stronghold of Rajgad is said to be its finest point and can be reached with some effort. Once you enter the main gate you can see the palace ruins, the *janani* and the Bramhrishi temple and a water tank. There is quite a wonderful view from the top. You can see various mountain ranges and spot several forts from here including the Mahabaleshwar Raireshwar plateau, Raigad, Makarandgad, Lingana, Torna, Visapur, Tung, Sinhgad and Purandar.

Rajagad is built on a hill named Murambdev which was not captured for a long time. In 1702 Aurangzeb laid siege on Rajgad and changed its named to Najibgad.

Around Rajgad are the rivers Velwandi, Kanandi and Gujavani, so that all the routes to the fort are across rivers. The main gates to the fort are Alu Darwaja, Gunjavane Darwaja, Pali Darwaja and Chor Darwaja.

How to get to the gate:

1. To enter the fort from the Alu Darwaja from Pune you have to go to Bhor. Near Bhor you board a launch at Basrapur at the Bhatghar dam. A five-hour ride will take you to Bhutonde, which is at the foothill of Rajgad. From here, it is a three hour climb to the Alu Darwaja.
2. To get to Gunjavane Darwaja you take the Pune-Velha bus to Margasani village and from there you go via Sakhargaon to Gunjavane village. From here, it is a six to seven hour climb to the Gunajvane Darwaja.
3. The easiest route is via Vinzar village from Vazeghar or from Velha to Pali and thence to the Pali Darwaja. This takes about 5 hours to reach the top. The grandeur of this gate is well worth seeing.

4. Another favourite route is through the Chor Darwaja. To reach here you take the Velhe bus to Vinzar village, cross the Kanandi River and climb up via Sakhargaon. This takes about 4 hours, the last part of this path being quite rocky. When you enter

from here you reach the Padmavati Machee. Here it is possible to spend the night at the Padmavati temple. Some trekkers have drawn a map of the fort within the temple. It is necessary to carry all requirements like food and water with you. If you leave Pune in the morning you can climb to the top by the afternoon, spend the night there, returning the next day.

Torna

Fact File

Best time- June to March

Location - Village Velha or Keland near Pune

Getting there - ST buses from Pune to Velha or Keland.

Where to stay- Pune

Where to eat - Carry your own food and water.

This is the first fort that Shivaji captured. He is said to have quietly occupied the fort without any bloodshed in the monsoon of 1646. Legend says that when he began reconstructing the fort, which had fallen into disrepair, he came across a hidden treasure, with which he built the fort of Rajgad on the hill opposite to Murumbdev.

The height of Torna is 4,604 feet. The expansive plain at one end of the fort, the Budhala Machee, has given the fort its name of Prachandagad (The Huge Fort). Torna has two main gates – the Bini Darwaja and the Kothi Darwaja. Just inside the Kothi Darwaja is a small temple dedicated to Toranjai while another temple, the Toraneshwar, the Toran rank and the Khokad tank are nearby. The main temple in the fort is the Mengai temple. To the east of this stronghold is the Zunzar Machee. You can see a few water tanks and ruined buildings while walking towards this plain. The Brahmapishaccha (Ghost) stone is also here. On the way from the Kothi Darwaja to the Zunzar Machee lie the Hanuman bastion and the Bhel bastion.

At the other end is the big stretch of plain known as the Budhala Machee. While walking towards it, the Takmak bastion, the Thibthiba and the Konkan Darwaja are plainly visible. From the top of Torna, you can see the Khadakwasla dam, Sinhgad,

Raireshwar, Bhatghar, Mahabaleshwar, Raigad, Pratapgad and Makarangad. In 1704, Aurangzeb is believed to have seized control of Torna and renamed it Futuhulkhaib.

There are three routes to reach Torna:

1. Catch the bus to Velha. From here it is a 2 to 3 hour climb to the top.
2. Take the Pune-Keland bus, disembark at Keland village, and then proceed to Bhatti village. From here, you can climb to the Budhala Machee on Torna.
3. From Torna, it is also possible to reach Rajgad. From the Budhala Machee you take the path to Sanjivani Machee, roughly a 7-hour walk.

Sinhgad

Fact File

Best time- June to March

Location - Outskirts of Pune

Getting there - PMT bus from Pune to Kondhanpur. Walk to Kalyan village.

Where to stay- Pune.

Where to eat - Carry your own food and water.

Almost every child in Maharashtra knows the story of how Tanaji Mahisure captured Sinhgad Kondana for Shivaji. One of the most heroic and exciting stories in Maratha history, the tale of how he used an iguana to climb this mountain has been told again and again. Shivaji was said to have remarked that "We won the fort but lost the lion", and thus the name of the fort was changed from Kondana to Sinhgad.

There are several things of interest in Sinhgad. If you enter though the Kalyan Darwaja, you reach the Dev tank, which has clean, refreshing water. To the west is the Donagiri cliff, now popularly known as *Tanaji kada*, the side from where Tanaji is said to have climbed the hill. The Zunjar bastion, the Kalavanti bastion and the Tanaji memorial are all places worth seeing. To the east is the Ganesh tank while a memorial to Rajaram Maharaj has been erected to the north. At the centre of the fort are the

Amriteshwar temple and the ruins of the palace. The Zilla Parishad maintains a rest house here.

Sinhgad can be easily distinguished from among the hilltops which surround the city of Pune because of the television tower atop it. Sinhgad is about 26 kilometres southwest of Pune City and there is an excellent tarred road right up to the top.

While travelling from Pune to Sinhgad you pass the Khadakvasla dam before you reach the Panshet junction. Drive towards Donje village and then straight up to Sinhgad. If you take this route, you enter through the Donje Darwaja.

If you take a PMT bus from Pune to Kondhanpur, you then go to Kalyan village and climb up to Sinhgad, entering through the Kalyan Darwaja. This climb is less steep. For trekkers there is a third route. Climb down near the Karjat tunnel, climb the hill to the right and then keep walking across several hills till you reach Sinhgad. This is a 13-kilometre trek.

Since there is a tarred road right to the top there is no problem obtaining food or water here. This is a day's outing from Pune.

Rajmachi

The Rajmahi point at the hill station of Khandala is very popular with tourists. From this point you can see the Rajmachi fort atop two peaks close to each other. The taller peak to the right is the Shrivardhan fort, while the slightly shorter one is Manranjan. There is a pass or *khind* between the two peaks. A Bhairoba temple nearby is the spot from where one can climb to the top.

Fact File

Best time- June to March

Location - Khandala is a one and a half hour drive from Mumbai by road, two hours by train.

Getting there - Climb down Tungarli hill from Lonavala and then walk.

Where to stay- Villagers of Udhewadi accommodate travellers for a night.

Where to eat - Carry your own food and water.

If you climb down Tungarli

hill from Lonavala, you will reach Udhavane village after about 13 kilometres. Another 6 kilometres ahead, just short of Walwand village, is a small canal to the left, across which is the Rajmachi plateau. Rajmachi is part of the same range of mountain as Lonavala and Khandala. It is joined to the main Sahyadri range by a mountain only 300 metres long. Once you cross the canal you reach the foot of Srivardhan and after walking around it you reach the Bhairoba temple. The residents of Udhewadi village will accommodate you for the night if you wish to stay. Shrivardhan, which is the taller of the two peaks is 910 metres high and is therefore the stronghold (about 3,000 feet). There are regular steps to climb but they wind around the mountain. There are some water tanks here, one of which has an iron pillar lying in it. There is hardly anything in the way of construction here, only a small rampart, which was probably used to guard the area. The fort was probably used only as a look out to control the ghat region.

Manranjan is about 2,700 feet high and has massive ramparts and three gates. Only the ruins of the fortkeeper's house are seen here besides some water tanks. From Manranjan you can see the River Ulhas and its valley. Visible to the far side is the Duke's Nose, the railway line in the Khandala ghat, as well as Karnala, Matheran, Mahuli and Bhimashanker in the main Sahyadri range of mountains.

At the bottom of Rajmachi are the ancient Hindu and Buddhist Kondhane Caves. Because they are directly below the mountain, the rain-water falling from the top has eroded the caves significantly. After seeing Rajmachi you can climb down via the Udhewadi plateau and catch a bus to Karjat. The other way to get to these caves is from Thakurwadi railway station from where you walk to the River Ulhas and take the road to the left which goes straight to the caves. It is also possible to take the road to the right and go to Rajmachi via Udhewadi.

While the walk to Rajmachi is long (nearly 18 to 20 kilometres), it is not arduous and is ideal for people just starting on their first trek. The path takes a circuitous route near the River Ulhas and round the narrow mountain which joins Rajmachi and Khandala. You can spend the night at Udhewadi. The entire route is very beautiful, ideal for people of all ages.

Sudhagad

Fact File

Best time- June to March

Location - Near Ghat near Lonavala, an elevated portion of the Sahyadris or Pali in Konkan which is famous for the Ashtavinayak Ganesh.

Getting there - Pali to Mumbai is two hours by road via Khapoli or Nagothane: 13 kms. from Pali. Or from Lonavala a motorable road takes you via Koraigad to village Telbaila. Then get down to Vazri pass to Bhairampada.

Where to stay - Temple on top or Pali

Where to eat - Pali or carry food

This is probably among the better-maintained forts in Maharashtra. Like Rajgad, Rohida and Sarasgad, this fort too was controlled by the ruler of Bhor. It was well- maintained right till the British times and even today the ramparts of the 2,030-foot high fort are intact. Sudhagad is to the west of the *Ashtavinayak* pilgrim centre of Pali. The village of Bhairampada is 13 kilometres from Pali. The Dhondse-Nadsur-Wada State Transport bus takes you here. The slope to Sudhagad begins from Bairampada village. While entering from this route, you go through three gates. The first, the Mahadarwaja, is the largest and in good condition. On the plateau is a Shiva temple while to the east of the fort is a large stable. The main goddess on the fort is Bhorai, the family deity of the Pant Sachiv family, the erstwhile rulers of Bhor State. There is a large lake here set in an enormous grassy plateau. Takmak Point and Echo Point are the other places you can visit, while here.

While Sudhagad can be approached from Pali, it can also be approached from the Mulshi dam. You have to go via Kori Fort to Telbaila. From here you pass the Vazari Khind and reach Bhairampada.

En route from Pali to Bhairampada is the village of Nadsur. About 9 kilometres from here is the village of Thanale where there are some Buddhist caves. There are also some caves at Khadsamble, a village south of Sudhagad. In the forest, at the foot of the hill, there are many *Pandharichi Kathi* trees, well-known for providing the raw material for the famous walking sticks of Matheran.

There are several places which can be covered on a three-day visit to this area – the Pali Ganpati, Sarasgad, Sudhagad fort, the caves at Khadsamble, and Thanale, the newly developed hill station of Tadgaon as well as the hot water springs at Unhere.

Raigad

Fact File

Best time- All year round.

Location - Konkan, close to Mahad.

Getting there - Four and a half hour drive from Mumbai, ST buses ply from Mumbai and Pune. A new ropeway from base village takes you to the top in ten minutes.

Where to stay- MTDC resort, Jog Ropeways and hotels atop the fort

Where to eat - Eateries atop the fort.

This is the centre of the erstwhie Maratha Kingdom and Shivaji's capital; this is also where his coronation was held and where he breathed his last. When I first started trekking, like many others I was confused between Raigad, Rajgad and Rajmachi fort. The easiest way to remember the difference is that Raigad is in the Konkan, Rajgad on the Deccan plateau and Rajmachi in the ghat region. It was Raigad and Rajgad which were the jewels in Shivaji's crown. He stayed at Rajgad for nearly 25 years, but after his coronation moved to Raigad for the next seven years. Shivaji chose Raigad for his capital after surveying various forts and discovering that this particular one was virtually impregnable. He had captured this fort, once known as Rairi, from Chandrarao More in April-May 1656. There is a large plateau on the hilltop and the hill face is practically inaccessible on three sides.

The Chitta Darwaja and the Khublada Bastion are among the places still remaining. Near this bastion are three large caves called the *Waghbile* (Tiger's Hole).

The height of Raigad from the Khublada Darwaja is 1,200 to 1,500 feet while from mean sea level it is 2,900 feet. Even if you drive up to the top, the last stretch of steps, which you have to climb to the Mahadarwaja, are so steep that they leave you exhausted. This door is huge and is still in a good state of repair. On entering there are a few more steps before you reach the Hatti Lake (Elephant Lake). A short climb from here takes you to Gangasagar Lake, near which lie the ruins of the palace. The plateau here is covered with the remains and ruins of a number of buildings, cisterns and rock-cut reservoirs. The walls of the main *darbar* or the King's court are still standing and within it you can see a low mound where Shivaji's throne was placed. Just below this, the MTDC has built a rest house.

The Hirkani Bastion is to the western side of the fort. Legend has it that a milkmaid, Hirkani, climbed down this precipice in order to reach her child and home, after the main gates had been closed for the night. Later when Shivaji heard of her feat he rewarded her and blocked the loophole by erecting a bastion. Looking at the sheer fall, it is difficult to believe that anyone could have climbed down from here.

Just below the Hirkani bastion is the Nana Darwaja. If you walk from here to the Gangasagar Lake and take the path to the left, you will reach the northern part of the fort. This is the famous Takmak point, a vertical cliff face, and looking down from here is thrilling, but equally frightening. It was from here that traitors or those given the death sentence were thrown to their death. It has now been fenced off. From this point, you can see houses in the small village of Nizampur, which was the village where Hirkani came from.

Just near the Takmak point is a ruined building which was once the arsenal. Another village visible from this point is Panchadgaon, where the residence of Rani Jijabai can be seen, while at the centre of the fort is the Shirkai temple. A statue of Shivaji has been recently erected here. Close to this are the ruins of what historians think was the market place, nearly a mile long, and at the end of that is the Jagdisheshwar temple. The Koli Laka and the Samadhi of Shivaji are nearby.

To the east are the remains of a house where a foreign tourist, Henry Oxenden, is said to have stayed. This is Bhavani point. From here, you get a view of the Sahyadri range, at the centre of which is Lingana. This is thought to be the most difficult fort to scale, and at 3,000 feet, it is slightly higher than Raigad. Just behind Lingana you can spot Rajgad and Torna. Nowadays a popular trekking route is to scale Rajgad, then Torna, Lingana and then move on to Raigad.

If you walk on the western edge of the mountain from Bhavani Point, you reach Wagh Darwaja (Tiger Gate) behind which is the Kushavart Lake. From here you can see the Sahyadri ranges including Raireshwar, Kolheshwar and Mahabaleshwar.

A ropeway at Raigad enables you to reach the top within minutes. Even otherwise with steps going right to the top this is not too difficult to climb, and makes for a pleasant trek. Since Raigad is at a considerable height, the climate here is always pleasant. Raigad could be described as a historical hill station, and while it is possible to see the entire fort in a day, it is also a pleasant place for a brief stay.

Pratapgad

Fact File

Best time- All year round.

Location - 45 minutes from Mahabaleshwar

Getting there - Regular tourist buses from Mahabaleshwar which is a five hour drive from Mumbai (221 kms.)

Where to stay- A rest house available if booked in advance, or at Mahabaleshwar.

Where to eat - Small eatery atop.

Straight ahead of the Elphinstone Point at Mahabaleshwar is a flat-topped, high, rocky mountain, known in the pre-Shivaji era as Bhorpya or Gudhya Dongar. It was here that Shivaji built the great fort of Pratapgad. This fort, standing at a height of 3,540 feet, took two years to construct.

The Poladpur-Mahabaleshwar stretch is nearly 40 kilometres of ghat road. The part between Poladpur and Paragaon is known as Parghat, then from Kumbharoshi to Mahabaleshwar it is known as Ambneli ghat. At the top of this ghat, to the left, is a road to Pratapgad. This fort is wel-known in history because of the infamous Afzal Khan episode. Afzal Khan was the general of Adil Shah of Bijapur and his main strength was his cavalry and heavy artillery. Surrounded as it is by the rugged terrain and the thick forests of Javli, the terrain around Pratapgad made it difficult for Afzal Khan's troops to function. Shivaji won the battle against Afzal Khan when he succeeded in luring him to Pratapgad.

The fort was built by Moropant Pingle, who later became Shivaji's Prime Minister. The construction was completed in 1658. It was a year later that Afzal Khan attacked Pratapgad and was killed by Shivaji who went on to conquer the region up to Kolhapur and Panhala. This was the beginning of Shivaji's domination over the southern region.

It was here that Shivaji consecrated the Bhavanidevi idol. The idol of the goddess was made from a special stone brought from the Gandaki river in Nepal. There is also a *shivling* in the Mahishasurmardini Bhavani Devi temple. This temple lies immediately to the left after you enter from the Mahadwar (main gate). To the right is the Jivamahal or the Tehelno bastion. If you look down from this point you can see Afzal Khan's grave, while straight ahead is Mahabaleshwar. There are steps from this plain to reach the stronghold. To the right of this is the statue of Hanuman installed by Samarth.

The stronghold is actually quite small. The place where Shivaji's palace stood now has his statue. This statue was unveiled by India's first Prime Minister, Pandit Jawaharlal Nehru. The Afzal bastion, the Surya bastion, the Kadelot bastion, the Dakshin bastion, the Rede bastion and the Kedar bastion are all part of the strong ramparts of the fort. There are two lakes, the Naske Lake and the Devi Lake. At one place you can see a large vessel containing water, placed deep into the earth. It is said that this was made for horses. Today, there is a small garden in the fort, behind which is a rest house.

Since the fort gets plenty of tourists, food and water is easily available. Pratapgad is 45 minutes from Mahabaleshwar. Three hours is sufficient time to see the fort and its environs. There is a regular 'Pratapgad darshan' tourist bus from Mahabaleshwar.

Lohagad-Visapur

> **Fact File**
>
> *Lohagad-Visapur*
>
> *Best time- June to March*
>
> *Location - Malavali on the Mumbai-Kasara suburban train route.*
>
> *Getting there - Train to Malavali from Mumbai and walk from there to Bhaja village.*
>
> *Where to stay- There is no place to stay atop the fort.*
>
> *Where to eat - Carry food and water.*

Just after Lonavala on the road from Mumbai to Pune you can see two forts next to each other on the right. These are the forts of Lohagad-Visapur. To get here by rail you have to alight at Malavali station. Bhaja Village is 3 kilometres from the station. There is a path through the Gaimukh *Khind* (narrow pass)between Visapur and Lohagad. After heading for a while in the direction of Visapur, the path turns and goes towards Lohagad.

Lohagad is 3,412 feet while Visapur is 3,567 feet in height. At the base of Lohagad is the village of Lohgadwadi. From here you can enter the fort through four well-built gates. The first gate is the Ganesh Darwaja, followed by the Narayan Darwaja and the Hanuman Darwaja; the fourth and final gate is the Maha Darwaja. There are inscriptions on this gate. Once inside, you can see the remains of a building and a blacksmith's forge.

At the centre of the Lohagad fort near the building which looks like a mosque, is a slightly raised area with two store rooms, the Khajindar Kothi and the Laxmi Kothi (treasuries). There is also a lake here which does not have much water. To the west is what is called *Vinchukata.* This rampart resembles a scorpion's fangs, hence the name. (Vinchu means scorpion). From here you can see a range of mountains which have a rampart on them. From behind Lohagad you can see Pauna Dam and Umbarkhind.

Lohagad has a peculiar gap on one side, therefore it is easy to recognise even from a distance. It is believed that both Lohagad and Visapur were built as lookouts for the Bhor ghat.

The Visapur hill lies in-between the Lohagad and Bedshi hills.

To get to Visapur you have to go through the Gaimukh Khind from Lohagad. These forts were built in the Satavahana reign. After being under the control of Nizamshah and Adilshah, the forts were then conquered by Shivaji. Later in a treaty signed by Shivaji with Mirza Raje Jaysingh, he handed over twenty-three forts to Aurangzeb, one of which was Lohagad. Subsequently he attacked and recaptured it, but after his death it again came under Mughal rule before Kanhoji Angre won it back. During the time of the Peshwas this fort was used quite a lot. The lakes on the fort were built by Nana Phadnavis. Around 1818, Col. Prother took over these forts.

While visiting Lohagad and Visapur it is also possible to visit the Bhaje and Bedse caves. The Buddhist caves of Bhaje are one kilometre from Bhaje village. The Bedse caves are in the triangular hill near the Visapur fort. This is a day's trip from Khandala.

Sajjangad

Among the various forts in the vicinity of Satara is Sajjangad. This was well-known because Shivaji's Guru Shri Samarth Ramdas Swami stayed here. Earlier known as the Parli fort, Shivaji won it from the Bijapur rulers in 1673. Samarth Ramdas stayed here till his death in 1682. Shivaji is known to have visited the fort several times for discussions on various matters with Ramdas Swami. After Samarth Ramdas Swami's death, Sambhajiraje built a *samadhi* for him on this fort.

Fact File

Best time- All year except April and May when there is a water shortage.

Location - Close to Satara

Getting there - Satara to Mumbai is a seven hour drive (260 kms.). ST buses ply from Mumbai, Pune and Satara

Where to stay- Pilgrim hostels atop the fort.

Where to eat - Food and water available at the top of the fort.

Sajjangad is just 15 kilometres from Satara, and there is a regular State Transport bus service connecting the two places. It is also possible to get here by taxi or autorickshaw. There is a good tarred road right to the top of the fort. Thereafter, take a few steps up and you enter the two main gates of the fort. The path takes you to the Shri Ram Temple. The idols in the temple were sculpted by a blind sculptor named Arnikar. They are made out of *Panchdhatu* and were gifted to Ramdas Swami by Vyankojiraje. In the basement of the temple is Ramdas Swami's *samadhi*.

On the outer walls of the temple are boards detailing the history of Sajjangad and the important events which took place here. The different places of interest in the fort are also outlined. Near the temple is Ramdas Swami's ashram. Here you can see the well-preserved bed, his water glass and other personal items and some things gifted to him by Shivaji. To one end of the fort near the ramparts are the temples of Maruti and Anglai Devi. It is said that Shivaji consulted Swami Ramdas in privacy within these temples.

There is an expansive view of the surrounding area from the top of Sajjangad. The Urmodi river, Ajinykatara and Yavteshwar can be easily spotted. The fort is 3,000 feet from mean sea level. There is place to stay and food is also available in the fort. The fort is quite clean and with its serene atmosphere and pleasant climate, is well worth a visit.

Naldurg

Fact File

Best time- June to March

Location - 45 kms. from Sholapur and 47 kms. from Tuljapur in Osmanabad district.

Getting there - Eight hours by road from Mumbai, Regular ST buses to Naldurg

Where to stay -- Sholapur

Where to eat - Eateries aplenty.

The forts of Maharashtra, though boasting excellent garrisons and of immense strategic value, have little to show in the way of architectural craftsmanship. This is unlike the forts built in northern India, where architectural excellence went side by side with security when forts or palaces were built. Many of the northern forts have also remained in good condition because the rulers sought the protection of their conquerors instead of fighting back. This helped preserve their forts. In Maharashtra, however the attitude was to fight to the end. The result was that the forts suffered great damage. Only the ramparts of a few forts and some of the buildings within have remained intact. Even these have suffered neglect over the years, so that now only ruins remain.

Naldurg is one fort which is in reasonably good condition. This is one of the few land forts in the Tulzapur taluka of the Usmanabad district. The fort has strong ramparts with several bastions and gates. The river flowing to the east of the fort was diverted to flow through the fort. The bund built here is an excellent example of architecture skill — the Pani Mahal (the water palace). The fort was apparently named after King Nal who is credited with having built this place. However, historical records show that this fort was reconstructed during the time of Adil Shah around 1561. Earlier, it was under the Chalukya and Bahamani kingdoms.

The fort has several bastions. Of this the Upali bastion is the main one, about 150 feet high and with 70 steps. On top is a massive gun with a long range. There is a palace here as well as an arsenal. Among the other larger bastions is the Sangram Bastion which has in it a gun made of five metals (*Panchdhatu*), the Bandanawaj Bastion and the Paranda Bastion

Seven gates lead into the fort. The main one is called the Hulgun Darwaja. This massive wooden door has nails on it to prevent an attack by elephant-borne troops. The other gates are the Hazzarotti Darwaja, the Pani Mahal Darwaja, the Ramana Darwaja, the Hatti Darwaja and the Panthat Darwaja.

Immediately after entry through the main gate, to the right are seen the quarters of the fort keeper. This has now been converted into an office. Here a vandalized gun made of *Panchdhatu* is seen lying around. Further ahead is the mosque. Near the ramparts is another building called the Baradari, from where you can see the Bori river and dam. The eastern flank of the fort is known as the Machi Tat. From here you get a wonderful view of the water falling from the Bori dam, beyond which is visible the Ranmandal hill.

The Pani Mahal has been built in the dam wall below the falling water. The view of the water from this place is wonderful. The most beautiful view is during a heavy monsoon flood, for, as the water hurtles down, the suns rays glitter on the water to form a rainbow. The interior of the Pani Mahal is also worth seeing. Next to the Pani Mahal is the Panchakki (water wheel). Here water power was used for grinding grain on a large scale.

The fort appears to be virtually invincible due to the high ramparts around it, coupled with the clever use of the river. In addition to the usual security aspects, the construction of the Pani Mahal adds a beauty of its own to this unusual fort.

This fort is about 45 kilometres from Sholapur and 47 kilometres from Tulzapur, and approximately an hour's drive will bring you here. Regular State Transport bus services go to Naldurg. There are good restaurants in the vicinity where you can stop for a meal.

Dhakoba

Fact File

Best time- June to March

Location - Village Amboli near Junnar

Getting there - Mumbai to Junnar via Malshej ghat is a four and a half hour drive (170 kms.) ST bus to Amboli.

Where to stay- Amboli

Where to eat - Carry own food and water.

The hills and fortresses in the Sahyadris have stood as silent sentinels for years. The area around Junnar is particularly steeped in fascinating history. Forts like Harishchandragad and Shivneri have already captured many people's imagination. Few, however, are aware of the other, lesser known places of interest, like Hadsardurg and Dhakoba.

Amboli is an hour's drive from Junnar. To the west of Amboli village, stands a Ganesh temple, frequented by the villagers, yet isolated from the hamlet's human settlement. A narrow road takes you from one side of the temple right up to the Darya ghat. A short walk reveals a fork in the road. Continue along the left, and you come upon Dhakoba, (the right turning continues to the Darya ghat.)

A beautiful scene awaits you here. Flanked by a vast plateau on its left, and jagged cliffs on the western side, Dhakoba is pristine Nature. The foothills of these ranges mark the beginning of the lovely Konkan coast. Throughout this walk, one is keenly aware of the glorious view of Amboli ghat. To the south, a path leads to the Durg fort and the temple of Dakeshwar. It is a good two-hour walk from the temple up to the fort, which is surrounded by thick forest. The temple owes its existence to the people of Durgwadi who have constructed it using local manpower and material.

It is a thrilling, difficult trudge through the dense undergrowth to reach the top of Durg hill. What makes it worth the effort is the whistling, clean, breeze and a virtually unmatched view of the rolling hills. Dhakoba itself is a good 2-hour walk from Durga fort. From a distance, the crown of Dhakoba resembles Nandi--Lord Shiva's bull. It is actually easier to scale Dhakoba peak from the north. This is the highest point in that ridge of the Sahyadris that acts as a barrier between the coast, and mainland Maharashtra. The distant forts of Harishchandragad, Siddhagad, and Gorakh-Machindragad are visible from here. Spend another half an hour strolling the periphery of the peak. You'll never tire of the panoramic view that greets you at every turn.

Prabalgad

For the driver cruising on the Pune-Mumbai highway, the ruggedness of Prabalgad is an overwhelming sight. As you leave Panvel behind, keep looking to the left. It is difficult to miss the V- shaped formation to the west of the fort. The gigantic Prabalgad is not alone. Irsalgad, standing at the edge of its larger cousin, is distinguished by a canoe-shaped sheet of rock at its

Fact File

Best time- June to March

Location - Close to Matheran and Panvel.

Getting there - One hour drive from Mumbai to base of Prabal.

Where to stay- No place to stay on top.

Where to eat - Carry your own food and water.

Kaalbhairav Temple

Upper Deck, Lonavla

Sunset at Moti Daman

Sadashivgad

crown. These 'siblings' are extremely well- known to hundreds of travelers who whiz by on the highway. Yet, due to lack of proper information, the duo of Prabalgad and Irsalgad rarely find themselves on the tourist map.

The mountain that makes up the hill station of Matheran rises just behind Prabalgad. The famous sunset point of Matheran lies along the same line of vision as the V-shaped gorge on the left of Prabalgad. One can reach this fort from Matheran, via the small village of Arkas. The road ultimately leads to Shirdi, starting from the temple of Pisarnath, near Matheran's renowned Charlotte lake. The valley that nestles between the hills of Matheran and Prabalgad is a thick green blanket. Leopards and wild boar are common here. Anyone with a keen eye and a pair of binoculars can, standing at the edge of the valley near Charlotte lake, spot the fortifications and ramparts of Prabalgad.

Prabalgad stands at an altitude of 2300 feet, nearly as high as Matheran. Here is a thickly forested tableland. These forest tracts are a known habitat for many species of plants, including the rare Karvy, a beautiful flowering plant . The area around Prabalgad would have made an ideal hill station, except for the absence of a sufficiently large reservoir of water. For this reason alone, the Maharashtra Tourism Department dropped plans of converting the fort into a commercially viable tourist attraction. Actually, this is one reason why these virgin hills have stayed undisturbed and beautiful for years.

Prabalgad is accessible from the Konkan by taking a turn at the Poinje Phata. This road branches out from the Panvel road, just six kilometres short of the Panvel crossing. From Poinje, you can trek to the top of the fort, passing Thakarwadi. The fort has some ruins of stone walls and ramparts. There is a small water tank and a Ganesh temple. A map guiding you around the fort has been displayed recently. Still, it is wise to take the help of a local guide at Thakarwadi. This way, you can be assured of finding your way amidst the wild tracts of Karvy. The only traces of humans are the cowherds who take their cattle and goats to graze in and around the fort. A tiny lake also provides these animals with drinking water.

There are few records mentioning the historical or geographical importance of Prabalgad, save that in 1826, the freedom fighter, Umaji Naik, along with his companions, had made the fort his home for a brief period. The fort is close to Mumbai as well as Pune, making it an excellent place to go for a weekend trek. With its misty monsoons and cool summers, the massive image of Prabalgad will leave you with happy memories.

Dhodap

Fact File

Best time- June to March

Location - About 25 kms. north east of village Chandvad in Nashik.

Getting there - Mumbai to Nashik is a three and a half hour drive, also by train

Where to stay- Caves at the top.

Where to eat - Carry food. Water is available for drinking in tanks atop the fort.

Dhodap fort is the tallest fort in the mountain range of Ajintha, with an altitude of 4750 feet above sea level. It lies about 25 kilometres to the north-east of the village of Chandvad, in Nashik district. The road leading to either Chandvad or Satana will pass via a hamlet named Vadali-Bhoi. The peaks of the fort are visible here, to the west of the village. From Vadali-Bhoi, it is 7 kilometres to the village of Dhodambe. From here, it is a walk of 4 kilometres to the foot of Dhodap fort. Halfway up the fort, one reaches the temple of Lord Goraknath. The path then continues to the 'Sonar Wasti', a settlement of locals. The slopes of the fort are home to two kinds of residents- the Sonar Wasti, and on the other side, Golwadi, whose people are all Hindi speaking and have been staying here for years. A road connects both stops.

The path going to the top of the fort skirts the Sonar Wasti. After a considerably steep climb, the door of the fort is visible. Here, two towers have been built in extremely difficult terrain. A set of 30 rock-hewn steps take you to a high wall. The wall serves an important purpose—to provide a catchment area for water. Here too, one has to negotiate 20-odd steps that take you to an oblong tableland. The entrance door of the top fort leads to a kind of tunnel. Some more steps, and finally you begin to catch sight of the peak—the highest point of the fort.

Amidst thick undergrowth, one has to climb the rock face using the niches on the wall. At a little height above, a semicircular cave shows signs of attempts at creating a cavernous hall. A path leads from this cave some distance away and the pinnacle comes to an end. Here, an enormous cavity in the form of the letter V is seen. A wall, a natural rock formation, measuring more than four metres in thickness and 350 metres long, stands here, with a south-west orientation. At the end of the wall, a large splinter has dislodged itself from the main wall, and it is here that a tower has been deftly filled in.

Walking to the point where this massive rock wall actually connects the fort, makes interesting viewing. If you look at the spire or the Shikhar from here, a needle's eye about 75 feet tall and 3 feet across is clearly visible. It gives the appearance of a naturally carved tunnel. The eastern mouth of this tunnel opens out into a cave where there is a huge water tank, carved out of the rock itself. This cave has a remarkable reputation for being home to many a trekker. With its cool interior, ample space inside, and clean, clear water, the cave is better than a three star hotel! The cave is 35 feet long and 25 feet across. In addition to this large 'hall', there are 3 more caves inside, 10 feet by 12 feet in size. At one end of the cave, a narrow path leads out, and at the other end, there is a broken sheet of rock 4,000 feet high. Look down from here, and nature surrounds you in all its glorious colours. One can spend hours here; in fact, many trekkers do.

In the same range as the Dhodap fort, to the east, a sheer cliff rises up, 4,000 feet tall. It peaks at the top and has jagged edges. It is called the Ikhara peak. It is a constant challenge for daredevil rock climbers who are often seen here with all their equipment.

The Dhodap fort has a colourful history. Originally in the hands of Burhan Nizamshah, it was probably built sometime before 1550. Later, in 1635, it fell into the hands of Allavardi Khan, who captured it for the Mughals. During the Peshwa rule, Raghunathrao Peshwa, in a strong show of protest and rebellion, made the fort his home in 1778. Peshwa Madhavrao took an army and soon after, arrested the offender in his lair. This short but definite Peshwa influence is evident in many facets of the fort, such as in the entrance doors and the construction style of the temple.

For hundreds of years, the outskirts of the fort have been home to the 'Bhaiyyas', a gentle, Hindi–speaking people who trade in milk and milk products. It is now more popular as the home of the Khoya-making community, and not surprisingly, the place is known far and wide for its excellent quality of soft, delicious Khoya (milk solids, the main ingredient for making most Indian sweetmeats, like *gulabjamuns, pedas,* etc.)

Amidst the barrenness of rock and dust, a fort like Dhodap lives to this day, filling its visitors with awe and respect. A trip to the fort is like going back to its days of glory.

Mahuli

One can drive down to the Mahuli fort from Aasangaon, located near Shahapur in Thane district. The most enjoyable way to reach the top is of course, by trekking up. The fort is famous for its intricately carved entrance door along with very elaborately arranged porches and pavilions for a ceremonial guard. This main door is flanked by two towers on either side and wide steps take the visitor through the huge opening. The entire area is covered by a thicket of 'Kevda', a fragrant twig specially favoured by Lord Ganesh and hence highly valued. Making your way through the shrubbery is a minor tussle, so thick is the growth. Follow the path and a high iron ladder, ten feet long, greets you. The top of the fort is accessible by climbing this ladder. Of course, this route is almost 300 metres away from

Fact File

Best time- June to March

Location - Asangaon in Thane district.

Getting there - By road on the Mumbai-Nashik route; suburban train to Asangaon and drive to Mahuli fort.

Where to stay- Caves atop the fort.

Where to eat - Carry your own

the formal entrance of the fort. The fort has a fresh-water reservoir here, from where you can again backtrack to the ceremonial entrance. Here too, there is a water tank. The large pavilions and porches are good enough for an overnight stay.

Like other forts, Mahuli too has a temple, water reservoirs, and stone steps to negotiate the sometimes steep climbs. The fort is also noteworthy for some exquisite stone carvings. From the main door, if you continue straight ahead instead of turning to the right, you come to a place known as Namazgir. It is here that there are slabs of stone, some with carvings, and some with written text engraving. To the north, there are traces of a *wada,* probably an ancestral home belonging to either an officer of high rank or some royalty. There is a bamboo grove here which forms a kind of entrance to Palasgad.

Another interesting spot to visit is the temple of Shri Mahuleshwar. Take the left track from the water tank near the ladder, and continue westwards until you reach a big lake, on the bank of which lies the temple. Once again, the stepped entrance to the temple is flanked by engraved stone images of a pair of women in armour. These sculptures probably depict the fact that women too were allowed to form some kind of military force. It is here that you reach the edge of a valley.

The Mahuli fort is separated from Bhandargad by a deep gorge. A good trekker can descend the pass and again climb up a rough and energy sapping slope to reach Bhandargad. The prominent door of the fort, the Kalyan Darwaza, is to the west. The inner side of the stone entrance displays some inscriptions in the Devnagari script. There is a large water reservoir here. A spiralling peak named ' Karangli' (little finger) is a focal point and immediately attracts the eye.

On the return trail to Mahuli, the dilapidated remains of another doorway can be seen on the eastern face of the crown of the fort. This Hanuman Darwaza has sculptures of Lord Hanuman and Lord Ganesh.

A couple of disputes apparently resulted in the fort being split up into 3 parts. To the north is Palasgad, to the south, Bhandargad, and between the two, Mahuligad. The top of the Mahuli fort, at a height of 762 metres, offers a beautiful view of the twin lakes of Lingi and Tansa. Mahuli also has a good water supply, very advantageous for avid wildlife enthusiasts who want to stop over for a day or two. In addition to the convenient porches at the entrance, there are also a few caves dug out nearer the ramparts where a small group of trekkers can easily pitch camp.

Chandan-Vandan

Fact File

Best time- June to March

Location - Off Pune-Satara road.

Getting there - Mumbai to Satara is seven hour drive(260 kms.)

Bus service from Satara to Village Vanvadi

Where to stay- Satara

Where to eat - Carry your own food and water.

These twin forts lie off the Pune-Satara highway. About 24 kilometres before you reach Satara, a road branches out from the village of Bhuinj and heads towards Lagadvadi. Ten kilometres of driving, and you reach the foothills of Chandan-Vandan. There is a bus service that allows you to come right up to the village of Vanvadi, situated here. If you come via Bhuinj, the road will take you to the western side of the valley that touches Chandan Vandan. If you come from Satara, you will reach the eastern side of the fort. Strangely, from Vanvadi, only the Chandan fort is visible. Vandan lies hidden behind its sibling and is not seen from the village at the bottom.

At one end of Vanvaadi stands an ancient Shiva temple. The sanctum sanctorum, where the Shivalinga is housed, is deeply recessed in the stone and is submerged in water the whole year round. The prayer hall in front is connected to a tunnel that opens out into the fort. It is here that the climb to reach Chandangad actually begins. At a height of 2500 feet, the trek is a good one. A small lake is situated centrally and from here one can also see the dam of Arabwadi. Folklore has it that during the reign of Adil Shah, there was a large Arab cantonment here, from where the name originates. To the left, a flattish hill, shaped somewhat like a counter, is visible. For some mysterious reason, it has been named *Bhoot tekdi,* the haunted grove, by the locals.

A walk of about 45 minutes will bring you to a completely derelict tower. An arch stands behind this, framing a small temple of Lord Chakreshwar. The top of the fort is distinguished by two pillars. The pillars stand on a flat area and have been constructed by arranging huge slabs of stone on each other. A little distance off is the Gospak Darga, where each Thursday, devotees flock to pay obeisance. Just behind this Darga, stand the ruins of what was once the proud mansion of the fort's caretaker. A well next to this is an almost perennial source of sweet, cool drinking water. The taste of the water instantly reminds one of the water drawn from the Devgad lake at Sinhagad. The Chandan-Vandan forts must have been of some importance, because one corner of the fort shows signs of an ordnance depot. There are cellars beneath this very building, and one can still enter with the help of a flight of stairs. The precipice of the fort is not far away. The skyline in front of you now showcases Vandangad, while to the right, down below, are the hamlets and little settlements of Belmachi, Tal, and others. To the casual observer, Vandangad seems just across the valley, but the experienced trekker knows that with pieces of stone giving way over the years, the gorge is a jagged and treacherous mass that one may find impossible to descend. In fact, the huge gap between the two opposite faces is a challenging arena for many expeditions of ace rock climbers and trekkers, who can bridge the breach with a rope. For the tourist out on a ramble, though, it is best to climb down Chandangad and, following the route around it, ascend Vandangad, even if it means taking a detour. Thus, the twin forts Chandan-Vandan have something to offer both to the serious adventurer and the leisurely tourist.

Jeevdhan

Jeevdhan has the unique distinction of being one of the foursome that seems to guard the Naneghat terrain. Shivneri, Hadsar, Chavand, and Jeevdhan, form a set of 'watch towers' that stand many hundreds of metres above the landscape and offer their

Fact File

Best time- June to March

Location -27 kms. north of Junnar.

Getting there - ST bus to Junnar and from there to Ghatghar at the foothills of the fort. The other road comes from Kalyan-Murbad to Nanetale.

Where to stay- No place to stay atop the fort.

Where to eat - Carry your own food and water.

stolid protection. The Junnar–Naneghat route was an important trade connection in ancient history. This area is about 27 kilometres to the north of Junnar. Today, however, the natural beauty of this belt is its most important asset. Jeevdhan stands at the very beginning of the Naneghat, and acts as a bodyguard to the stretch ahead.

The fort occupies an illustrious page in history. One of the descendants of the Nizamshahi dynasty had a son who was imprisoned here by the Mughals. Shahajiraje, father of Shivaji Maharaj, rescued him and moved him to safety at the fort of Pemgiri near Sangamner. He also had him formally installed as the Nizamshah in a ceremony atop the fort. He installed himself as his prime minister and began to oversee the administration. Pemgiri was renamed Shahgad. When the news reached Shah Jahan, emperor of Delhi, he commanded Mohammed Adil Shah to overturn this rebellion. So Adil Shah set out to attack Pemgiri and break the partnership of the Nizamshah and Shahaji. With his wife Jijabai and young son Shivaji, Shahaji retreated from the vicinity of Pemgiri and Jeevdhan, and fled to Mahuli in Thane district, where he sought refuge along with the Nizamshah. The plan did not work, and Shahaji met with defeat. He had to surrender the fort as well as the custody of the Nizamshah to the enemy.

There are two routes that take you to Jeevdhan. There is a regular bus service from Junnar that reaches Ghatghar, at the foothills of the fort. The other road comes from Kalyan- Murbad and skirts the village of Vaishakhe, before stopping at Nanetale. The mountainous climb of Naneghat begins here and ends at Ghatghar. A road then climbs 70 feet, from the jungles at the bottom, to a sheer rock face. This road ends at the eastern doorway of the fort. There is a water tank right next to this doorway. Much of this fort has collapsed, including the arch at the main entrance.

Within the fort, adjacent to the doorway, there is a sculpture of Goddess Gajalaxmi. The only other standing structure is the godown. The year 1818 was witness to one of the last battles between the British and the Maratha forces and saw a devastating fire that set ablaze many hundreds of tons of grain stored here. Amazingly enough, the ash in the building is more than a foot deep and has stayed untouched for over 200 years!

The summit of the fort is long and extensive, at a height of 600 metres. The south again shows ruins of masonry and structures. The Tulsi Vrindavan that Jijabai worshipped everday, still stands, sad witness to the ravages of time. The vista at this spot encompasses Hadsar to the east, along with Matheran. To the east is 'Nana's thumb', and Naneghat. To the north stands in lonely grandeur, the peak of Mount Kalsubai. Paying respect to her height are Ratangad, Aajoba, Harishchandragad, and Bhairavgad. To the south is Dhakoba. The fort also has a huge fresh-water reservoir to its north.

The fort is ideal for a day-long excursion, but there are no structures on the fort, and hence no place to stay.

Pandavgad

This fort is situated in sylvan surroundings and yet close enough for a day visit. It is an hour and a half from the little town of Wai, on the Pune-Mahabaleshwar highway. At 1400 metres, the fort is accessible and close to major towns like Pune, Wai, Satara, and Bhor. King Bhoj the second, of Kolhapur's Shilahar dynasty, was the patron of this fort and it was constructed under his supervision. Prior to 1673, the fort was controlled by Adil Shah of Bijapur. More than twenty five years later, the fort was captured by the Maratha forces.

The fort encompasses an area of more than 10 square acres. The flat summit of the fort is surrounded on all sides by natural rock formations that rise a few metres high. The strong fortifications

Fact File

Best time- All seasons

Location - North of Wai and south of Bhor town.

Getting there - Mumbai to Pune is three hours by road, four hours by train. ST buses from Mumbai, Pune and Satara to Wai.

Where to stay- Hotels in Wai.

Where to eat - Hotels inWai. One has to carry food and water to Pandavgad.

and doors add to the well-protected environment of the fort. There are remnants of a man-made lake at the eastern end of the top of the fort. Sadly the small temple of Shri Pandjai at the central point of the fort is on the verge of collapse, and until efforts are made for its conservation, will fall into decay like so many other heritage structures. The fort was built to accommodate as many as 18 small and large water reservoirs. Of these, barely two or three actually yield water. The rest are dry.

The crown of the fort offers a picture perfect view. The region includes Mandhardev, Wai, the area around the town of Menavli, Mahabaleshwar, while the tablelands of Panchgani, and Raireshwar. Kamalgad, Kenjalgad, Chandan-Vandan, Makarandgad, Pratapgad, and Vicitragad are all visible from here. Arm yourself with a pair of binoculars, and hours will slip by before you realize it, so picturesque is the scene atop the Pandavgad fort.

In the vicinity of Pandavgad, the Dhavdi village has some interesting sights. To its south-east are some caverns. One such cave measures a massive 7m x 2 m. x 3m. Another deep cave, probably excavated, is adjacent to this cave. It houses a shrine of Lord Shiva. Next to this is a huge Buddhist prayer hall with 7 rooms. A water tank completes this mini complex. Like the rest of the structures on the fort, these too, are in a highly dilapidated state and overgrown with weeds.

The lovely hill station of Mandhardev is a very good place to visit. It is 12 kilometres from Wai and 21 kilometres to the north of Shirwal. The trek from Pandavgad to Mandhardev is a very interesting one, especially in the monsoon, when the entire terrain wears a misty look and there are rivulets and tiny waterfalls everywhere. Every full moon in the Hindu month of Paush,

Mandhardev is thronged with devotees and pilgrims. They flock to two temples here, one of the Goddess and the other a temple of Lord Hanuman. Two days are enough to scour each little hillock in the trek from Pandavgad to Mandhardev. A trip here is a must for any passionate tourist who wants to have a taste of the outdoors and yet take time off to relax.

Hadsar

Fact File

Best time- June to March

Location - Junnar taluka

Getting there - Get to Junnar by ST bus via Pune.

Where to stay- There is no place to stay on top of the fort.

Where to eat - Carry your own food and water.

Few people are familiar with this fort, which lies in Junnar taluka. The famous Lenyadri caves are on the road that connects Junnar to Hadsar. The river across which the Manikdoh dam stands, faces the village of Hadsarwadi. The fort dates back to the Satavahana era. When, in 1637, Shahajirao Bhosale handed over five forts to the Mughals, this was one of them. With the arrival of the British the fort, along with the region in and around Junnar, fell into their hands.

There is an unbroken flight of stone steps to the fort. The original fort occupies an entire hill by itself. On the east, it is only in the gorge that it comes into contact with other hills. On all other sides, it is surrounded by rock faces. To the west, there is another mountain as high as Hadsar. The pass between these two peaks is interspersed with steps carved out from the rock at regular intervals.

Beyond the village of Hadsar, a rough track leads to where the hill has a cylindrical projection. The hamlet of Mundhewadi is nestled at its base. The path continues ahead along the projection till you reach the sheet of rock that marks the boundary of the fort. There are two water reservoirs. A narrow depression with about 100 steps is seen here. The steps take you to a massive wall. Carved out of solid rock, a grand entrance greets the visitor. This door has been chiselled out of a monolith. Another set of stone steps, and the margin of this wall is visible. From here, deep drops are seen both on the east and west, and a pathway has been roughly cut out along the hill slope.

A walk around the periphery of the fort reveals rough, torn rock edges and jagged shards of rock all around the fort. Probably for this reason, there are no signs of any major fortifications, since the fort is naturally well protected. The top fort is in the centre of the fort. At the foot of this hillock, there is a temple of Lord Mahadev in surprisingly good condition. The vast expanse of the Kukdi lake is clearly seen. There is a large dry water tank behind the temple. It takes an hour to walk around the circumference of the fort.

The flat part of the fort at the western edge has a tank. One can enter the tank with the help of convenient steps on one side. The water is clear and sweet. A little distance off, to the right, a sort of tunnel seems to have been dug out from the rock. At the other end, there is an underground clearing. Just opposite, a huge dark dungeon has been similarly carved out. Not just one, but actually three such underground cells exist. All of them have steps on one side. No light enters these rooms and they seem to have been constructed specially to serve as either secret cellars, or torture chambers for criminals and prisoners.

The locals have made an ingenious and no-fuss arrangement to reach the top of the fort. The eastern face of the fort shows a successive series of iron bars hammered into the hard rock wall. The height of over 100 feet can be negotiated by grabbing these bars, and finding footholds in the crevices and projections of the rock. Climbing up this way is an energy-sapping, but extremely thrilling experience. The inexperienced climber, however, is cautioned against attempting this climb, for it is slippery and the footholds are hard to negotiate. When you come up this way, the stone-walled water tank and the flat plateau at the top are seen. The western side of the fort offers a splendid view of distant and not-so-distant forts like Bhimashankar, Dhakoba, and Jeevdhan.

With your base as Junnar, a trip to Hadsar fort can be completed in a day. A visit to this little-known fort promises an altogether different experience.

Purandar

> **Fact File**
>
> *Best time- June to March*
>
> *Location - Close to Saswad near Pune*
>
> *Getting there - Motorable road till base of the fort, then an easy climb*
>
> *Where to stay- Saswad or Narayanpur*
>
> *Where to eat - Small canteens above but better to carry own food*

This is the mighty Purandar, pride of Maharashtra and the theatre of one of the most landmark victories for the Maratha empire. When Mirzaraje Jaising, with the help of Diler Khan, launched his campaign against Swarajya, this fort was a prime target for the rebels. With the capture of Vajragad, the noose around Purandar tightened. It was then that the legendary commander Murarbaji, with just 700 Maratha troops, faced the mighty strength of Diler Khan. The tale of this battle not only exists in folklore, but is celebrated in song and dance in Maharashtra.

Till as recently as 1976, there was an army post on the fort. Its strategic importance and the presence of soldiers on top made it out of bounds for commoners and tourists. Today, there is still a strong military presence on top, but the fort is open for trekkers, groups of tourists, and the local population. There is a motorable road right up to the top. You can also go up crosscountry. It takes an hour. The Murar Gate has sentries at attention. If permission is requested, they will let you in. The gate opens into a plain which has the Rajal lake. This was the stage where the lion-hearted Murarbaji, wielding two swords at a time, inspired his tough, wiry band of Mavlas to counter a big army with skill and bravery. A jet black statue, 5 feet tall, is installed here. It is an emotive sculpture, that floods one with poignant emotions and makes the mind wander back to the time when men like Murarbaji made the Maratha army the most feared and respected force of its era. The face of the statue seems flushed in the heat of battle, the passion of a man for whom nothing came before his pride and his supreme commander. It is extremely difficult to tear yourself away from this place, and when you do, it is with moist eyes and a heavy heart.

Purandar is close to Saswad, near Pune. The fort lies on the same mountain range as the Sinhagad fort. This ridge continues for around 15 to 20 kilometres and terminates at Bhuleshwar. The mountains contained by this ridge are crisscrossed by various passes like the Katraj ghat, the Bapdev, Dive, and Bor ghats. Close to the Bapdev ghat, the hills branch out in the north-south orientation, and a few kilometres on, there is a ridge perpendicular to this one. The two important bastions of the Maratha empire, Purandar and Vajragad, are situated in this mountain range.

The village of Narayanpur, or simple *Pur*, as it is casually referred to, was a prosperous town during the time of the Yadavas. The temple of Lord Narayan, nestled in a grove, is beautiful. The temple is designed in the Hemadpanti style and is believed to be at least 700 years old. There are some inscriptions in stone at the left side of the main door. There is a distinct connection between this text and the preachings of Changdev, a revered saint whose presence here is recorded around the same time as Sant Dnyaneshwar.

Purandar and Vajragad stand on the Indranil mountains. The Bhairavkhind pass acts as a natural barrier between the two. There are sentry posts throughout the area between the top and the bottom of the fort. These posts are called *Met* or *Chowkey*. The Teen Taki post lies to the east, Bavchi Met and Nirgud Met to the south, and Misal Met to the north-east.

Of the two routes to the top of Purandar, the one on foot will take you to the doorway. The Sar Darwaza will let you in. The Kandakada hill here stretches a 100 metres long but is just 3 to 4 feet wide. There is a water tank here and the informal, secret doorway to the north. The Sar Darwaza is followed by the Bini Darwaza. Going west, you can go around the entire fort and see the Nishana Buruz, Shendri Buruz, Hatti Buruz, Fatteh Buruz, and Konknya Buruz. The last of them, the Konknya Buruz, has a strong room constructed in stone and was probably used to detain prisoners. To the south of Fatteh Buruz stands the Kedar Darwaza. The Bor water tank too is nearby.

Apart from the Kandakada hill, the top of the fort also has two hillocks – the *Rajgadi* and the *Kedar Tekdi*. They stand at an altitude of 1500 metres. There used to be a mansion belonging to Chhatrapati Shivaji, on Rajgadi. Today it seems undisturbed by any human presence. The Purandar fort has an ample supply of potable water, for there are almost 50 water reservoirs here, some small, some larger. Notably, most of these are in good state. The fort also has the distinction of being a destination for the devout, with the shrines and temples of a number of gods and goddesses. Temples of Lord Kedareshwar, Narayan, Mhasoba, Hanuman, Ganesh and Goddess Lakshmi and Padmavati are located in close proximity to each other and dot the fort.

Though extremely derelict, one can still see remnants of the glory of Purandar in its heyday. The main hall atop the fort and the bungalow belonging to the Peshwas, are two of the many residential structures that stand, some of them merely stone plinths. The armoury, stockyard and godown, granary, ordnance depot, and check posts, are other buildings. These, together, made up a completely self-sufficient city that was well-equipped to face any invasion. The fort of Purandar is very long and extensive. Its age and time of construction dates back to the Yadav era.

The fort of Vajragad is a great deal smaller. It has a north-facing doorway flanked by towers on either side. Immediately after you enter this, there is another north-facing doorway. It is an arched structure with borders like tongues of fire. The doorway leads into the main fort of Vajragad on top. The area suddenly opens out to a number of sharp, tapering shards of rock and gigantic boulders. Purandar is easily visible from here. This place is the best location on Vajragad, from where you can spend some time looking at the magnificent walls of Purandar fort. One can descend from here by a small doorway – the Dindi Darwaza – to a lake. There are two temples—one of Lord Maruti and the other of Lord Rudreshwar. Both are placed to the south.

The fort, though small, is very well-protected by fortifications and five towers. There are three water tanks, of which only the one next to the temples, yields water. The other two are full of dirt and weeds.

Purandar, one of the oldest forts, was built during the Yadav era and as such, has witnessed many regimes. The Bahamani,

Nizamshahi, and Adil Shahi empires established supremacy from time to time and the fort eventually passed into the hands of the Marathas, under the leadership of Chhatrapati Shivaji, and subsequently, into the Peshwas' control. Sambhaji Maharaj, the son of Shivaji, was born here. In the years of Peshwa rule, the fort was the birthplace of yet another son of Maharashtra's Swarajya—Sawai Madhavrao Peshwa. As the Peshwas' sovereignty began to fade, it became the home for Gangabai, wife of Narayanrao Peshwa. It was because of this constant habitation that the fort was well maintained. The English, too, could not resist setting up a military outpost here. Today, the Indian Army has a strong contingent stationed here. However, today the areas outside the military jurisdiction, like the water reservoirs, the temples, and the buildings which still stand, are sadly derelict. Thus, despite its sheer size, a large and once well-equipped fort like Purandar, today, is desolate and wears an abandoned look. The Purandar fort, though massive and dominating the entire landscape, is surprisingly easy to climb and free from any dangerous curves or barriers. This, amongst many other reasons, makes a trek to Purandar one that you will never forget.

Ajinkyatara

Fact File

Best time- All seasons

Location - On the outskirts of Satara

Getting there - 15 minute drive from Satar town. ST buses to the top of the fort from Kolhapur.

Where to stay- Hotels in Satara

Where to eat - Hotels and eateries in Satara

Ajinkyatara was built in 1150, under the patronage of Raja Bhoj II. In a history spanning more than 800 years, the fort has witnessed regimes that changed from the Bahamani rule to the Adil Shahis, and ultimately, Maratha rule under Shivaji Maharaj. This fort, which is near Satara, is better known for being an important venue during the small and large battles waged during the reign of Rajaram Maharaj and later, Shahu Maharaj. In 1698,

Rajaram Maharaj made this fort his capital. It was around the same time that Aurangzeb, the emperor on the Delhi throne, personally led an assault on this fort. Unfortunately Rajaram Maharaj passed away at Sinhagad, but Ajinkyatara was defended valiantly by the fort's commander, Prayagji Prabhu. The Marathas were numerically no match for the massive infantry of Aurangzeb. Still, the Mavlas persisted, and it was only when the granary was empty, the armament exhausted, that Prayagji Prabhu conceded defeat. It was a typical battle of the Marathas, where no amount of statistical inferiority could dampen the passionate fighting spirit of these sons of Maharashtra. So it was that in 1700, the fort fell into Mughal control, and as was the practice, was promptly renamed *Azamtara*. The Marathas had not forgotten their loss, for a little later, the soldiers of Tararani, under the cover of disguise, entered the fort and claimed it. This time their leader was another fine warrior, Annajipant Shahir.

The fort, though now out of Mughal hands, was still to see a change of guard. The same Tararani, who wrested one of Maharashtra's best forts from Muslim rule, was ousted by Shahu Maharaj in 1708. He proclaimed himself king and his coronation was held in a grand ceremony atop the fort. Tararani was tragically destined to live a considerable part of her life in imprisonment within the same fort where she once reigned. The seeds of the Peshwa rule were sown here when the Bhat clan was given the designation of Peshwa and appointed the king's premier decision- makers. Bajirao I, whose tales inspire glowing chapters in Maharashtrian history, was accorded great honour and bestowed with fond gifts and praise.

In 1818, the British continued their domination over the entire country with the capture of Ajinkyatara. They installed a puppet governor, Pratapsingh, who later became a hostage of the British. This imprisonment has an intriguing tale. From 1840 to 1853, for 13 long years, an intrepid citizen named Rango Bapuji set up home in London and pleaded the cause of Pratapsingh, trying to convince the British Parliament that this decision had to be reviewed. He managed to collect 60,000 signatures and worked hard to make public all the details about this gross injustice. Around the same time, in 1847, the king of Satara passed away while in jail. Six years later, Rango Bapuji left the shores of London and returned to his country. All his resources, financial and otherwise, were finished and he was a broken man. It was a sad end to a valiant struggle, and perhaps in tribute of his unstinted show of support for his country, there is a memorial dedicated to him. It is located opposite the fort and is referred to as *Char Bhinti* by locals.

The fort has two doorways at opposite ends. There are temples of Manglai, Hanuman, and Mahadev. The collapsed walls of a building here hint at the palatial floors that it once housed. A huge storage for oil and ghee is kept nearby, along with a couple of reservoirs. The main doorway has an entrance porch with a stone plinth, on which is a tableau depicting the hand-to-hand fight between Vali and Sugreeva, a famous scene in the epic Ramayana. The adjacent towers display carvings of cobras.

Ajinkyatara is famous for an extremely moving statue of Chhatrapati Shivaji Maharaj. The usual depictions unfailingly show him astride his horse. The statue at this fort, however, is remarkably vivid and a splendid manifestation of all that this liberator of the Deccan achieved, and everything that he inspired in his land of hills and forts. It is truly unique and unduplicated anywhere else. A visit to the fort just to see this statue alone is well worth the effort. From the ramparts of Ajinkyatara, one can view the forts of Chandan-Vandan, Kalyangad, Yavateshwar, Jaranda, and Sajjangad.

Shivneri

The birthplace of the founder of Hindavi Swaraj, the site where the young Shivaji was deeply influenced by the teachings of his mother Jijabai – this is the fort of Shivneri, glowing with the tributes paid to it throughout its history.

The fort is three kilometres from Junnar. At an altitude of 1100 feet, there are two routes to the top of the fort. One path takes you via stone steps dug out from the natural strata. These steps date back to the Satavahana era. The second is a rough pathway that was extremely hazardous a few years back, but has been

Fact File

Best time- All year

Location - Three kms. from Junnar

Where to stay- MTDC resort.

Where to eat - MTDC restaurant, other eateries

improved in recent times with the help of a parapet and chain barricades. The fort has a total of seven doors – Maha Darwaza, Parvangicha Darwaza, Hatti Darwaza, Peer Darwaza, Shipai Darwaza, Phatak Darwaza, and Kulambkat Darwaza. The Maha Darwaza is closely followed by the Parvangicha Darwaza. The arched doorway has carved elephants on either side. The fifth doorway- the Shipai Darwaza, is halfway up the fort. It is an outstanding specimen of robust fortification. If you turn left from here, an arched doorway leads to the Shri Shivai Mandir. Until 1925, this fort too, was left to the vagaries of nature and was in a state of utter decline. That year, however, some attempt at conservation was made and after the formation of the state of Maharashtra, a good motorable road was made that reached right up to the main door of the fort. The year 1960 saw the unveiling of the statues of Jijamata and the little Shivaji. Every year, the birth celebrations of Chhatrapati Shivaji Maharaj take on colourful hue here; this is an excellent occasion to visit.

The fort tapers to one side. Its northern face is called Kadeloat. To scale the fort, you will have to negotiate a climb of 300 metres. A little before the northern face is reached, one comes to a huge lake — the Badami Talav. Around the lake are remnants of quarters and bungalows. It is here that Shivaji was born and spent some of his formative years. A considerable amount of renovation work has been carried out and a new two storeyed structure stands here. Its top floor has windows which afford a magnificent view of the landscape surrounding the fort. Perhaps, about 350 years ago, Shivaji and his mother Jijabai talked about many things here, in a time and era much removed from ours.

Shivneri has a number of underground caves. A road also traverses this fort, along the south of the Kala Thamba hill, and reaches Bhimashankar. By the side of the Mangni hills, nestles the Tulja hillock, providing a cosy backdrop for the temple of Goddess

Tulja. Shivneri is surrounded on all sides by forts and the top of Shivneri is a perfect place for spending a wonderful hour peering at these sights through a pair of binoculars. To the North lies Narayangad and Harishchandragad, to the west, Hadsar, Chavand, Jeevdhan, Bhairavgad, and to the south, Rajmachi point, Gorakshagad, Siddhagad, and Machhindragad. There are five dams in and around Shivneri — Vadaj, Yedgaon, Pimpalgaon, Manikdoh, and Dimbhe.

There are a total of 187 large and small forts in Maharashtra. A map showing the location of all these forts has been displayed atop the Shivneri fort. The speciality of this map, however, is that it is engraved on the ground. This map, the only one of its kind in the state, is more or less a physical representation of both, the geographical importance of such mighty sentinels, and an enduring symbol of a gallant history that saw the flag of Hindavi Swaraj flutter far and wide. Standing at the foot of this map, it is easy to imagine the mighty power of the Maratha regime under Chhatrapati Shivaji Maharaj.

In a strange irony, the very fort where Shivaji was born and took his first steps, could never be later claimed by him. In fact, his repeated attempts at the conquest of the fort proved futile. In 1673, Shivaji brought about the defection of the fort's keeper, Azizkhan, to the Maratha side. Not only this, in 1678, he laid siege to Junnar and marched ahead to mount a massive assault on the fort. Both these well-planned campaigns were in vain. The fort continued to be under the control of the Mughals. Finally, it was not until 1716, that Shahu Maharaj brought the fort back into the Maratha fold. Like other bastions of Shivaji's sprawling empire, Shivneri too, was controlled by the Peshwas for a brief period before falling into the hands of the British.

The Maharashtra Tourism Development Corporation (MTDC) has made good arrangements to stay atop the fort. Breakfast and lunch is also available. There is much for the tourist to see. An arch shows Mughal influence, towering over a water tank that is heavily reminiscent of the Yadav era. The Ganga-Jamuna reservoir, and the Idgah at the central square of the fort, are some of the sights that will make your sojourn here a highly enjoyable one.

Besides, the fact that you are in the very place where one of India's greatest kings was born, is an exhilarating feeling.

Devgiri

> **Fact File**
> *Best time- June to March*
> *Location - On the road connecting Aurangabad and Verul.*
> *Getting there - Aurangabad is a 12 hour drive from Mumbai; by road from Aurangabad to Verul.*
> *Where to stay- MTDC tourist home, a forest rest house, a PWD guesthouse at Khuldabad.*
> *Where to eat - Restaurants at the resorts and tourist houses*

A heavily-guarded and impregnable fort, Devgiri is unmatched anywhere else in Maharashtra for the methods used by its rulers to deceive, mislead, and ultimately rout an advancing army. Its ramparts are almost two kilometers long, and with a good motorable road reaching up to the top, it provides an exciting tour.

Devgiri lies on the road connecting Aurangabad and Verul. The massive stronghold that you see on the left, becomes clearly visible as you ascend the ghat that heads towards Verul. The fort at the top stands on a hillock roughly 700 feet high. Right in front is a 200 feet tall *minar* in light pink. This tower has four floors and tapers towards the top. There are steps to go up and until a few years ago, tourists were allowed to climb the minaret. Recently, however, this has been disallowed.

The Devgiri fort possesses three doors and a sturdy set of ramparts. At the top, the Hatti Haud was a place reserved for tying up elephants and allowing them to rest. There is a Bharatmata Mandir with a well next to it. As you go towards the fort, the Chinese Mansion is hard to miss. It once served as a prison for Yesubai and Shahu Maharaj, who were kept here under house arrest. From here, the thrills begin. Before you can enter the gates of the fort, a 45 feet-deep trench has to be bridged. This moat had a wooden drawbridge which can be lowered and raised. A little ahead, there is a tunnel, 125 feet in length, with the disquieting name of *Andhari* (darkness). There are a number of paths beginning here that lead nowhere-they were obviously meant to confuse an approaching band of soldiers. The correct path leads to a huge iron pan. This pan could be heated red hot to either kill the enemy or drive them away in terror. Besides, there is a concealed set of openings just above this spot from where boiling oil or water could be poured to badly scald the enemy army down below. And if the unfortunate enemy escaped the dual attacks of insufferable heat and jump into the moat below for relief he would be torn into bits by the waiting jaws of the many crocodiles that lurked in the dark waters below. A more formidable arrangement is not to be found in any other fort in Mahararashtra. Apart from these obstacles, the host army at the fort would be waiting to welcome the invaders with cannon, while foot soldiers were always in readiness, armed with swords, spears and fireballs. Against today's backdrop of technological warfare, it takes a lot of imagination to understand the kind of hostilities that existed 700 years ago. The typical army man had to be a physically tough and an expert in his weaponry, but also had to have the psychological motivation and high morale required to brave such a barbaric end.

Even now, it is with a flaming hand-held m*ashal* that the guide will lead you up this *Andhari* tunnel to the top of the fort, after, of course, stepping over the huge iron pan. The summit has a formal *darbar,* the royal court, and a cannon — the Durga cannon. There is also a *samadhi* of Janardan guru, the mentor of Sant Eknath.

The fort is said to have been completed in the reign of Bhillam Yadav. It was built on plain land, unlike most of Maharashtra's hill forts, and was originally named Devgiri. The fort was deemed impregnable, until in 1294, the ruler, Ramdevraya, along with his son Shankar Dev Raya, had to face a humiliating defeat at the hands of the Muslim commander, Allauddin Khilji. The fort was looted and its treasury laid bare. The fort then came under the Nizamshahi rule.

Devgiri is halfway along the road from Aurangabad and Verul. At Khuldabad, which is close to the fort, there is an MTDC tourist home. One can also stay at the Forest Rest house, or the PWD guest house. A trip to both, the Ajanta caves, as well as the Devgiri fort, can be completed in a day. At the fort, leisurely scan every corner, and you'll come out feeling you've been in a totally different world !

Kothligad

> **Fact File**
>
> *Best time- June to March*
>
> *Location - Ambivali*
>
> *Getting there - Two hour drive from Mumbai or by suburban train; ST bus from Karjat via Kashele to Ambivali.*
>
> *Where to stay- No place to stay atop the fort.*
>
> *Where to eat - Carry your own food and water.*

The Sahyadris extend from Bhimashankar to Rajmachi. The fortress of Kothligad is a little removed from this main artery of the Sahyadri mountains. It is also smaller compared to the more massive, dominating forts of this range. Nevertheless, its importance as a strategic point for reconnaissance was matched only by its usefulness as a specially-designed place to stock armaments and ordnance.

The little village of Peth, at the foot of the fort, is itself at a considerable height. The climb from here to the fort, is therefore not much of an ascent. The fort resembles the fort of Karnala and has a cave and a water tank. The mouth of the cave reveals a temple of Lord Bhairoba. There are 5 delicately carved pillars within, with an idol of Goddess Janai. The summit of the fort shows some ruins and a water tank. From here, one can clearly see the side of Sahyadris that meets Bhimashankar, along the east. Kothligad is joined to this primary branch of the Sahyadris, by the Vandre pass. To the west, the ridge from Hajimalang to Matheran is seen. The fort was constructed in the Satavahana era.

One can drive up this fort or take a State Transport bus from Karjat, via Kashele, and stop at Ambivali. From there to the hamlet of Peth, it is a climb of 3 kilometres. From Peth, you can scale the summit in half an hour. Peth is famous for its fresh *khoya* and its milk. A trip to the fort can be completed within a day from Pune or Mumbai.

Chanderi

Chanderi is distinguished by its razor sharp edges and the degree of difficulty in climbing it. It lies on the Sahyadri ridge

Fact File

Best time- June to March

Location - Panvel, between Matheran and Haji Malang.

Getting there - Alight at Vangani on the Mumbai-Karjat suburban train route and walk to Chincholi.

Where to stay- Caves at the top.

Where to eat - Carry your own food. Water is available in tanks atop the fort.

between Matheran and Hajimalang. The fort is almost as high as Matheran, about 2500 feet high. Chanderi comes under the taluka of Panvel. If you alight at the railway station of Vangni on the Karjat-Mumbai rail route, you simply have to follow the railway tracks until you reach Goregaon. Take the left track to Chincholi. A path from here will take you inside a cave adjacent to a sheer rock face. The cave contained a *Shivalinga* and a statue of Nandi the bull. The *Shivalinga* is now in a very dilapidated state, while the idol of Nandi has disappeared. Near the cave, there is a water tank which even today has clear water.

Walk ahead and you can reach the base of this cliff. There is another cave here with a water reservoir. The cliff is narrow and steep. Recently, a large part of the rock wall simply gave way, and since then it has become even more dangerous to access this part of the fort. The east shows the union of the two rivers – the Lendi, and the Gaadhi. The fort is completely devoid of any sort of elaborate fortifications. There are no signs either of any man-made structures atop the fort. While the east has Matheran, Prabalgad, and the lake of Konadle Pajhar, the west shows the plateau of Bhimashankar, Siddhagad, Gorakshagad, the fort of Peth, and Vishalgad.

Though the fort is very desolate, it is possible to spend a night in the cave, with its supply of water. The *Chanderi* restaurant on the way to the fort, too, offers excellent hot meals. The fort's rugged loneliness alone makes it a favourite for the diehard trekker or rock climber. Once on the top, you have only the whistling breeze and the clouds for company—therein lies its true beauty.

Manikgad

Fact File

Best time- June to March

Location - Very close to Karnala, visible from the Mumbai-Pune Expressway. .

Getting there - On the old Mumbai-Pune highway get down at Chowk, a 10 km trek from here

Where to stay - Day trip. There is no place to stay.

Where to eat - Carry your own food and water

As you cruise along the Pune-Mumbai highway and go towards Pune, the stretch after Panvel begins to reveal the summits of a number of familiar forts. To the left you will see Prabalgad, Matheran, Irsalgad, and to the right, the 'Thumbs Up' sign of Karnala, and the dome of Manikgad. After the expressway, this fort seems even closer now.

The fort, which is 1900 feet high, rises a straight 1200 feet from its foothills. Vehicles can be driven until you reach the village of Vadgaon. The Patalganga bridge connects this small hamlet from the Chowk village. A road skirts Chowk, which is on the Mumbai- Pune highway, and turns to the right to join the Patalganga bridge. There is another route that continues from the Khopoli- Pen road, via the Varsai-Ghote village, to the fort. The western side of the fort shows a rock face, 150 feet high. The valley on the east of the fort can be reached by trekking along a western projection and continuing along the edge of the rock wall. This valley is thickly forested. It now takes half-an-hour to reach the top of the fort. There are signs of some fortifications and a water tank. The main entrance of the fort has the image of Lord Ganesh carved here. To the north, Matheran, Prabalgad, and Irsalgad dot the landscape. Far below, the large expanse of the Reliance Industries plant is seen faintly. Karnala's thumb shape juts out to the west. The principal mountain range in the Sahyadris lies to the north-east. A path taken through the Ghote village can also give you a tour through the fort of Sankshi Badruddin.

The entire area of Manikgad fort is ideal for a day-long trek from Mumbai. The Savne lake to the western foothills of the fort is an excellent and convenient picnic spot.

Bhairavgad

> **Fact File**
>
> *Best time- June to March*
>
> *Location - Close to Chiplun and Koynanagar.*
>
> *Getting there - ST to Koynanagar via Karad and to Helvak.From Helvak it is a one day trek*
>
> *Where to stay- Bhairav mandir close to the fort*
>
> *Where to eat - Carry own food*

The Pune-Kolhapur highway and Mumbai-Goa highway both connect Chiplun to the stretch of Karad Koynanagar-Helwak. Bhairavgad is located at an altitude of around 1000 metres to the south east of Navja.

There is a State Transport bus service from Koynanagar to Helvak. In half an hour you can cross the river here and reach Kondhavle. The hamlet of Mendheghar lies on the way. Follow the stream and you reach Ramghal. This place has a perennial source of water in the form of a natural spring. The basin of the Koyna river makes a lovely picture from here.

The road to Bhairavagad is a nature lover's dream, with its thick undergrowth. The jungle gives way to the village of Vaghne. To the left is a spot where the stream originates, and Patharpunj to Bhairavgad is a broad stretch that leads to the mouth of the spring. At the end of the ghat, stands the temple of Bhairoba. Not far away, is a small brook whose water can be used for drinking. The hill on which Bhairavgad stands is a little removed from the main ridge of the Sahyadri mountain range. One can descend the valley on the left and emerge from the right side of the brook.

The western face of Bhairavgad has a water tank. The fort of Prachitgad is seen to the south. From the temple of Bhairoba, you can walk down the Bhairavghat to reach Durgavadi, from where a State Transport bus will take you to Chiplun.

Alibag

Fact File

Best time- All year round

Location - Alibag

Getting there - Two hour drive from Mumbai (110 kms.) ST bus to Alibag. Except during monsoon by motorboat from Bhaucha dhakka to Revas. Then by bus to Alibag (Two hours totally)

Where to stay- Several good hotels.

Where to eat - Restaurants and hotels at Alibag.

The Alibag fort is a fine example of a stronghold that is almost amphibious in character. At high tide, the fort is surrounded by the foaming Arabian sea, and its turrets keep an eagle eye on oceanic traffic. During low tide, the fort assumes the identity of a territorial bastion. Also, it then seems surprisingly close to the coastline and accessible too. This rock steady sentry beckons the first time visitor and is an irresistible tourist attraction.

The fort was conceived in 1681, when Shivaji Maharaj took a personal interest in the construction of this Maratha naval base, which was built near an island in the seas of Mauje Navghar. The fort replaced what was earlier a military post under the command of Bhivji Gujar. Half a kilometre from the beach, Kulaba is within walking distance during the ebb, and one can even take a ride in a horse cart, right up to the stone walls.

The principal doorway faces north-east. There are carvings of a peacock, elephant, deer and tiger. The doorway at the terminal end even has a pair of crocodiles engraved on it. This carving makes a strong statement, symbolic of the supremacy of the Marathas on land and on the high seas. Immediately after the first doorway comes a second one. A temple of Devi Padmavati stands here. Some distance away there is a man-made lake. Today a thick layer of moss and silt clouds the surface, but the nearby well receives water from the lake, water that is filtered and purified many times over. It is sweet to taste and fresh. It is one example of the amount of thought that went into the planning and design of a seafort. The rear side of this rectangular tank shows ruins of what was once the ancestral home of Kanhoji Angre, the legendary naval commander who outfoxed his foes and virtually ruled the seas. The Angres, whose exploits and naval prowess were unmatched, took pride in the upkeep and maintenance of Kulaba, which was in fact, one of their favoured forts.

A walk around the fort is humbling, forcing you to pay obeisance to nature. The sea breeze that blows from the west spatters you with spray, while the eye travels endlessly beyond the blue expanse, where sky meets the ocean. The not-so-distant beach and tree-lined shores blend perfectly.

Today, save for the devotees who come to the two temples in it, there is hardly any human presence on Kulaba fort. Yet, its grandeur and strategic importance are immediately evident from the nature of the buildings that still stand there and the battlements at the edges. The Angres gave the fort affluence and a prestige that made it one of the most influential naval bases of the time. The fort was ravaged not once, but three times by a fire that consumed the Angre's *wada*, leaving nothing in its wake. There was a period of neglect and the slow slide into decay began. It is a tale that has been repeated rany times over at most of Maharashtra's forts. Amazingly, two temples, one of Devi Padmavati, and the other of Lord Ganesh, are still well preserved and in fact important places of worship. The Ganesh temple is the fruit of the efforts of the local fisherman community who took it upon themselves to restore the temple, by installing a few modern amenities.

The Kulaba fort is accessible, but it is extremely important to have accurate information about the exact timings of low or high tide. The period of high tide can be calculated by multiplying the date on that particular day (according to the Hindu calendar) by three- quarters. Four hours after this, one can safely go into the fort. This 'safe period' lasts for between two to three hours. After that, however, the waves start hitting the shore and it is high tide. I would like to caution the reader about the treacherous water by citing the experience that our team had whilst shooting for the travel serial *Bhatkanti*.

We went into the fort with all the paraphernalia for filming and everything went as planned. Our task completed, we retraced our steps and found to our dismay that high tide had begun to

Saandan

Saaswad: darshan of Kaanifnath

Bhuleshwar: where the *pedhas* disappear!

Atop Nanacha angtha

Green Valley Resort

come in. While the sandy banks had welcomed us when we arrived, there was now water making its way to the shore in rising waves. Alibag beach seemed tantalizingly near, and we fearlessly began our way towards land. What followed was a nerve-racking drama that haunted us for a long time.We were wading through the salty water and slowly but surely inching towards the beach. The water was now chest high. The waves were crashing in ominous monotony, but we continued. Now, in the sandy shallows of the patch between the fort and the coast, there is a slight depression which goes unnoticed at low tide. At high tide, however, the water gathers around this ditch and what results is a treacherous whirlpool lurking to trap the foolhardy swimmer. Unawares, we began to advance towards this and it was only the yelling and shouting of our guide from the fort that stopped us in our tracks. We looked around to see him desperately waving his arms and signalling to us to return to the fort. We immediately turned around and began to half swim, half walk back to the fort. The waves thudded against our bodies and refused to let us progress, but we held on to each other and to this day, I'm not sure how we came back to the safety of the fort. Every sense was tingling, and when the guide explained the situation to us, we realized that we had, well and truly, come back from what was a certain, watery, death. It was a sobering experience and one that none of us is likely to forget.

The Alibag fort has a secondary fort-like bastion, called Sarjecoat, which also has ramparts. There is a water reservoir in the centre. To the north, Khanderi, Underi, and to the south, Kornai, are three sea fortresses that are visible from here. The fort still has two cannons at one corner. The cannons once boomed right across the vast blue expanse of the sea, and their gun power and accuracy ruled the waves, instilling fear into any audacious intruder who dared to challenge the mighty Maratha naval might. The cannons have their English markings intact, and one can't help but linger here for a few minutes to touch them, and feel their strength.

I have been to Alibag on numerous occasions in the past, and have seen the city evolving from a primarily fishing and trading community post that it was, to a modern city growing with the times. Six-seaters and rickshaws have spawned and hotels, resorts, and eat-outs have added to the ambience of Alibag as a destination for an invigorating weekend. The famous Birla temple and the exquisitely – planned temple campus is also a very good place to visit. The Birla Ispat factory is an important plant that turns out steel coils, and the temple has been built under the patronage of the Birla company. It has a unique design and is spread over several acres.

Apart from the leisure activities that are slowly putting Alibag on the tourist's list of 'must see' spots, another institution that has made the place famous is the Magnetic Observatory. The first director of the academy, N.A.F.Mus, graduated from the Government college of Engineering, Pune, in 1896, and devoted the next twenty three years to the observatory. There is a small museum here, with exhibits mainly including the instruments that Mus and his team of dedicated scientists used to study magnetism. There are a number of rare manuscripts, the first issue of *Nature* magazine, a huge pair of binoculars, and even the skeleton of a dinosaur. The academy has sent a team on an expedition to Antarctica. The specimens they collected there are displayed here, and include the bones of the krill fish, and some rocks. Like the rest of the world, the observatory now uses computers on a large scale, but in its formative years and later too, many hands and minds worked in tandem to achieve results of studies that ranged from the oceanic movements to the tidal waves. The spirit of Dr.Mus's work continues to inspire present-day academicians at the institute and the current director is determined to continue the mission that his illustrious predecessor began.

Alibag has much to offer, and to satiate your appetite, it is essential to set up camp here for a day or two. The numerous beaches of Alibag have a character of their own - some of them are quiet and tree-lined, some are commercial hot spots with the ubiquitous *bhel puri* stalls and Chinese food shacks. The Alibag fort, the Birla temple, the Magnetic Oservatory, and the recently established excellent resorts give a tourist a wide choice. For the large group on a tour, there are several two-star hotels like the Meera Madhav that will offer good food and good service. The beautiful Kihim beach has an MTDC resort. Such is the magic of this coastal town that you will want to return again and again.

Sindhudurg

> **Fact File**
>
> *Best time- All year round*
>
> *Location - Sindhudurg*
>
> *Getting there - ST bus to Malvan or by train*
>
> *Where to stay- Resort on the fort.*
>
> *Where to eat - Eatery at the resort*

As the flag of Hindavi Swaraj began to be unfurled in one area after another, the reach of Shivaji Maharaj spread far and wide. Most of the territory in and around Maharashtra, right up to the Deccan, was under Maratha rule. In this scenario, foreign invaders like the English, Portuguese, Dutch, and the Siddis, were waiting to oust the Marathas from their forts and fortresses. Shivaji, therefore, decided that if Hindavi Swaraj was to have a truly national presence, it was not enough to rule the land – it was imperative to have control of the large coastline. With this in view, he decided not only to capture seaforts held by the enemy but to build a strong, impregnable fort that would give him invincible access to the seas. In 1664, the plans for such a stronghold were finalized, and the construction continued until 1667. This was named Sindhudurg.

The circumference of the fort measures 3.5 – 4.0 kilometres. There are 42 turrets and the ramparts rise upto a massive 35-40 feet. As in the Janjira fort, one has to reach the fort by a ferry. The sea between the fort and the shore is beset with jagged rocks and undercurrents and it is only an experienced boatman who can negotiate these hurdles and safely carry his passengers to the huge black walls of Sindhudurg.

The main entrance faces east. On entering, there are two temples in close vicinity to each other. One is the temple of Maruti and the second is a shrine of Jarimari. To the right, a tower has two dome-shaped structures. In the upper dome is embossed the right palm of Chattrapati Shivaji and in the lower dome, the print of his right foot. A coconut tree stands between these domes and the temple of Shivrajeshwar. This temple was built by Rajaram. This fort is noteworthy for preserving some of the objects that Shivaji actually used. The temple has a statue depicting the Chhatrapati in a *Veerasan* position. Shivaji's sheathed sword is also kept here.

One needs little imagination to conjure up the vision of a fiery Shivaji wielding the sword and inspiring his band of Mavla fighters to great victories.

There are a number of freshwater wells on the fort, by the names of Dudhbav, Sakharbav, and Dahibav. One can climb the ramparts, there being a total of 45 sets of steps. To the rear of Dudhbav, there is a lake and the Nishan Buruz. There is a small path leading to a small sand bank. This was the lagoon which served as a bathing pool for women of the royal family. It is called *Ranichi Vela*.

It takes two to three hours to see the fort properly. Fortunately, one can stay at this fort, which doubles the enjoyment. With the vast sea on all sides, even a few hours, halt is exciting .

Vasota

Fact File

Best time- June to March

Location - 35 kms. from Satara

Getting there - Boat ride from Bamnoli that is 35 kms. from Satara town.

*Where to stay- Satara***

*Where to eat - Satara****

Deep within forest covering on all sides, the Vasota fort was once a penal colony. Its history dates back to 1170, when Raja Bhoj of Kolhapur's Shilahar dynasty began to construct a fort. Twenty three years later, in 1193, the fort was complete. In 1665, the fort was captured by Chhatrapati Shivaji. During the Peshwa rule, the fort was used to keep jailed British soldiers. In 1817, the British forces launched an all-out attack on the fort, and the effort paid off. The fort fell into the hands of the English invaders. The British, in a spate of bombardments, destroyed all structures on the fort. One of the dwellings that suffered this onslaught was a palatial bungalow belonging to a danseuse called Tai Telin. All that remains of this once luxuriously-appointed house, is the plinth.

Vasota, surrounded by thick forest cover and a number of water bodies, is accessible by boat from Bamnoli, which is 35 kilometres from the town of Satara. A 15-kilometre boat ride will take you to the foothills of Vasota fort. The lake is the Shivsagar lake, one mouth of which forks into the forest around Vasota. The rivulet that flows down the sides of Vasota empties into the Shivsagar lake. Following the rivulet takes you to the Handal post. This was an important toll gate and checkpost. Today, only stone ruins remain. The canal continues further to snake past a dilapidated temple of Lord Hanuman.

The climb to the fort begins here. For a good three kilometres, it is a steady climb. The climb further on, however, will test your fitness, for the path is now overgrown with weeds, and there is no beaten track, leaving the trekker to find his own way. The path stops at a *Dindi-Darwaza* – the door within a door. The fort has a temple of Lord Maruti here, and a small freshwater spring. The water in this natural lake is fresh and sweet, making your climb well worth the effort. There are lots of trees within the fort, including mango and gooseberry. The thicket of shrubs and grass spreads all over the fort.

A walk up from here leads you to the precipice of the fort, the Babukada. This is at a height of 1800 metres above sea-level. The old Vasota fort can now be seen, beyond this side of the ridge. It has excellent forest cover on top. The fort is surrounded by naturally well-planed edges of rock that fortify it and make for naturally-formed ramparts. The precipice shows a distinct red pattern in the rocks. This red belt continues and can be seen in the Sahyadri range, right upto Nashik.

At this height, all that one hears is the whistling breeze and the silence of the forest. The view is simply astounding. The wind can blow away a blanket and comes straight at you like a hurricane, rising up the valley with a speed that can jolt the unprepared. A coin, tossed down, will swish right back. To the left, the dense jungles of Redeghat are visible on a clear day. The Konkankada, a sheer cliff on the fort of Harishchandragad, is the highest ridge in Maharashtra, with the Babukada the second-highest. On the western façade of Vasota, stands the broken masonry of Tai Telin's bungalow. A path leads from here to a stone temple of the Mahadevi Chandika. The battlement tower in front of the temple offers a magnificent view of the Shivsagar lake and the entire Koyna reserve forest area. The temple is one of the most serene places from which to watch a sunset. For this and its pristine isolation, the centuries-old temple is often used by true nature lovers as a stopover. The night sky is aglow with a million stars, and its sheer beauty and splendour is hard to describe.

Since the Vasota fort is situated within the Koyna forest reserve, part of the fort's natural wealth is shared. After descending part of the fort, the path forks to the left. It is this route that will take you through a forest that is not only rich in its trees and plant life, but will take your breath away with its isolation. For a good five kilometres, the forest path will bring out the true wanderlust and footloose spirit in every trekker. Absolutely removed from all worldly things, it's just you, the elements, and this forest cover. Where the path reaches an edge, there is a cave—the shrine of Lord Nageshwar. The rock that makes the roof of this cave lets in a steady trickle of drops in the rains, offering *Abhishek* to the Lord. In the summer, the cool insides of the cave are ultimate bliss. Down below, the valley shows the expanse of Chiplun. Look to the left, and you can see the fort of Vasota that you had just visited.

The road down the cave quickly leads to the place where you left your boat. The same ride back, and you are in Bamnoli. Vasota is a fine example of a fort that complements its wild setting. In any season, this fort, situated right amidst the vast Koyna forest reserve, is something that you will treasure for its past and present glory.

Vishalgad

There are three main places of paramount historical importance that are said to have shaped the fortunes of the glorious Maratha history. Panhala, Pavankhind, and Vishalgad, in the monsoon of 1660 were to become immortal in the Maratha annals of bravery and martyrdom. It was the twelfth of July of that year. Shivaji was held captive by Siddi Johar, and with daredevil planning, it was decided to place Shiva Nhavi, a lookalike of Shivaji, in the palace while the real Chhatrapati was whisked out. The quick exchange took place but Siddi Johar's troops got wind of the escape and set off in hot pursuit of the fugitive. The pass of Pavankhind stood between the Chhatrapati and the advancing Siddi army.

Fact File

Best time- June to March

Location - Kolhapur (385 kms. from Mumbai)

Getting there - Drive from Kolhapur via Malkapur and Pandarpani.

Where to stay - Small sanatorium on top

Where to eat - Small eateries at the fort

What followed was a chapter written in letters of gold but drenched in the blood of hundreds of soldiers who perished in the pounding rain and resounding battle cries of that *Ashadi Poornima*. Bajiprabhu Deshpande, commander-in-chief, requested the king to carry on while he held off the pursuing army as long as he could. Shivaji and his retinue hurried towards Vishalgad, after promising to signal their safe arrival at the fort with the sound of cannonfire.

It was clearly a fight to the finish. The furious Siddi army met the Marathas head on. Bajiprabhu Deshpande was like a man possessed — the life of his supreme commander was at stake, his *Matrubhumi* was clamouring for his courage, and steely resolve coursed in his veins. Amidst rain that blinded the vision and lightning that made communication impossible, Bajiprabhu and his handful of gallant Mavlas fought like demons in the treacherous terrain of that mountain pass. As the violent fighting raged on, the skies resounded with the distant booms of cannons, in the direction of Vishalgad. The Chhatrapati had reached safely! It was the signal Bajiprabhu had been waiting for. Wounded but victorious in his mission, he succumbed to grievous injuries and fell fighting. There were many bravehearts who died with him that dreadful night. It was the end of a giant among warriors and the legend of Bajiprabhu Deshpande of Pavakhind will be retold to children for many more centuries. Such is the aura of Vishalgad and Pavankhind, where even the breeze whispers memories of the twelfth of July, 1660. One's heart and mind are completed enraptured just gazing at the rocks and soil where this scene was enacted more than three centuries ago.

The road from Kolhapur to Vishalgad meets the one coming from Panhala. Kolhapur-Malkapur is 45 kilometres while Malkapur to Pandharpani is 13 kilometres. Vishalgad is 18 kilometres from Pandharpani. Malkapur is thus about 31 kilometres from Vishalgad. The road continues to the foothills of Vishalgad and you can drive up and park here. There is sufficient parking space at this point. It is only when one comes very close to the fort that it emerges from the shadows and cluster of surrounding cliffs and mountain ranges and becomes visible. Vishalgad itself is connected0 to the main Sahyadri range by a narrow projection. From this point, there is a climb of 300 steps. It takes about half an hour. The ascent also includes two iron ladders. Vishalgad is at an altitude of 3500 kilometres above sea-level; 14 kilometres short of Vishalgad, a rough cross-country track leads to the Pavankhind pass. There is also a path, two kilometres from the nearby village of Gajapur from where one can reach this mountain crossing. The pass is a difficult one, even in broad daylight, and the uneven and craggy edges deter even normal climbing. How such a fiery combat could take place in darkness, with rain pelting down, and with so much at stake, is beyond comprehension. Even a few moments spent here make you salute the memory of those brave men, before you continue to the main fort.

The main doorway has disappeared with time, but to the right, the Mundha Darwaza is still visible. The tomb of Malik Rehan, surrounded by smaller kiosks, attracts a lot of devotees both Hindu and Muslim. The kiosks provide food and shelter. To the rear of the tomb, a path carved out of the rock passes by a temple of Lord Mahadev, to enter the Patal Lok valley. At the summit of this valley, a small field has memorials of Bajiprabhu Deshpande and Phulaji. This valley has thick green cover, and from the top, near the memorials, the entire valley can be seen. In the monsoon, the heavy rainfall rejuvenates many lofty waterfalls. To the north of the tomb, a brisk walk reveals the memorial of Ahilyabai, the wife of Chhatrapati Rajaram who immolated herself after the latter's demise. A little below, one can see the edge of Vishalgad that protrudes into the Konkan. This precipice has a number of small and large naturally carved upright stone slabs. The locals call this tableau a *varaat* or a wedding procession. It is said that an ancient sage cursed a wedding party and as a result, they were transformed into stone. The crown of the fort has a crescent-shaped lake and another, Bhupal lake, credited to a King Bhupal who is said to have dug it. The bank of the lake has a temple of Lord Shiva. The temples of Vaghjai, Narsoba, Maruti, are among many other temples found on the fort.

Vishalgad was built by Raja Bhoj of the Shilahar dynasty. In the year 1689, it was captured by Aurangzeb. Much later, the fort was gifted by the ruler of Kolhapur to the family of Pantpratinidhis. A path leading down the tower of Pusati at Panhala continues 7 kilometres to the flat land of Mhasai. From here, Mandalakhadi is 13 kilometres away. Pandharpani, which is 5 kilometres from Pavankhind, is 12 kilometres from Mandalkhadi. If you take the route via Gajapur, it is a 55-kilometre-long trek.

Every year, scores of young trekkers, brimming with enthusiasm, choose the pouring rains of July to make a commemorative trek from Panhala to Vishalgad, via Pavankhind. It is this spirit that helps us appreciate the true harmony between historical and natural wealth. At Vishalgad, both are in abundance.

T E M P L E S

TEMPLES

Kankeshwar

Fact File

Best time- All year round

Location - Alibag

Getting there - From Alibag ST bus to village Mapgaon on Alibag-Rewas road

Where to stay- Dharmashalas and private residences provide food and lodging

Well-known for its pleasant climate, Kankeshwar is also famous for its ancient temple. There are two ways to get there from Alibag. Near the Munivali junction on the Alibag-Rewas road, about 4 kilometres away from the Karle Khind is a small road to the left marked by a signpost saying 'Kankeshwar-3 kms'. This 12-kilometre stretch of road takes you to Mapgaon. Plenty of State Transport buses ply on this route. Mapgaon is the village at the foot of the hill on which Kankeshwar is located at a height of about 1,200 feet. Just beyond the railway line are the 700-750 steps leading to Kankeshwar. After a short climb you come across two samadhis (tombstones) of Mohanagiri and Balgiri, two sadhus (holy men) belonging to the Karnatak Gosavi Sect. Another 500 feet later is the Nagobacha Tappa. According to folklore the resident cobras congregate at this spot for the festival of Nagpanchami. Further up is the Jambhalica Tappa and about 100 feet further, is the Devachi Payri (God's step). On this step is embedded a footprint. A rich devotee Govind Revadas built these steps in 1764. He was the treasurer to Sardar Raghoji Angre, the Governor of Alibag. It is said that on completion of these steps God himself visited the place and gave it his blessing by leaving behind a footprint!

Near the top of the hill is Gai Mandi where there is a sculpture of a cow. There is a drinking-water tap near here. Looking south from this spot you can see Sagargad, also known as Kheddurg fort. The road from Gai Mandi to the Kankeshwar temple is through a dense growth of trees. Just before the main temple is a Maruti Temple and a bramhakund (water tank). The actual location of the temple is very interesting. The stone temple is built in the Hoysala style of architecture. There is an octagon-shaped tank that contains water all the year round.

To the west of the temple is the residence of the temple priest Mr. Vaishampayan. A short walk away are the temples of Patrubai and Mahayogini Manamata. There is a dust path, which goes down to the Alibag-Rewas road through a thick forest. There are a few dharmashalas (ashrams) and private residence near the temple. It is possible to stay here at a reasonable cost.

Just behind the temple is a path leading into the forest. A ten-minute walk down this path leads to Gaimukh where water falls into a tank from the mouth of a stone cow. The view from here includes the sea and the forts of Khanderi and Underi and the Rashtriya Chemical Fertiliser plant at Thal. There is a big plateau known as Vyaghreshwar Pathar to the east of Kankeshwar. The highest point in the area, it also has a small temple. The Department of Railways has leased out land from the temple authorities for a Microwave Link Station. There is another route from Narangi village to Kankeshwar, via this plateau, but it is not greatly used. Kankaeshwar boasts a very pleasant climate all year round but is especially enjoyable just after the rains. The entire area is very similar to Mahabaleshwar and Bhimashanker. A lovely place for a short two-day break.

Pateshwar

There are several tourist spots near Satara. Of these one of my favourites is Pateshwar. I fell in love with this extremely peaceful, ancient town on my first visit. To the south-east of Satara, this 3,500 foot-high hill is clearly visible from the additional MIDC area of Satara City. A 14-kilometre stretch of road from Satara goes directly to Pateshwar. About 4 kilometres from MIDC is the village of Degaon Pateshwar, another 2 kilometres ahead is a *kuchha*

Fact File

Best time- All year round

Location - South East of Satara

Getting there - A good tarred road till MIDC Satara, then a kutcha motarable road to village Degaon Pateshwar

Where to stay- Temple on top

Where to Eat -- Temple staff provide food on order but it is better to carry your own food

ghat road. A motorcycle or jeep can reach this point. The one-kilometre stretch after this point has to be completed on foot. An abundance of trees, with the Sagwan quite prominent, covers the hill. Behind the hill on a slight slope is a dense forest in which a large variety of birds can be spotted, among them the Red Vented Bulbul, Crested Lark, peacocks and skylarks. As the path begins there are several small temples dedicated to Ganesh,

Riddhi and Siddhi. A short walk through the forest on the plateau brings you to an ancient pond full of lotus flowers.

After this to the right, are the steps of the ancient Pateshwar temple. It is possible to see the entire temple if you climb a little further. Encircled by trees, the architecture of the temple and its sculptures is quite astounding. Outside the temple Nandi the Bull in black stone makes one marvel at the skill of the workmen who sculpted it.

The most unique aspect of this temple is the numerous *shivlings* sculpted here. To the east of the main temple in what is called the Varhad ghar (groom's residence), are literally thousands of *shivlings*. From a tiny one the size of a thumb to a huge one nearly five-foot high, the shivlings fill the room. No one knows who the sculptor was.

Villagers tell an amusing tale about the thousands of statues. In ancient times, they say there were several thousand gods residing here. A devotee came with a sack of rice grains. He began placing one grain on each god's hand. Unfortunately he ran out of grains when there was just one god left. He promised to return with more grains of rice, but never came back. The god however continued to wait for him with one hand stretched out. The statue of this god can be seen even today with one hand stretched in front. Another story told by the villagers is that of the Varhad ghar and how the groom's side of an entire marriage party disappeared but left their utensils behind The stone pots can still be seen in this room. Atop the Pateshwar Hill is the ashram-cum-residence of Govind Maharaj. It is possible to spend the night in one of the smaller temples that surround this ashram. A fair is held here every Monday in the Hindu month of Shravan. If you visit Pateshwar during this period there will also be plenty of food available!

Pateshwar has all the ingredients to make the place interesting for tourists - a salubrious climate, plenty of trees with a variety of birds singing in them and the ancient temples pervading the place with a spiritual serenity.

Saptashrungi

About 40 kilometres north of Nasik is a stretch of the Sahyadri mountains known as the Ajantha-Satmala range. The average height of peaks here is about 4,500 feet. The tallest (around 4,600 feet) in this group is Dhodap towards the centre of the range and Saptashrungi towards the western side. Saptashrungi is well-known because of the temple atop the hill, dedicated to the goddess Saptashrungi.

Fact File

Best time - All year round

Location - 40 kms. north of Nashik

Getting there - ST bus to village Naduri via Vani

Where to stay - At the temple complex

Where to eat - At temple complex

There are two routes to Saptashrungi, the first is via Vani, Chandakpur on the Nashik-Saputara road. The distance between Nashik and Vani via Dindori is 39 kilometres, while via Pimpalgaon it is 51 kilometres. Going by this route means you have to climb up all the way to the top of the mountain. There are steps to reach the temple. An easier alternative is the road via Nanduri village, 14 kilometres after Vani. Nanduri village is in the foothills of

Saptashrungi, and a regular minibus service run by the State Transport Corporation plies from here to the top of the plateau. From the plateau it is a relatively easy half-hour climb up 250 steps to the temple. The temple is situated within a slight hollow in the mountain and is not visible, even from the plateau. The sight of hundreds of devotees, from the very young to the very old, making the long, tiring climb up to this temple is very moving. The statue of the goddess is on the top floor of this two-storeyed temple. During the nine days leading up to Dassera, an annual festival is held and all routes to the temple are literally choked with devotees. Since the temple is at a height it affords a splendid view of the surrounding hills. While climbing down from Saptashrungi, near the Nanduri village, the Mohindri Mountain with its gaping hole can be seen. Villagers say that after winning a fierce battle the goddess Saptashrungi disappeared through the mountain, leaving behind a gaping hole!

The height of Saptashrungi ensures that it has a cool climate throughout the year. In winter it can get quite cold. It is possible to stay the night in the temple complex and arrangements for food can also be made here. This is one place that is not only attractive to the devout but even to the ordinary tourist.

Tungareshwar

While several places in the south-western part of the ghats have become popular hill stations, few are aware of the equally beautiful northern end of the western ghats. In this northern part, quite close to Mumbai and just off the Mumbai-Ahmedabad highway is one such place-Tungareshwar. At the foot of the Tungareshwar hill is the Tungareshwar temple. Fifty kilometres from Bandra on the highway is a sign post pointing in the direction of Tungareshwar. The tar road runs for just a kilometre, thereafter you have to take the *kuchcha* road through dense forest. Two kilometres down this road is the Shri Seshnag Maharaj Temple after which the climb begins and 3.5 kilometres after the Tungar junction is the grand Tungareshwar temple. Set against a backdrop of the green hillside and encircled by trees the temple surroundings are certainly inspiring. Every Mahashivratri, large crowds gather here.

> **Fact File**
>
> *Best time- June to March*
>
> *Location -- 50 kms. from Bandra on Western Highway*
>
> *Getting there - By road on the Mumbai-Ahmedabad Highway, one hour drive to Tugareshwar*
>
> *Where to stay - Sadanad Maharaj Math*
>
> *Where to Eat - Small eateries near temple, but better carry own food*

A deep lake formed by erosion of the Tungareshwar river behind the temple is called Ramkund or Gupt Ganga (the secret Ganga). People are known to have drowned here. As a precaution, railings have now been put up around this natural lake and swimming has been forbidden by the government. The view from this point however is really wonderful. The green valley set against the flowing water is a sight worth seeing. After crossing the bridge, to the right of the temple there is another smaller Dutt Temple and the source of the Gupt Ganga.

While most visitors to Tungareshwar visit all these spots, many do not bother to climb to the peak of the hill. This is about 7.5 kilometres from the temple and the red mud path leading through dense undergrowth reminds one of Matheran. Except in the rainy season and the three months after it, it is possible for private vehicles such as jeeps to reach this spot. At a height of 2,200 feet, it gets cooler as you climb. At the end of the road is the ashram of Sadanand Maharaj. This is an ideal place for meditation. The peaceful, ascetic atmosphere is a welcome respite after the tiring climb. To the east in the valley below is Vajreshwari. The road in front of the ashram goes down the hill to Ganeshpuri.

Near this ashram are several ponds called Parshuram Kund. From this point the Tansa river valley below and the peaks of the Takmak Fort look beautiful. Just before you reach the Ashram is the Pelhar Lake and from there the cliff drops straight down about 800 feet right into the Konkan. The lake is a popular picnic spot. The small Chinchoti waterfall near the Kaman junction just before reaching Tungareshwar is also well-known among tourists. There are several buses plying between Vasai and Tungar.

Kundal : A religious place of the Jains

> **Fact File**
>
> *Best time- June to March*
>
> *Location - 30 kms. from Karad, 9 kms. from Sangareshwar by road*
>
> *Getting there - By ST bus*
>
> *Where to stay- At the temple Dharmashala*
>
> *Where to eat -- Food and water is available at the temple*

After the decline of the Satavahana dynasty, several small states came into existence. One of these was Devrashtra near Sagareshwar. The capital of this state was Koundinyapur, or what today is known as Kundal.

Kundal is 30 kilometres from Karad and 9 kilometres from Sagareshwar. It has gained significance today as an important religious shrine for the Jain community. A southern-facing ancient temple belonging to the Digamber Jain sect can be found here. A five-feet tall black coloured statute of Parshvanath is installed in the temple. Of the two most important religious shrines of the Jains in Sangli district, one is the Vashi Parshvanath and the other is this one at Kundal. The well-known litterateur Vyankatesh Madgulkar lived near this temple. Two kilometres from the village on a small hill is the smaller west-facing Zari Parshvanath temple.

To the south of the temple is a pond with perennial water supply. From here you can see the Karad-Tasgaon road running below. From behind the Zari Parshvanath temple is a small dust path leading to the peak on the mountain where the Giri Parshvanath temple is located. It takes a 30-minutes climb to reach the top where the footwear of Shridhar Swami can be found. Nearby is the Giri Parshvanath temple. Behind the temple are 4 or 5 caves belonging to the Lingayat sect. Anyone taking time off to visit Sagreshwar should make it a point to come here. After the rains the view from the Zari Parshvanath temple is really memorable. In 1985 this area was declared as protected forest area. While there are no hotels or rest houses here, it is possible to spend a night at the Jain Dharmashala. Drop them a line at the Jain Dharmashala, at Post Kundla, Tasgaon taluka, District Sangli.

Shri Gondeshwar Temple at Sinnar

Fact File

Best time- June to March

Location -- 26 kms. from Nashik, 190 kms. from Mumbai

Getting there - By ST bus, by road

Where to stay - Nashik or Sinnar

Where to eat -- Mnay eateries at Sinnar

On the Shirdi-Nashik road, 26 kilometres from Nashik and 190 kilometres from Mumbai is Sinnar, an important industrial town.

About 1.5 kilometres from the State Transport bus stand at Sinnar is the Shri Gondeshwar temple. Spread over a large area this is actually a temple complex of five temples. After entering the main door, you see the Shiva temple with its 125-feet high spire full of carvings. Around thc main Shiva temple are the temples of Ganpati, Vishnu, Suryanarayan and a Devi. On the outer walls of the temple are carved tales from the Mahabharata and Ramayana.

In addition to this, the Meshwatheshwar temple in the Chalukya style just outside Sinnar is also worth visiting.

Our temples are often treasure troves of history. These shrines were places that were not merely restricted to being religious sanctuaries, but were important centres of knowledge, research and debate on local policies. Temples like Trimbakeshwar, Kukdeshwar, Shegaon, of Maharashtra are sites of paramount importance. The degree of skill that went into making the carved panels, the elaborate shikhars, and the entire design of the temple still arouses awe.

Shegaon

This is the hallowed town of Gajanan Maharaj, where devotees flock in thousands to pay obeisance. Shegaon, an important pilgrimage centre, lies in Vidarbha. The stretch of Central Railway's Mumbai-Nagpur route lying in Buldhana district, passes via Shegaon. The temple is a 10 minute walk from the railway station. The place receives pilgrims from as far away as Denas, Indore,

Fact File

Best time - All year

Location - Vidarbha

Getting there - Overnight by Central Railways on the Mumbai- Nagpur route or by bus, one hour by plane from Mumbai

Where to stay - Temple complex

Where to eat - Temple Complex

Paithan, Pandharpur and Baroda. All these are connected to the town by private and state-owned buses.

The temple has a walled compound all around. The temple of Gajanan Maharaj is situated right in the centre. The compound has doorways to the north and west. The shutter in the main doorway is always kept open. The memorial or 'Samadhi' of Gajanan Maharaj is in a crypt deep down below the temple. There are idols of Lord Ram, Laxman, and Sita on a platform here. There is also a statue of Lord Hanuman. On the southern side of this temple, there is a place where a few objects that the saint used are kept. This is also the spot where he departed from his mortal body to attain the state of samadhi. It was where he lived for many years, and visitors come to this place to pay their respects to the great soul.

There is a temple of Nagdevta to the north of the temple. There are two marble memorial temples of two of the Maharaj's most trusted and devoted followers, Narayan Maharaj and Balabhau Maharaj. Gajanan Maharaj had experienced a divine vision which informed him of the time and date when he would have to free his soul. In 1908, there was a meeting held at a shop owned by one Kadtaji Patil. The meeting included several devotees, villagers and local businessmen. The formation of the Gajanan Maharaj trust was a result of this mutual discussion, and in the presence of the Maharaj himself, this association was formed. Today, the trust looks after a variety of social activities and manages many educational, medical and environmental programmes. On the Khamgaon road, there is a lovely garden maintained by the trust. It has been named Shri Gajanan Vatika in memory of the saint who enriched this land with his preachings. There is a statue of Gajanan Maharaj exuding total serenity situated in the centre of this park. The jets of fountains sprinkle coloured water on the statue. The garden spreads over four acres, and includes an animal park, a plant nursery, and a children's play area.

Shegaon is a place which I visit at least once a year. I come here and pay my respects at the feet of Gajanan Maharaj, an unfailing annual ritual ritual for many years now. Once I have completed my little pilgrimage to the sacred places of Shirdi and Shegaon, my mind feels refreshed and purified. It's as if something deep within the environs of these places rejuvenates my soul. Perhaps it does the same for many other people like me!

Theur

Fact File

Best time - All year

Location - 13 kms. from Pune

Getting There - To Loni on the Pune Solapur Road

Where to stay - Pune

Where to eat - Theur

This shrine, one amongst the Ashtavinayak sites, has been immortalized by the almost legendary tales of Madhavrao Peshwa and his wife, Ramabai. The village of Theur is situated on the banks of the Mutha, just 13 kilometres from Pune. The Pune-Solapur road will take you to Loni, from where one can go on foot or hitch a ride in an autorickshaw. The temple is 3 kilometres from here.

The deity at Theur is Shri Chintamani. The entrance faces north, while the idol of Lord Ganesh faces east. The idol is said to be swayambhu (self manifest). The Lord, sitting cross-legged, looks serenely upon his devotees. For the devout it is an extremely moving experience. This was the place where Morya Gosavi of Chinchwad, an ardent devotee of the Lord, attained purity of soul.

The late Madhavrao Peshwa breathed his last in these very premises. In a period of extreme illness, the Peshwa tried to please the Lord by offering a perennial Abhishek of milk. In his last days, this illustrious ruler-one of the most benevolent that late Maratha history has seen - took refuge in the all-encompassing presence of Shri Chintamani. His young wife, Ramabai, immolated herself on his funeral pyre. There is a memorial dedicated to this couple.

Every year, in the Hindu calendar month of Kartik, a little ceremony is held here and the glory of the late Peshwa is revived.

Trimbakeshwar

Trimbakeshwar is one of the five Jyotirlingas in Maharashtra. It sits at the foothills of the Brahmagiri mountains that shelter the village of Trimbakeshwar. This village is 45 kilometres from the Nashik Road junction on the Central Railway route. There is a frequent bus service from Nashik to the temple. It takes just an hour to reach it.

Fact File

Best time- All year

Location -- 45 kms. from Nashik Road Junction

Getting There - By bus

Where to stay- MTDC resorts, private hotels

Where to eat - Many good eateries around temple

The entire temple is built of dressed stone masonry. The premises of the temple are impressive and large. Along all four boundaries, the temple is protected by rock fortifications. The main shrine is situated on an elevated square platform. On the anterior side of the premises there is a Kund or sacrificial quadrangle of Kushavarta. It is accessible on all four sides by steps. The niches at the rear house several deities. The temple of the holy Godavari stands here. The river, second only to the Ganges in Hindu scriptures, has its origins in the Brahmagiri hills, and then continues unseen throughout. Mythology tells us the story of how the Ganga, trapped in the matted locks of Lord Shiva, came to purify this land. Gautam Rishi, a revered sage, had an ashram here, where he performed his religious rites. There was also a field where he cultivated paddy. One day, a cow strayed into the fields and began chewing the crop, ruining it in the process. Enraged by the sight, the sage flung a blade of grass at it. This darbha (sacred grass) killed the cow instantly. Realizing that he had committed the grave sin of killing a sacred animal, the Sage Gautam performed a series of unrelenting penances till he invoked the blessings of Lord Shiva. To cleanse the region of this sin, Lord Mahadev commanded the holy Ganges to descend to earth. She refused, and in anger, the Lord lashed the earth with his locks. The rocks of Bramhagiri hills are said to bear the marks of this punishment. Just above this site is the spring where the Godavari originates. Ultimately, Ganga relented and came down to wash away the sins of the Sage Gautam. Since one of the streams of the river flowed over the dead cow to bring it to life, this particular part of the Ganga began to be called as Godavari. From its beginnings at the site of Chakrateerth, the Godavari continues along the country to meet the Rajmahendri with its seven mouths, in the Bay of Bengal.

The hills of Bramhagiri stand at a height of 4250 feet above sea level. To reach the place where the Godavari first emerges, one has to climb almost 700 steps. The pathway forks to the left here. Again, 300 steps are carved out of the rock which leads to the crown of the Bramhagiri. There is a small fort-the Trimbakgad, with a south-facing doorway.

The entire range including the Bramhagiri hills receives good rainfall. Hence there is thick greenery all over. The temple of Trimbakeshwar hosts a huge fair every Mahashivratri. Also, the area is famous as the site of the Kumbha Mela every 12 years. The importance of Nashik as a pilgrimage centre ranks second only to Allahabad. The sacred Jyotirlinga of Trimbakeshwar, along with the surrounding spots of Bramhagiri and Trimbakgad can be visited in a day, provided you start early.

The Temples of Chaul

Chaul is half an hour's drive from Alibag. Earlier known as Champavati, it was the capital of a kingdom ruled by King Champ. It is believed that the name derives from the fact that this entire region was full of Champa trees. There is hardly any relic of the kingdom that once graced this picturesque land. Surprisingly, however, many of the temples have survived intact.

Many chapters of history have been devoted to Chaul's colourful past. It was once an important port, and hence, the arena for battles waged between the Portuguese, the Marathas and the Moghuls from time to time. The Chaul of today is an extremely pretty little hamlet, with its wadis, ancestral homes, coconut trees, and the ebullient Konkan spirit.

Fact File

Best time- All year

Location -- Half hour's drive from Alibag

Getting There - By road or by ST bus

Where to stay -- Alibag

Where to eat - Chaul has small eateries which specialise in fish

Each temple in Chaul has an accompanying legend. The temples of Lord Datta, Devi Shitaladevi and Hingulja Devi are charming. There are so many temples here that the village seems to have been built around them. The temples have characteristic styles and all of them are excellent examples of the temple architecture that was prevalent in that day and age.

Ranjangaon

Fact File

Best time- All year

Location -- 46 kms. from Pune

Getting There - An hour's drive from Pune by car or by ST bus

Where to stay - Pune

Where to eat -- Ranjangaon

Ranjangaon is one of the five Ashtavinayak (the eight cardinal Ganapatis) temples that come within the Pune district, and lies in the Shirur taluka, about 46 kilometres from Pune. There is a legend surrounding this temple. The cruelty of Tripurasura and his evil deeds had terrorized the three worlds to such an extent that the destroyer, Lord Shiva, had to be approached to put an end to the Asura's power. Lord Shiva did so, and on Tripuri Poornima, the evil Rakshasa was killed and the worlds liberated from his tyranny. Before he achieved this triumph, Lord Shiva had propitiated the god of success, Mahaganapati. The site where he did so was called Manipur. It was later renamed Ranjangaon.

The temple faces east. Some parts of the temple complex, including the Sabhamandapa, have been reconstructed by Sardar Kibe of Indore.The Shinde and Pawar families who held posts of prominence under the Peshwa rule, have built parts of the temple. Some say that the inner chamber or sanctum sanctorum was built under the patronage of Madhavrao Peshwa himself.

The idol of Lord Ganesh also faces east. This means the idol's trunk is turned towards the right (Davya Sondecha Ganapati). The idol is flanked by the twin statues of his consorts, Riddhi and Siddhi. Some sources also claim that there is yet another idol hidden in the cellars of the temple.

Every Ganesh Chaturthi, devotees flock to this temple and there is a hugely popular festival. For puja offerings and abhishek to the lord, one must correspond with the temple authorities much in advance, we are told. Of course, this can now also be done on the Internet.

Pali

Fact File

Best time- June to March

Location -- Khopoli on the old Mumbai Pune Highway or Mumbai Goa road via Nagothane

Getting there - Mumbai to Pali is a two-hour drive by car, ST buses

Where to stay - At the temple

Where to eat - Food is available at the temple

One of the deities amongst the Ashtavinayaka, this is the seat of the Lord Ballaleshwar. The town was earlier called Pallapur. An interesting legend forms a backdrop for this temple. A trader who owned a shop here had a son named Ballal. The child was the fruit of a long period of vows undertaken by the trader. The boy was religiously inclined from a tender age. He often spent hours making little temples of clay. He adopted Lord Dhundivinayak as his deity, and would offer fervent prayers to Him. One day, the trader received a few complaints about his son's behaviour. Furious with the boy, the trader caned him and, in the process, destroyed the clay temples that the little boy had painstakingly made. When Ballal regained consciousness, he prayed to his lord and begged Him to manifest Himself. Lord Ganesh was pleased with the boy's earnestness, and He gave him

KOYANA FOREST RESERVE

ROSE AT VISAWA RESORT

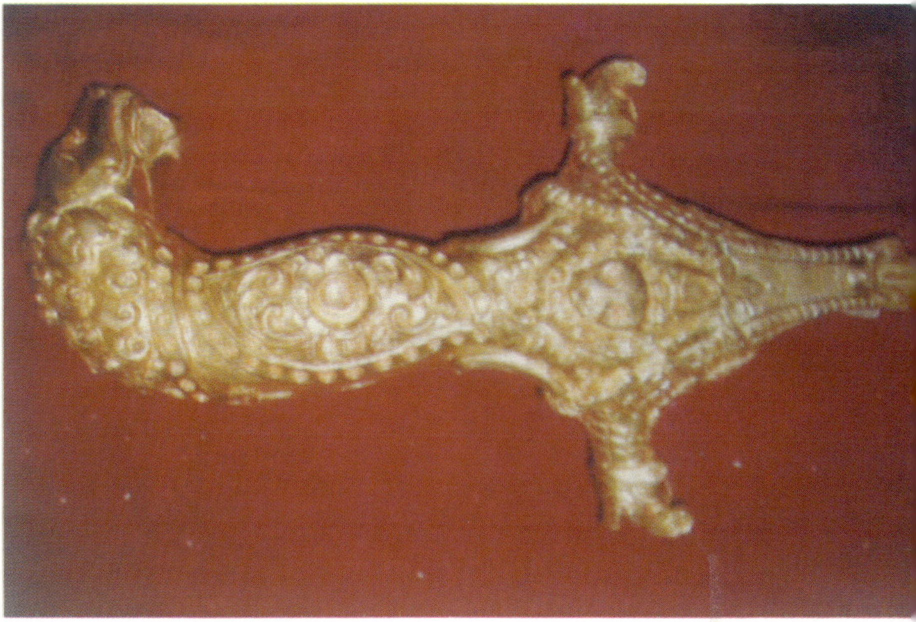

KADAMB FAMILY HEIRLOOM

SILVASSA MUSEUM

a promise that he would to remain in this land. To the boy's delight, the Lord told him, " I shall be known as Ballalvinayak ." The deity is thus, called Ballaleshwar. It is claimed that the Ballaleshwar deity originally installed in the region of Murud Janjira's Nandgaon village, was moved to Pali.

The temple of Ballaleshwar, as also the idol, faces east. The Lord is seated on a stone throne, and the idol is one metre tall. There is a diamond in each of the eyes and the navel. A very attractive part of this temple is the huge bell that hangs outside. The massive bell is said to be part of the booty that came to Chimaji Appa when he looted the prosperous town of Surat. This bell is said to be one of the five that he took. It has Portuguese markings on it and is made of an alloy of five metals.

Pali lies along the Lonavla-Khopoli road and is 110 kilometres from Pune. From Mumbai, one has to travel along the Panvel-Khopoli route for a distance of 124 kilometres. About 4 kilometres from Pali, the hot water springs of Unhere are famous for their curative properties. The water is said to be the answer for many skin ailments. The village of Sarasgad is very close to Pali. To the east is the fort of Sudhagad. Both these forts are good places to visit.

In the Hindu months of Bhadrapad and Magh, there are two important festivals in this temple town. A procession dedicated to the Goddess is also arranged. The lord is said to satiate His hunger around this time.

Pali has adequate facilities to offer to the tourists who come here. Besides its importance as a destination for Ganesh devotees, Pali is also a good place for tourists to combine a visit to the temple with a trip to the springs of Unheri and the twin forts of Sarasgad and Sudhagad.

Ozar

Ozar is just 85 kilometres from Pune and 180 kilometres from Mumbai. The temple is situated along the dam that spans the Kukdi river. The temple, facing east, is surrounded by a walled compound. The premises contain two tall deepmaals. The temple has a spire sheathed in gold foil.

Ozar is a small place but does have some convenient places to stay over. There are a number of other places to visit in the vicinity, like Junnar, Shivneri, Parvatgad, the Chavand fort, the temple of Kukdeshwar and Lenyadri. The radio telescope centre at Arvi too is an interesting place.

Fact File

Best time- All year

Location - 85 kms. from Pune, 180 kms. from Mumbai

Getting there - ST buses, private taxis

Where to stay - Pune

Where to eat - Eateries in Ozar

Siddhatek

This is the shrine of Lord Siddhivinayaka, one of the most revered of all the Ashtavinayak sites in Maharashtra. The temple, surrounded by thick green trees of Babul, lies in the village of Siddhatek. The village lies in the Nagar district on the eastern banks of the Bhima river. The eastern bank of the river runs along Pune district, and the temple of Siddhivinayak is roughly 1 kilometre from the village. That the temple has enjoyed a long period of royal patronage is evident from the fact that there is a paved path right up to the main doorway of the shrine. The creation of this road is attributed to Sardar Haripant Phadke, an official of thc Peshwas.

The temple faces north. The threshold of the main shrine has a small sculpture depicting the head of an evil asura. Legend has it that there were two evil demons, Madhu and Kaitab. Lord Vishnu tried to free the region from their cruelty but his efforts were fruitless. Ultimately, the Lord performed severe penance at this spot and invoked the blessings of Shri Vinayaka. The lord attained siddhi or divinity and the asuras were killed.

The temple, constructed in black stone, was built by Rani Ahilyabai Holkar. The roof of the sabhamandap, the public hall, too is built of stone blocks. It is a good example of the craftsmanship of that day and age. There is another Sabhamandap which was added later. The principal entrance to the temple has a

Fact File

Best time- All year

Location -- Nagar District, Sidhdhatek village

Getting there - By road, by bus

Where to stay - Siddhatek village

Where to eat - At Siddhatek

Nagarkhana. It is said to have been made under the directions of Sardar Haripant Phadke.

The inner chamber is flanked by the idols of the valorous pair of Jay and Vijay. The idol of Lord Siddhivinayak facing north, is installed here. This chamber has a domical ceiling in stone. The idol has the rare right-turning trunk of Lord Ganesh. It is commonly believed that to please this deity, an extremely rigorous set of vows has to be strictly adhered to. The idol is sheathed in brass and the lord is depicted sitting on a stone throne. The deity sits cross-legged, with his consort Siddhi seated close to the Lord. The saffron paste and puja offerings, however, sometimes obscure this part of the idol.

On the auspicious day of Ganesh Jayanti large crowds visit this shrine. There is a festival and jatra(folk play) every Vijayadashmi and on Somvati Amavasya. As you enter the village, a slightly raised hillock can be seen, with a Vishnu temple atop it. It is believed that this temple was built during the Adil Shahi rule, in fact, under the very patronage of the rulers. The Muslim style of architecture adds credibility to this theory. In any case, it seems possible that the inauguration and initial religious rites of this temple were undertaken before the temple passed into the protection of Rani Ahilyabai Holkar. Who actually performed this task and exactly when, is still unknown, for the temple is ancient and no records exist. The area in and around the temple is also called Deulwadi. The remains of the ancestral wada (manor) of Haripant Phadke and its surroundings bear witness to the fact that the temple dates back many hundreds of years ago.

Mrutyunjeshwar

The Karve Road of Pune seems a strange place to have a temple, but its true that this arterial road, always choked with traffic, has one of the most ancient temples in this area. The temple of

Mrutyunjeshwar was built during the reign of the Peshwas, when this area just had wooded tracts.

> **Fact File**
> *Best time - All year*
> *Location - Karve Road, Pune*
> *Getting there - City transport*
> *Where to stay - Pune*
> *Where to eat - Pune*

Since a major improvement and restoration campaign was undertaken a few years back, much of the temple appears to be newly built. The sanctum sanctorum, however, is still the same as it was two hundred and fifty years ago. This temple of Lord Shiva depicts Him in the form of conqueror of death Mrutyunjeshwar. This is yet another of the many forms in which Mahadev is portrayed. This deity is said to be swayambhu (self manifest).

Morgaon

Morgaon is 80 kilometres from Pune. You can drive along the Pune-Solapur highway and continue up to Supa along the Neera, when you reach Morgaon. There is no direct bus service to Morgaon from Pune, though one can go to Jejuri and catch a bus to Morgaon from there. The Shri Moreshwar Mandir at Morgaon is one of the Ashtavinaayak shrines that lie in Pune district.

One legend tells us that Lord Ganesh, astride a peacock, destroyed the evil Kamlasur, which is why he is known as Lord Mayureshwar. Another story says this town was so populated with peacocks, that it became Morgaon and hence, the lord was called Shri Moreshwar.

The main entrance faces north, though the deity faces east. The idol has four arms and three eyes. The eyes are encrusted with diamonds. A serpent protects the Lord with its hood raised above His crown. The forecourt of the temple has two huge Deepmal (receding towers with niches for lamps). There is also a sculpted mouse, 6 feet high. The space around the sabhamandapa (public hall) consists of a systematic arrangement of 23 different idols and depictions of the Lord. Known by his various names, these are the idols of Sinharudh, Vakratunda, Mahodar, Ekdant, Vikat,

Fact File

Best time - All year

Location - 80 kms. from Pune on Pune-Solapur highway

Getting there - ST bus service via Jejuri

Where to stay- At the temple

Where to eat -At the temple

Dhumravarna, Vighnaraj, Lambodar, the octet of Lord Vinayaka, and Gajanana. Some of these idols have been installed by followers of the Yogendra Ashram.

There is a more recent sabhamandapa with idols of Lord Vishnu and Goddess Laxmi. This leads to a central hall constructed by King Kurundwad Patwardhan. The ceiling is carved out of a single rock. The idol of Lord Moreshwar is flanked by sculptures of his consorts, Riddhi and Siddhi. These idols have been made from an alloy of five metals. The deities are skilfully covered in silver revealing ace craftsmanship. The temple has an impressive boundary wall and interestingly, four minarets that speak of a Muslim influence somewhere in the temple's history.

On the Pradakshina (the ritual circumbulatory) path, there is a tree next to the Kalpavruksha mandir. This is the tree under which the devotee Morya Gosavi is said to have performed penance. The temple of Morgaon is full of devotees every year on Ganesh Jayanti and in the month of Bhadrapada when a procession of pilgrims arrives all the way from the 'Mangalmurti' temple of Chinchwad.

A sacred pilgrimage to the eight holy Ganapati temples that comprise the Ashtavinayaka, begins from this temple. The tour is deemed complete when the devotee comes back to Morgaon to pay his obeisance. There are a few other places around Morgaon, like Jejuri, Lavleshwar, and the Varah mandir of Loni. One can stay overnight at Morgaon after making reservations. To book a room, you will have to correspond with the Shri Morgaon Devalaya Trust, Chinchwad, Pune.

Marleshwar

Often called the 'Trimbakeshwar of the Konkan', this temple is a said to be a Svayambhu (self-existent) shrine. The name

Fact File

Best time- All year

Location -- 14 kms. from Devrukh in Konkan

Getting there - Direct ST bus service

Where to stay- At Sangameshwar or Devrukh

Where to eat --At the temple

Marleshwar comes from the village of Maralgaon, where the temple is situated. Maralgaon is 14 kilometres from Devrukh, which, in turn, is 18 kilometres from Sangameshwar. From Mumbai, Sangameshwar is 289 kilometres by road. From Mumbai, there is a good bus service to Devrukh. The bus continues to Marleshwar. One can stay at either Sangameshwar or Devrukh.

From Maralgaon, the temple is 3 kilometres away. A part of the distance can be covered by vehicle, and only the last kilometre is a climb. The flat area allotted for parking overlooks a valley called Powai. There is a rough pathway along the edges of this face that will lead to the temple. To the left and far beyond, the ridges and towering peaks of the Sahyadris watch over the area. The spray of the Gangotri river rises into the air and the river gushes along the gorge created by the surrounding cliffs. The mist, the green of the hills, all make for a rambling walk, and before you realize it, you are at the entrance of the temple.

The deity of Marleshwar is housed in a cave. At the forecourt, there is a canopied hall. It has a Deepmal (traditional lamp tower)and a Tulshivrindavan (the holy basil grove). To the right is the mouth of the cave. This entrance is flanked by an idol of Lord Ganesh and a pond filled with cool, clear water. The Shivalinga is installed in the cave. A silver cobra guards the deity. On one side, there are images of the five heavenly deities, the Panchdevta. The nooks and corners of the cave are occupied by snakes. At times, one can actually see a cobra silently coiled in a crevice. Strangely, though, there have been no incidents of snake-bites. The rear side of the cave unveils what is, undoubtedly, the most rewarding part of coming to this place. From high above, the Dhareshwar waterfall thunders down to drop with a deafening roar into the Karambeli gorge. The falls originate from a height which the eye cannot follow. The front of the cave too offers a magnificent vista of the white foam.

An ancient legend surrounds the shrine of Marleshwar. At the beginning of the eighteenth century, the Shivalinga was installed in Muradpur, which was infested by the unruly army of one Sardar Murad Khan. The men looted the commoners and nothing was safe. Alarmed at this vandalism, some devotees decided to take the Shivalinga to a place where it would be safe from marauders. They carried the lingam in a bag and brought it to this cave, deep in the heart of the Sahyadris. There is another facet to this story. One myth says that the deity himself moved to the cave, sick of the atrocities of Murad Khan. In the guise of a wandering mendicant, the Lord walked into Maralgaon. A tanner took pity on this newcomer and showed him the way to the cave. The mendicant walked into the cave and became invisible. Later, when a group of hunters somehow found their way here, they witnessed a humbling sight - at the centre of the cave was a Shivalinga, with snakes and cobras coiled around its circumference. It was Makar Sankrant. To this day, the villagers celebrate, with much joy and pride, the wedding of Lord Marleshwar to Girijadevi. There is a great festival here, on every Makar Sankrant day. In tribute to the tanner who helped the Lord find a safe haven, his descendants are given the great honour of leading the procession that makes its way to the shrine. Even today Mr. Pavar and Mr. Narkar carry out this duty with great devotion.

Like in most shrines of Lord Shiva, there is a big Jatra or festival every year on Mahashivratri and on Tripuri Poornima. The devotees who make their way here from far-off places are catered to by the volunteers of the Shri Marleshwar Seva Sangh, who offer them facilities like drinking water, medicine, and lodging.

The village of Kundi lies just before you reach Maralgaon. The fort of Mahimatgad, in the principal mountain range of the Sahyadris, is seen from here. Beyond Marleshwar, at the base of the Amba ghat, lies a small hamlet, Sakharpa. The massive walls of Vishalgad are visible from this village. Both these forts can be attempted by trekkers. The verdant landscape and the mysteries surrounding the shrine, make for an extremely interesting trip to the sacred site of Lord Marleshwar.

Mahad

At a distance of 6 kilometres from Khopoli, Mahad is close to both Pune and Mumbai, around 85 kilometres equidistant from each. There are frequent buses coming here. Mahad is also well equipped to offer lodging and boarding facilities to tourists.

Fact File

Best time- All year

Location -- 6 kms. from Khopoli

Getting there - Direct ST bus service

Where to stay- At Mahad

Where to eat --At the temple

The beautifully carved temple of Mahad faces east. The temple is surrounded on four sides by skilfully crafted sculptures of elephants. The western side of the temple has a water reservoir, the Dev lake. In 1690, it was in this very lake that an idol of Lord Shrivaradvinayak was discovered. Facing east, the deity presides on a throne which is delicately carved in stone. The idol was installed ceremonially in 1725. Since 1892, a perennially-lit lamp has been placed in front of the Lord. It is never allowed to go out. To the north of the temple, a massive niche gouged out of an equally large rock is something that will hold your attention.

In the Hindu months of Magh and Bhadrapad, the temple complex is host to two major festivals. In the waning period of the month of Magh, the fourth, fifth and sixth day are noteworthy. On all these days, the rays of the sun fall directly on the idol, a phenomenon considered especially auspicious.

Lenyadri

Lenyadri is one of the Ashtavinayak temple sites. Via the Mumbai-Kalyan-Otur route, this shrine, which comes under the Junnar taluka, is 179 kilometres from Mumbai. Buses that operate on the Pune-Junnar, Talegaon-Junnar, or Mumbai-Junnar routes, will take you to Lenyadri. There is no state transport for the last 5 kilometres, but local transport will reach you to the entrance of the temple complex.

Fact File

Best time- All year

Location -- Junnar Taluka, 179 kms. from Mumbai

Getting there - By Road

Where to stay- Junnar

Where to eat --Carry your own food and water

The shrine at Lenyadri is seated deep in a cave. One has to climb about 300 steps to reach the hollow in the hills where the deity is installed. Just next to the shrine, there is a tank with cool, clean water. The entire cavernous region is looked after by the Archaeology Department. Sardar Deshpande of Junnar is in charge of the day-to-day activities of the temple; he has also been nominated as the Sarpanch of Lenyadri. After leaving Junnar, there are no arrangements to halt for a cup of tea, so tourists are advised to carry along water and some food when embarking on a visit to Lenyadri. The climb up the steps becomes hot in the afternoons, and there is no place to take a break. It is ideal, therefore, to start very early or later in the day.

The area around Lenyadri makes an ideal spot for looking around the surrounding landscape with a pair of binoculars. The forts of Shivneri, Chavand, Jeevdhan, Hadsar, and Narayangad are visible from here. The temple of Kukdeshwar and the Naneghat can also be spotted. The radio telescope at Khodad, and the satellite communication centre at Arvi; are other interesting sights. All these places can also be visited from nearby Lenyadri. The temple of Vighneshwar at Ozar too is close by. A week would be ideal to cover these interesting destinations.

Kukdeshwar

This temple is situated where the river Kukdi originates. It is steeped in an ancient aura. With its carvings, exquisite frescoes, and green environs, the temple of Kukdeshwar is an amazingly well-preserved monument. The site is about 15 kilometres from Junnar, and lies in Pune district. The closest place to the temple is the village of Pur, where buses from Junnar ply the whole day. A better way for the nature-lover, is to get down at the Khadakwadi

Fact File

Best time- All year

Location -- 15 kms. from Junnar

Getting there - By Road

Where to stay- Junnar

Where to eat --Carry your own food and water

turning on the Ghatghar - Aajnavale road, and to make it on foot. From here, it's just 6 kilometres, amidst lush green forest. In an hour or so, you can easily make it to the temple.

The temple of Kukdeshwar is encased in thick green cover. The entrance to the temple will greet you with a picture perfect brook cascading between gnarled branches of trees, to fall into a pond below. The pond continues to overflow and a little ahead continues as a stream. At the far end of this brook, there is a paved path leading to the temple. The road is interspersed with carvings and rock-hewn images. The river Kukdi splits into two at the entrance to the temple. The two branches flow around the temple and rejoin to continue as one. There are hills behind the temple, with the fort of Dhakoba visible. The fort can be reached by negotiating a mountain pass and following the pathway. To the east of the temple are seen the strong ramparts of Chavand fort. To the left, a series of even hills is interrupted by a mound which resembles the Shivalinga. It is, for this reason, called the Shambhu hill.

The temple is situated in a depression. It is protected on all sides by strong parapets. To enter, you have to descend a few steps before the beauty of the temple stands revealed. Every inch of the temple bears an artist's stamp, with its intricate carvings, wooden engravings and unique layout. The design of the temple is distinctly of the Hemadpanti style. The sanctum sanctorum is a study in detail. The roof is sculpted like a lotus with a thousand petals. The walls and pillars of the inner chamber are full of detailed rock-hewn images. A niche to the right contains an idol of Lord Ganesh.

The sabhamandapa is equally beautiful. The niches on the sides showcase images of Shivaparvati. In one corner, there is a statuette of Lord Shiva in a dancing pose. It seems to possess a strange magnetism. This anterior chamber is crowded with a number of columns. The central pillar is remarkable for its wonderful carvings in different styles. A look above will reveal that the pillar barely stands upright, a beam has come loose. The local populace has made a crude attempt to support the beam. The interior courts of the temple complex have been protected from the harsh effects of the sun and rain, with the help of asbestos sheets. Though this no doubt provides some protection, it jars with the classical beauty of the temple. It needs professional and aesthetic restoration urgently.

The ruins of sculptures in and around the temple complex give a fair idea of the regality with which the shrine was conceived. Every Mahashivratri, and also on Datta Jayanti, the temple comes alive with the chants of devotees, who come together for a huge fair. Kukdeshwar is, truly, a delight for the devotee, naturalist, and historian.

Jyotiba

The temple of Jyotiba is one of the most ancient shrines in Maharashtra. Its said that the twelve Jyotirlingas (sacred sites of Shiva) preside over twelve Upalingas (sub-sites) that are equally sacred. Jyotiba is one of them. There is an interesting mythological tale about this shrine. The Sage Paugand and his wife, after a long period of penance in the Himalayas, invoked God's blessings to have a child. The couple prayed to the Heavens and a child was born. It was Lord Kedarnath Himself! It was in the area of the Jyotiba temple that the Lord manifested himself, and this sacred part of the Earth came to be called Jyotiba, also sometimes referred to as Ravalnath.

The temple complex is about 18 kilometres from Kolhapur. With pilgrims thronging the shrine, there are frequent buses available. The Jyotiba hill is actually a projection of the Sahyadri range. The hill is elevated, with a height of 3100 feet above sea level.

As you alight from the bus, a high arch greets you. As with most temples in India, the road from the bus station to the temple doorway, is lined with kiosks and shops selling Puja offerings. The arch reveals the temple, sunk but accessible with 125 steps. The Mahadwar or principal doorway leads you in to what is a

Fact File

Best time- All year

Location -- 18 kms. from Kolhapur

Getting there - Frequent buses

Where to stay- At the temple

Where to eat -- At the temple

sprawling temple complex. Just near the entrance there are two temples on either side, one of Lord Harinarayan, and the other, of Lord Kashi-Vishweshwara. The entrance actually takes you from a direction which is opposite the face of the deity. Turn to the right to go to the Jyotiba temple. At the corner, there is a small temple of a pair of Nandis - the bull astride whom Lord Shiva invokes His might. One of the idols is slightly smaller than the first. You now enter a hall with an idol of Lord Badrikedar, facing north, with the temple of Goddess Chopdai just opposite. One story relates how Lord Jyotiba, with the aid of this Goddess, destroyed the evil Raktabhoj Rakshasa. Now the sanctum sanctorum of Lord Jyotiba shows a south-facing idol of the Lord. The idol is serene and emits a strange power. The idol has four arms, (Chaturbhuj), holding a khadag (sword), panpatra(betel leaf), a drum, and a trishul(trident).

This inner sanctuary also has two idols of Lord Ganapati and Lord Maruti, facing each other. A mandapa stands in the middle, supported on 4 columns. Each pillar is sheated in a film of brass, with beautiful inlays and carvings. As you step out of the inner chamber, you will notice a yagna kunda or sacrificial pyre. By its side, there is a sphere-like sculpture encased within a wooden frame. The locals call it the Dantai Dola (the eye of Dantai), and it is said to be one of the eyes of the Rakshasa Ratnasur, who was wiped out by Lord Jyotiba. This whole area of the temple complex and around, is also called Wadi Ratnagiri. In praise of this Lord who liberated the region of the tyranny of the Asura, devotees fervently chant bhajans and little poems. At the top of the temple complex is a small shrine with an idol of Lord Kalbhairav. Every year, on the full moon of the first month in the Hindu calendar, devotees flock to the temple for an annual ritual. The Chaitra Poornima is considered especially auspicious, and the place acquires an entirely new look on this occasion.

The circumbulatory pradakshina around the temple includes a narrow flight of steps carved into the rock, leading to the top. A bird's-eye view of the temple complex, the hills beyond and the colourful shops can be had from up here.

The Shiva temple of Ambarnath

Fact File

Best time- All year

Location -- Ambarnath

Getting there - Suburban train, an hours drive from Mumbai

Where to stay- At Ambarnath

Where to eat -- Hotels nearby

Dating back more than seven hundred years, the Ambarnath temple is a superlative example of the architectural style that Hemadpant, a minister in the Yadav empire, popularized. All designs that bear his distinctive symmetry and proportion are since referred to as the Hemadpanti manner of building. The Yadavs, who ruled circa AD. 1000 - 1300 AD. are responsible for many of the temples in Maharashtra.

Ambarnath is the third station if you start from Kalyan, along the Mumbai-Pune rail route. It takes about 20 minutes to reach this temple from the station. Buses and autorickshaws are easily available. The temple is situated on the banks of a stream. You will have to cross the bridge across this water course to enter the Shiva temple.

The temple consists of elaborate carvings that may remind you of the Ajanta -Ellora caves. The designs on the principal doorway are exquisite.

Directly in front of Nandi, Shiva's bull, is a large mandap or hall. Entrance doors open into this hall from three sides. The walls and columns of this hall are carved superbly. You descend to the inner chamber by a narrow flight of steps. The Shivalinga here is joined end to end. On all three sides of the temple, there are carvings and the rock has been etched in a continuous theme. Some of the engravings are large, some small. All, though, possess beauty of an astounding quality. The images in stone depict various animals, birds, flowers, decorative leaves, and of course, gods and goddesses. The sculpture of a trimukhi (three-headed) deity on the rear portion of the temple is particularly impressive.

The temple is believed to have existed since the days of the Mahabharata. It seems to have been set up in the hollow created by gouging out a large part of rock from a hillock. There is also a water storage tank nearby. A small shrine next to it houses a Shivalinga. The temple is at least 700 years old, and its art still speaks of the level of skill and craftsmanship of the men who worked on it. Sadly, there are signs of aging. The stones at the tip of the shikhar have become weak and are crumbling in places. There is an urgent need to preserve this magnificent heritage structure.

Amruteshwar of Bhor

Fact File

Best time- All year

Location -- 50 kms. from Pune

Getting There - On the Pune Satara highway

Where to stay- At Pune

Where to Eat -- At the temple

This temple of Lord Shiva is located on the periphery of the village of Mohri. As you cruise along the Pune-Satara highway, turn at the Bhor phata, you will reach a narrow bridge across the Gunjavni river. From the village of Kasurdi will branch out another road, the Hathway-Tambhad route. This road will take you to the temple of Amruteshwar. The site is 50 kilometres from Pune, and it takes one and a half hours to reach.

The temple is famous in the entire belt of Gunjal Maval. It is constructed entirely in stone masonry. Its walls display carvings of animals like the tiger, elephant, cow, bull. The lotus was also a favourite image for the engravers of those days. The temple is better known, however, for its sculpted images of the Gand Bherund. This is an imaginary, eagle-like creature with one trunk and two heads. The beast is said to be a good omen symbolizing strength and power.

The temple has always enjoyed the patronage of a family that tended to it. The village Sarpanch of Gunjan Maval, Mr. Shilimkar, owes allegiance to the temple, which is the kuldaivat or ancestral deity of his family. The shrine is said to be a wakeful deity, or jagrutisthan. Like many other temples, there is a myth surrounding the creation of this temple. It is said that a cowherd from the village of Mohri Budruk was grazing his cattle when he noticed two of his cows yielding milk at the banks of the riverbed. The place was cleaned of weeds and brushes, and the search revealed two Shivalingas. They decided to instal one of them in a temple dedicated to the Lord but all attempts to move it failed. Then a heavenly light was seen, and villagers were instructed to tie two young bulls to the yoke and the Shivalinga was moved to its new site. The Shivalinga was enshrined with prayers and chants, and this temple came to be known as Amruteshwar.

The temple is host to a hugely popular festival every Mahashivratri day. On the Tripuri Poornima, the deepmala in the front court of the temple is decorated with lamps. Every Chaitra Padwa, the locals set out on a pilgrimage to Shikhar Shingnapur on foot.

The temple of Amruteshwar is thus steeped in religious piety and mythology. A trip from Pune to this sacred site and back can be done in a day.

Amruteshwar of Ratanwadi

The temple of Lord Amruteshwar is situated in the village of Ratanwaadi. The village, composed of seven hamlets, nestles in the foothills of Ratangad, one of the peaks in the mountain ranges surrounding Mt.Kalsubai, the tallest peak in Maharashtra. The range includes the mounts of Kulang and Alang. In Ratangad, deep in the cave of Ratnubai is born Pravara - the river across which the Bhandardara dam has been constructed.

Close to the Igatpuri-Nashik route, the well-known tourist spot of Bhandardara dam needs no introduction. The lake, at an altitude of 2700 feet, is ringed in by the hills that make up the highest spot in the

Fact File

Best time- All year

Location -- Bhandardhara (180 kms. from Mumbai) off the Nasik highway

Getting there - By Ferry

Lodging- MTDC, Bhandardhara

Where to eat -- MTDC

state, that of Mt.Kalsubai. The temple of Amruteshwar is an extremely beautiful creation in black rock. Though less famous than its neighbour-the Bhandardara, every tourist with a love for the ancient beauty of Maharashtra's religious sites, must visit this shrine.

There is a rough track that skirts the Bhandardara lake. It passes by hilly forks like the Ghanchakkar, Aajoba, and others. The area is green and luxuriant and this makes the journey pleasant. An all-purpose vehicle like a jeep can easily traverse this path. However, this route is not accessible in the monsoon, when the waters of the lake inundate the surrounding area. In the rains, one can go to the village of Ratanwadi by ferry. The launch is provided by the MTDC. This boat ride is, to say the least, invigorating, and it takes just under an hour to reach the outskirts of Ratanwadi. From here, it is a half-hour trek up to the temple. The saffron of the flag fluttering atop the shikhar immediately attracts your attention.

The temple of Amruteshwar is more than a thousand years old, and was one of the twelve shrines of Shiva built under the patronage of King Jhanja. The rear doorway of the temple displays an astounding elegance of form and symmetry. It has carvings of loving couples. The roof of the temple also is carved. Various deities have been depicted as lovers, sometimes in serene solitude, sometimes dancing frenziedly.

The periphery of the temple is cloaked in dense forest, with the massive face of Ratangad visible clearly. It is this kind of luxurious setting that makes this temple an attractive jewel for tourists to discover.

Ganpatipule

> **Fact File**
>
> *Best time- All year*
>
> *Location -- Konkan coast, 50 kms. from Ratnagiri*
>
> *Getting there - By Bus from Mumbai, Ratnagiri, Kolhapur, Pune*
>
> *Lodging - MTDC, Private hotels*
>
> *Where to eat - Hotels nearby*

Ganpatipule is said to be swayambhu (self-manifest) shrine of lord Ganesh. The Konkan coast stretches in front of the temple, white sand all the way. Ensconced amidst coconut trees, Ganpatipule is truly a lovely place to visit.

The temple was, from time to time, under the protection of Shivaji Maharaj and Madhavrao Peshwa. The garbha graha or inner chamber was built by Shivaji, and the sabhamandap was built by the Peshwa Madhavrao. The temple faces west, towards the azure blue of the sky. The hill that forms the backdrop of this temple is itself in the form of a Ganesh idol and so a Pradakshina around this temple means a walk around the hill itself.

Ganpatipule is itself in the vicinity of a number of places of historical and tourist interest like Malgund, the birth place of Keshavsuta, one of Maharashtra's most famous poets, Jaigad and the temple of Karhateshwar and Laxmi-Keshav, at Kolisara. Fifty kilometres from Ganpatipule is Ratnagiri. The ashram of Swami Swaroopanand at Pawas is also not far from Ganpatipule.

The distance between Ganpatipule and Mumbai is about 375 kilometres. From Kolhapur, it is a 160-kilometre drive. Ganpatipule is close to Ratnagiri, just 50 kilometres away. Ganpatipule, virtually untouched until about ten years ago, is now a very popular tourist spot, and the MTDC offers excellent facilities. Bookings and reservations can be made at any Maharashtra Tourism office in Pune, Mumbai, Kolhapur, Ratnagiri, or in Ganpatipule itself. A visitor is sure to be dazzled by the white beaches, the amiable weather and a feeling of calm that the temple bestows upon its surroundings.

HILL STATIONS

HILL STATIONS

Maharashtra immediately brings to mind deep valleys and imposing mountain ranges, bubbling streams and lakes in a landscape that is unmatched in its beauty.

In Western Maharashtra several plateaux atop the hills have become popular hill stations, famed for their cool climate. Not only these hill stations but also the roads leading to them, provide an enjoyable experience. The roads wind their way through the ghats, bordered by rare and often breathtakingly beautiful flora.

Several of these places, like Mahabaleshwar and Matheran, are now well-known among tourists and trekkers but there is an equal number of less-known spots which dot these ranges, undiscovered and unsung.

On leaving the flat plains of the Konkan region behind, one begins to climb the winding ghat roads to reach the hilltops. The average height of peaks in the Sahyadri range is around 2,500 to 3,500 feet. The highest peak here is Kalsubai, which stands 5,500 feet tall. Kalsubai reigns over a range of hills called Balaghat or the Baleshwar Range. Most peaks in this range are around 5,000 feet high. Peaks like Harishchandra, Aajoba, Alang, Kulang and Madan make up this range. Combined with the graceful Bhandardara Lake, this region, in my opinion, is unrivalled for trekking, photography and nature-watching.

Several of the mountains in the Sahyadri range have forts atop them, while many have gained fame as hill stations. The view from these hilltops is really awe-inspiring. In the rainy season the entire landscape changes totally. The mist and the fog envelop the peaks, and just as you wonder what lies beyond the grey horizon, the sun peeps through the clouds, allowing a tantalizing glimpse of the valleys below and the peaks beyond. The clouds continue their game of hide-and-seek, and suddenly you glimpse the white foam of a distant waterfall crashing on to the rocks below. The peak known as the Duke's Nose is especially suited to this communion with the clouds. Once you have experienced the wonder of these fog-hidden peaks standing tall against the changing hues of the sky, the cool breeze blowing in your face, and, brightening up the path to the mountains, the small yellow flowers amidst blades of dew-laden grass, you are enslaved by the mountains for life. Anyone who has trekked through the forest at night, searching for paths and then sat at the top of the peak in the chill of dawn, looking out over the mist-hidden valleys, listening to the morning ragas of Lalit and Todi on a Walkman, knows what real pleasure is. As the morning mist lifts and the red orb of the sun becomes visible through the clouds the happiness one feels is indescribable.

It is not only the peaks that are picturesque; the roads leading to them have their own attraction. In ancient times India used to trade with several foreign countries. Most of the trade was done through the ancient sea routes. All the merchandise would be unloaded at the ports in the coastal regions of Maharashtra, some of which still exist. From here the merchandise would be transported hinterland to the bazaars of Paithan, Junnar and so on. Among the routes used for transportation were the Malshej ghat, Thal ghat, Ambenali ghat and the Varandha ghat, etc. These ghats are still used by villagers to travel on foot from the Konkan plains into the hills. These routes have now been developed into proper tarred roads. Imposing hills overlook these winding roads, one side of which plunges deep into the valleys below.

Chikhaldara

> **Fact File**
>
> *Best time- All year*
>
> *Location -- Amravati Dist, Satpura hills (Elevation: 3,564 feet)*
>
> *Getting there - By Bus from Amravati*
>
> *Where to stay- At MTDC, Private hotels*
>
> *Where to eat - Many eateries- being a popular hill station*

A glimpse into the ancient times of the Mahabharata is necessary to discover the origin of Chikhaldara, located in the Amravati district of the Satpura hills. It is said that during their period of exile the Pandavas stayed in a place called Viratnagari. Kichak, the king of this place, was a wicked person. Bhima, the strongman of the Pandavas, fought him and threw him into a valley. The valley came to be known as Kichakdara (dari meaning valley). With time that name became Chikhaldara (kichak meaning chikhal, meaning mud). Several of the valleys here are of outstanding beauty including the one in which Bhima is alleged to have thrown Kichak. The waterfall (Bhimakund) wherein Bhima is supposed to have bathed after carrying out the deed is also worth visiting.

Chikhaldara is 3,564 feet above mean sea level, so the climate is always cool and pleasant. Since it is the taluka headquarters, it is a fairly large town with several big buildings like the hospital and school. There are several places where one can stay including an MTDC guesthouse and the Government rest house. There is an excellent khanawala serving Gujarati-style food.

Chikhaldara is on the Melghat Mountain, one among the seven in the Satpura range. This whole range is a protected area and since hunting is banned the tiger population in this region is considerable. It is quite possible to spot a tiger in the Chikhaldara ghats or while travelling from Chikhaldara to Semadoha. There is also a large number of peacocks, fowls and bears. There is however one major difference between the Sahyadris and the Satpura range of mountains. In the Sahyadris there are a lot of evergreen trees making the forest not only dense but also very intensely green. The Satpura range has fewer evergreen trees and the green cover therefore is far less dense. The colour scheme in the forest here is more red and brown, blending in with the mountains of the same colour. The temperature, around 70 to 80 degrees Fahrenheit is suited to growing coffee which is among the major crops of the region.

Places of interest

Bhimakund: About 1 to 1.5 kilometres from the town. A motorable road right till the end. The waterfall leaps into a 3,500-foot deep valley.

Devi point: One kilometre from the town. You have to descend a few steps to reach the point. Towards the left is the source of the Chandrabhaga river. The river water collects in a small pond outside the temple and then falls into the valley. Right across from this point you can see the Gavilagad Fort, situated in a very peaceful and beautiful spot.

Mozari Point : Close to Devi point one can see the western part of the Gavilagad Fort. Also, the Mozari village in the west of the valley.

Hariket point : Close to Mozari point and with a similar view.

Nursery Garden : Planted by the Forest Department, this public garden has trees and plants of all kinds. A small toy train for children is an added attraction. Two leopards caught by the Department have been kept in this garden. There is a coffee plantation at one end of the garden.

Panchbol point : This point is off the road that goes from the nursery garden to Semadoha, about 4 kilometres from the town. From here you can see the four mountains which ring the valley below. This is a famous echo point.

Vairat Devi : This is probably the best of all the points here. About 11 kilometres from Chikhaldara, a temple dedicated to Vairat Devi has been built. At a height of 3,866 feet, the original statue of the goddess is actually located in a tunnel in the valley below. Since the original spot is virtually unreachable, the villagers from the surrounding villages got together and constructed a more conveniently-placed temple dedicated to the same goddess.

Gavilagad : 3 kilometres south of Chikhaldara, this fort belongs to the Bahamani era. A whole day is needed to see this fort. Architectural relics and old cannons can be found here. The moat and the security system are still in good condition.

Also worth a visit are the numerous lakes in the area, such as Shakkar Lake, Devi Lake, Machli Lake, Kala Pani Lake, and the several other smaller points including Monkey Point and Prospect Point.

From Mumbai you can take a train to Badnera Junction. Then a half an hour's run by State Transport bus to Amravati. From Amravati there is a direct State Transport bus service to Chikhaldara, which is at a distance of 94 kilometres.

Mandhardevi

Fact File

Best time- All year

Location -- In Bhor Wai region, Pune District

(Elevation: 4,500 feet)

Getting there - By road

Where to stay - At MTDC, Private hotels in Wai

Where to eat - In Wai and near temple

The hilly region of Bhor-Wai, near Pune, boasts several picturesque locations. Several mountains have large, well-developed plateaux, Mahabaleshwar, Panchgani, Kolheshwar and Raireshwar among them. Just before you reach Raireshwar there is the Mandhardevi temple, built at a height of 4,500 feet. Bhor is 45 kilometres from Pune. Eleven kilometres down the Bhor-Wai road is the Ambodeo Khind. 4 kilometres away, in a dense forest, is the Mandhardevi temple. The view from the Ambodeo Khind is spectacular. Spread before your eyes are the mountains of Pandavgad, Kamalgad, Rohida, Kenjalgad and Panchgani, and in the valley below are the waters of the Dhom dam. For a while, it is easy to forget that you have come to visit Mandhardevi and have to move on! The road is in a decent condition, permitting one to drive right up to the temple. The peak on which the temple is located is ringed with a dense growth of trees. To reach the temple you have to climb a few steps. The temple is small and has two stone lamps (deepmalas) flanking its entrance. There are shops catering to the devotees, selling articles for pooja, as well as tea stalls serving tea and snacks (pakoras). The path behind the temple leads to the edge of the peak. Since this peak is relatively higher than the surrounding peaks, it offers a wonderful view. The mountain peaks stand proudly in the sunlight while the small rivulets running down them glisten like molten silver. Towards the northern side, in the distance, you can see Rajgad and the Bhatghar dam, towards the east Purandar fort and the river Neera, towards the west Rohida, Kenjalgad and Kamalgad and towards the south, Pandavgad and Panchagani.

There is a large, tree-laden plateau atop the Mandhardevi hill. Even during mid-afternoon the weather here is quite chilly. It is said that the rulers of the erstwhile Bhor principality wished to promote this as a hill station and had even made some attempts to do so. Although their attempts failed, Mandhardevi still retains its beauty and can even now be promoted as an excellent tourist spot.

Varandha Ghat

There are several routes for people from the coastal region of Maharashtra to travel into the hinterland. In ancient times traders would bring their merchandise to Mahad, Kalyan, Nalasopara and other such small ports. From here they would transport their goods to the large market towns of Paithan and Junnar. Among the ghat roads they used to climb the mountains were Naneghat, Malshej, Bhorghat, Varandha, Ambenali-Amba, Amboli and Phonda. Several of these now have proper tarred roads and even today are used regularly to travel from the coastal regions. Varandha is one such route.

The Sahyadris stretch out to the east of Mahad. The average height of the mountains in this range is 4,500 feet. Mahabaleshwar, located on the Ambenali ghat on the Mahad-Pune or the Mahad-Satara road, is a famous hill station. Just before the Ambenali ghat

Fact File

Best time - All year

Location - Near Mahad (Elevation: 4,500 feet)

Getting there - By ST buses, four hour drive from Mumbai

Where to stay - At Mahad

Where to eat - Only tea and snacks available

near the Mahad MIDC, is a small road known for its dangerous bends and curves. Formerly the road was extremely narrow and travelling by State Transport bus meant sitting with your heart in your mouth! After the final turning at Varandha the valley below spreads out before your eyes, giving you a tremendous feeling of deja vu, so similar is it to the Khandala ghat.

Varandha is very strategically located and naturally, was of great importance historically. Several ancient forts can be spotted here. Towards the left peak of the ghat is the Kawlya Killa (approximately 2,000 feet high) standing like a guard at the edge of the ghat. As you climb the ghat, just before Varandha village you notice a small road which breaks off to lead to a place that has become famous, because Samarth Ramdas Swami once resided here, and is known as Shivthar Ghat. Just when you think you have reached the top of the ghat, you realize that there is still more to go. Another 900 to 1000 feet, in fact! At the top, you come upon a spectacular view of Rajgad and Torana. Towards the left, below you, is Raigad. As you begin the descent you will be able to see Kangori or Mangalgad and Raireshwar.

The road from Mahad to Varandha is about 20 kilometres long. Several State Transport buses ply on this route. While there is no place here where one can stay, there are several tea and bhaji (pakora) stalls en route. On leaving Mahad it is possible to take a night halt at Bhor which is approximately 40 kilometres away from Varandha.

Meera Hill

Located just 76 kilometres from Mumbai, Meera Hill was in the limelight some time ago for an attempt to make it another

Matheran. It certainly has all the necessary ingredients for a successful hill station - lots of open space, water all year round and easy accessibility, thanks to a good tar road.

Fact File

Best time- Monsoons

Location -- 76 kms. from Mumbai on the Mumbai-Goa highway (Elevation: 1,800 feet)

Getting there - By Road off Pen Khopoli road at Sopoli village

Where to stay - Day trip from Mumbai

Where to eat -- Carry your own food

Meera Hill is situated near Pen off the Mumbai-Goa highway. About 7 kilometres down the Pen-Khopoli road is the village of Sapoli, which lies at the foothills of Meera Hill. To reach the hill you have to cross a river. During the monsoon the river swells and the villagers have had to build a wooden bridge across it. Once you cross the bridge, stick to the path on the left till you come to the wide kuchcha road which takes you up the hill. Although not a very steep climb it is best done in stages. A first-time climber is sure to find it exhausting. During the monsoon the road is generously endowed with small and large waterfalls. At the first halt there is a small village called Bhormal. To the left you will see Manikgad, while Karnala is clearly visible from the rear of the village. The real climb begins at Bhormal; it can take over an hour to get to Thakarwadi at the top of the peak.

Meera Hill is about 1800 feet high, so the climate is quite cool. Since it is located in the Konkan region there is the usual splendid view of green fields below. Although the forest on top is not as dense as in Matheran, there is still quite a lot of greenery. The main places of interest atop the hill are the Vyagreshwar temple and the grand waterfall behind the temple. The hill, however, is so large, that even after reaching the top it can be quite difficult to locate the whereabouts of the temple. After the six-kilometre climb, you have to walk for about 3 more kilometres before you reach the temple. It can be quite nerve- racking to find your own way about especially during the monsoon when the villagers are busy in their fields and have no time to guide you. To reach the temple you follow the path through the fields leaving the village to one side.

The path leads right to the edge of the peak, where the temple is located. Well-constructed steps lead to the temple and a small water tank has also been built nearby. Sindoor-smeared pillars stand outside this large temple which houses a shivling. Although you can hear the sound of the waterfall in the temple, it is not immediately visible. Go behind the temple, climb down for a while and suddenly you will come upon an astounding sight. Falling from a height of approximately 100 feet, this breathtaking waterfall makes the long climb really worthwhile. To fully appreciate it, this one-day trek is best undertaken during the monsoon.

Igatpuri

On the Mumbai-Nashik road, just after the Thal Ghat, is the town of Igatpuri. Its location is similar to that of Khandala on the Mumbai-Pune road and both places are at approximately the same height of 1,900 feet. Igatpuri experiences a much colder climate however. While Khandala is well-known as a salubrious hill station, Igatpuri is better known as a large railway junction. Actually, there is much more to Igatpuri than its railway connection!

Fact File

Best time- All year

Location -- On the Mumbai-Nashik road just after Thal ghat (Elevation:1900 feet)

Getting there - By Road a three-hour drive (135 kms. from Mumbai) or three hours by rail

Where to stay - Private hotels

Where to eat - Many restaurants

Places of interest:

Bhatsa River Valley : Just as you enter Igatpuri after the Thal ghat, is a dense valley of trees towards the right, in the basin of the river Bhatsa.

Unta (Camel) Valley : Further down from the Bhatsa Valley is the Unta Valley which is formed by the partition of two mountains. The main attraction here is the 1,000-foot high waterfall, of which you can get a spectacular view in the rainy season.

Ghatan Devi : Prior to entering Igatpuri, a small distance from Unta Valley, is a small road towards the left. Half a kilometre down this road is the temple of Ghatan Devi. From behind the temple you can see the Tringalwadi Fort and the Utvad, Trimak and Harihar range of mountains.

The Five Level Waterfalls : A kuchcha road from the Ghatandevi temple leads you to the railway line. On the other side of the line, at a little distance, you can see a waterfall which falls in five stages. Although the path to the waterfall is not easy, the view is well worth the effort.

Lakes : There are three lakes in this area. The first is the one built by the Igatpuri Municipality at the foot of the hills. A little ahead, towards the left, after walking through the old parts of the town, is the Railway Lake. The third lake is 2 kilometres from the town and known as the Talegaon Lake.

Tringlwadi Fort : Just beyond the Mahindra and Mahindra Compound you can see the top of a fort shaped like a turban. The path at the foot of the hills will lead you to the fort which is at a height of 3,000 feet. Only parts of its steps and surrounding wall are still intact. There is a Maruti (Hanuman) temple on the other side of the fort. A panoramic view stretches in front; you can see the mountain ranges from Kulang to Kalsubai, the peaks of Utvad and Harihar and the lakes to the east.

Dhammagiri : Outside the town in the foothills of the mountain, is this monastery. People from all over the country as well as from other countries visit this monastery to practise Pashyana meditation.

There are several other places you can visit by making Igatpuri your base: Upper Vaitarna - 26 kilometres, Bhandardara - 35 kilometres, Randha - 40 kilometres, Khodala - 30 kilometres. For trekkers wishing to go to Kulang, Alang, Madan and Kalsubai, Igatpuri is a convenient place to halt.

Accommodation varies from the rather expensive Manas and Ambassador Hotels, to the cheaper Bombay Lodge. Several luncheon homes here offer both vegetarian and non-vegetarian food.

All railway trains stop at Igatpuri. State Transport buses on the Nashik-Manmad route also stop here. The distance between Mumbai and Igatpuri is 135 kilometres and can be covered in three and a half hours. This may not be a fashionable hill resort but for those wanting a relaxing holiday at an off-beat hill station, Igatpuri is the place.

Ajoba Mountain and its Surroundings

Fact File

Best time- All year

Location -- Off the Mumbai-Nashik road

(Elevation: 4000 feet)

Getting there - One and a half hour drive from Asangaon, ST buses from Shahapur

Where to stay -- Shahapur private hotels

Where to eat -- Carry your own food

Kalsubai : Dubbed the Everest of Maharashtra, this mountain stands tall at 1,646 metres, approximately 5,500 feet. Towards its west lie Madangad, Alangad and Kulandgad, while towards the south-west are Ratnagad, Ghanchakkar, Katrabai, Ajoba and Harishchandragad. All these mountains are higher than 4,500 feet. Called the Balaghat range or the Baleshwar range, these mountains are difficult to reach. With no motorable roads, only avid trekkers and mountaineers are familiar with the beauty of nature which is abundant here. Deep tree-filled valleys, meandering rivers and treacherous-looking overhanging peaks contribute to a type of terrain that is hardly seen anywhere else in Maharashtra but in Mahabaleshwar. In between the Ratangad and Harischandragad mountains, stands the Aaja Mountain, popularly known as the Ajoba (grandfather). Like an elderly statesman this huge mountain stands tall surrounded by the other peaks of the Baleshwar range. The western side of this mountain is approximately 3,500 to 4,000 feet high. Whichever side of the mountain you decide to tackle, it takes a day's walk to reach the top. It is not that difficult however to reach the Ajoba Dev temple or Rishi Valmiki's samadhi or the place known as Sita's Cradle.

80 kilometres from Mumbai on the Mumbai-Nashik highway is Shahpur village. Towards the right while travelling towards

Nashik from Shahpur is a road which takes you to Kinhavali. 29 kilometres down this road is the village of Dolkhamb. Towards the left on the Kinhavali junction-Dolkhamb road is the Bhatsa dam. Dolkhamb and Sakurdi (4 kilometres from Dolkhamb) are at the foothills of Ratangad, Katrabai and Ajoba. To reach Samarad from Dolkhamb you have to use the Karoli Ghat. To reach Kumshet on the Aaja Mountain from Sakurdi you have to travel via the ghat called Dara or Guyricha dara. Most amateur trekkers will find these ghats difficult and may like to use the 7-kilometre stretch of kuchcha road from Sakurdi to Ajoba Dev and Rishi Valmiki's samadhi. A motorcycle or jeep can also go up to this point. The path thereafter is very steep and through dense jungle. After an hour's climb you will reach the temple and Valmiki's samadhi.

Thick forest covers the area. Beyond the protruding edge of the mountain here is the area known as Sitamai's cradle. It takes half an hour through a rock-strewn path to reach this spot.

This is a day-long trip from Mumbai and you will be able to return only late at night. State Transport buses run from Shahpur to Dolkhamb. The view from the 4,500-foot Aajoba mountain is fantastic. Not only can you see the peaks of Kalsubai, Ghodishep, Ratangad and Katrabai but you can see right down into the Konkan as well. Trekking the mountain peaks through the ghat region is easier. The Malegaon junction near the village of Rajur takes you via Shirpunje village to the village of Kumshet in the foothills. From here for approximately 26 kilometres till Pachanai at the foot of Harishchandragad, there is only a kuchcha road. Most of these routes are for experienced trekkers. The distance from Mumbai to Rajur via Igatpuri is about 190 kilometres.

Aahupe Ghat

As you leave Murbad on the Kalyan-Malshej Ghat road, you will notice the majestic Sahyadri Mountains towards the right. If the weather is clear you will see the whole range from Siddhagad at one end to Kulangad at the other. Solid rock walls on one side and dangerous edges on the other overlook the deep valleys towards

Fact File

Best time- All year

Location -- Murbad on the Malshej-Kalyan road (Elevation: 4000 feet)

Getting there - Only by road

Where to stay -- Aahupe or at Ghodegaon

Where to eat -- Carry your own food

the coastal Konkan region. With an average height of 4,500 feet, this range has Maharashtra's tallest peaks Kalsubai (5,500 feet), Kulang (4,800 feet), Ratangad (4,200 feet), Ajoba mountain (4,600 feet), Harishchandra (4,700 feet), Jeevadhan (3,800 feet), Dhakoba (4,100 feet), Durga fort (3,800 feet) and Siddhgad (3,200 feet). When you reach Vaishakhare on leaving Murbad, you know you have reached the mountains. The black rock of the mountains set against the green of the fields gives this area a dramatic beauty of its own. There were several routes into these mountains from the coastal Konkan region. Many of these routes are still used regularly by villagers living in villages both in and at the foothills of these mountains. Only the Malshej ghat is a tarred road, which can be used by motorized vehicles, others remain footpaths for the exclusive use of the villagers. These paths include the Kasheli ghat, Darya ghat, Sakurdi ghat, Sadade ghat, Nane ghat, Amboli ghat, Bhorandyanche daar and Aahupe ghat.

The Aahupe ghat is used to travel from Dehari-Khopivali to the village of Aahupe in the ghat region. While the ghat road is not too arduous, it is covered in dense forest, and the first glimpse of it from Aahupe village can be frightening. The edges of the mountain are steep and are sheer drops right into the Konkan. The sight from this 4,000 foot high peak is intimidating. The forts of Gorakh and Machchindragad (both about 2,500 feet high) seem absolutely tiny from thi s point. There is a direct road from Dehari to Gorakhgad, through the Aahupe ghat.

Those used to climbing can take the Kalyan-Murbad via Dehri route and they will reach Aahupe after a two and a half hour climb. For the ordinary tourist there are now roads on which vehicles can ply. There is a road from Ghodegaon village on the Bhimashankar road, which goes via the Dimbha dam directly to

Aahupe. The distance between Ghodegaon and Aahupe via this road is 62 kilometres. The final 8-kilometre stretch from Tirpad to Aaahupe is through dense forest. Just 3 kilometres short of Aahupe towards the right, near Pimpargane, you can see the Durga fort and the peak of Dhakoba.

There are paths to the Durga fort and Dhakoba from Pimpargane via Doni, which will take two to three hours. Pimpargane is at a greater height than Aahupe. Just before you enter Aahupe village there is a thick mangrove forest. Towards the left of this is the source of the Ghodnadi River. It is quite a surprise to see that the source of the river and the large Dimba dam is only a tiny rivulet. Towards the left of the Devrai is a Bhairoba temple. A 5-minute walk behind the temple brings you to the edge of the mountain. From here you can see the entire Konkan region and the main mountains of the Sahyadri range. The villagers call this spot Dhag (cloud). Towards the right of Dhag is the peak known as Varada, while to the left is the Tekatvane peak.

The village of Aahupe has a population of 60. The people here mainly belong to the Mahadev Koli community. The villagers have little interaction with city folk and are very simple and hospitable. There are no urban facilities available here so, naturally, there are no hotels. On request, the sarpanch of the village will make arrangements for food and a place to stay. The main occupation of the villagers is farming nagli, varai and rice, and collecting honey which is later sold. For basic necessities like oil and salt they climb down to the shops in the villages of Adivare or Talghar, three hours away. The other alternative for them is to go to Dhasai in the Konkan via Aahupe and Khopivali. From here they can take the bus to Ghodegaon. The people here are so poor however that they prefer to walk 4,000-feet down the mountain and go to Kalyan via Dhasai rather than spend two rupees on bus fare. A two-hour climb down and a two and a half-hour climb up to save two rupees, makes us realize the value of money! The incidence of night blindness is very high among these villagers.

A thick forest surrounds the Aahupe village. This forest is known as Bhattiche Raan. About 8 kilometres from here is Kondhal which can be reached on foot. From there it is possible to take a State Transport bus to Bhimashankar. The distance from

Bhimashanker to Aahupe via this route is about 16 kilometres. Kokam, mango, jambhool and karvanda (berries) trees can be found in the forest. This has been declared a protected forest area so you can also see animals like foxes, leopards, deer, boar, monkeys and hares. Unique to this forest is a flying squirrel. There is also a large population of peacocks. A wide-ranging variety of birds including the Bhardwaj, peafowls, etc., can be seen here.

While going to the Bhattiche Raan from the village of Aahupe you will come upon a small waterfall known as the Waghmacha Waterfall. Just beyond this begins the Aahupe ghat. It offers an excellent view. The houses at the foothill in Khopivali village look like miniatures.

Normally cool and pleasant, during the monsoon there is heavy rainfall. The points here do not have westernized names like those at Mahabaleshwar and Matheran, and other than hard-core trekkers very few people venture this way. Most of the points are as picturesque as those at the better known hill stations. There are no hotels or modern conveniences here. While trekkers can request accommodation from the Sarpanch, the village headman, families should find amocomodation at Ghodegaon and after finishing the trek in a day, return to Ghodegaon for the night. If you make Ghodegaon your base it is possible to visit both Aahupe and Bhimashankar in a short trip of two to three days. Ghodegon is 200 kilometres from Mumbai via Junnar. Regular State Transport buses ply between Junnar and Ghodegon (25 kilometres). There are good hotels at Narayangaon, which is 18 kilometres from Ghodegaon.

If the government makes arrangements Aahupe can become a nice tourist spot. Presently, of the 62-kilometre road from Ghodegon to Aahupe, only 8 kilometres is tarred, therefore when it rains the State Transport bus service is irregular. For those bored with the popular but overcrowded hill stations, Aahupe provides a definite change.

Mahabaleshwar

The main Sahyadri range rises to the left after passing Mahad on the Mumbai-Goa highway. The plateaux of Raireshwar,

Kolheshwar and Mahabaleshwar form part of this scenic range. All three are hill stations although Kolheshwar and Raireshwar are not as well-known as Mahabaleshwar which gained popularity during the British rule. Mahabaleshwar also finds a place in history. Shivaji Maharaj is credited with having performed pooja at the Shri Kshetra Mahabaleshwar Mandir. Towards the west of Mahabaleshwar lies Pratapgad; the valley between the two is said to have been the site of Afzal Khan's ignominious defeat.

Fact File

Best time- All year except during monsoons

Location - Six hour drive from Mumbai. Turn at Mahad on the Mumbai-Goa highway, or via Mumbai-Pune or Mumbai-Bangalore highway (Elevation: 4700 feet)

Getting there - By Road or by the many tourist buses

Where to stay -- MTDC, Private hotels

Where to eat -- Plenty of eateries

The easiest route to Mahabaleshwar is via the Mumbai-Goa highway. Traverse the breathtaking Poladpur ghat after Mahad for 42 kilometres and you will arrive at this famous hill station. An alternative route is via the Mumbai-Pune or Mumbai-Bangalore highway. Cross the Katraj, Khambatki ghats after leaving Pune and take the right turn to Wai, heading for Panchgani. Both routes are equidistant, but the Mumbai-Goa road is recommended if you want to really experience the climb to the hill station which is at a height of 1,438 metres or 4700 feet. Since Pune is already at a height, the road from there will not offer the same kind of experience. There is a third route via Satara, as beautiful, but not very well-known and therefore less used. Leading from the Kanher Dam, along the banks of the river Venna, this 51-kilometre stretch is a visual delight.

Mahabaleshwar has thick forest cover and is known to receive the second highest rainfall in the country. Due to this heavy downpour Mahabaleshwar is closed for four months during the monsoon.

Mahabaleshwar and Matheran are both well known for their pleasant climate. However while the beauty of the Konkan still remains intact in the less-developed Matheran, Mahabaleshwar has become more commercialized. Even so, it has its own charm because it is twice as high as Matheran. The several look-out points scattered through the hill station offer an enchanting view of deep green valleys and rugged peaks. Since these points are at least 8 kilometres away from the marketplace and situated in different directions, it is advisable to drive to them.

Most of these points were discovered by the British and named after them. To the west is Lodwick Point, discovered by General Lodwick. Kate's Point, discovered by John Malcolm and named after his daughter, faces the neighbouring hill station of Panchgani. Arthur's Seat, discovered by Arthur Mallet is Mahabaleshwar's most precariously- situated point. The highest of all is Wilson Point.

The most ancient site in Mahabaleshwar is the Kshetra Mahabaleshwar, source of five rivers-the Krishna, Koyna, Savitri, Gayatri and Venna. The Savitri river flows down to the west through the Konkan while the others flow eastwards. The Koyna flows into Tapola lake which is 26 Kilometres away. The 51-kilometre long Shivsagar project, situated on this river, is the largest dam in the state. The famous Lingmala Waterfall is located on the Venna River.

The massive Krishna River valley is visible from Kate's Point. The Dhom Dam is located on this river.

Places of interest:

12 kilometres away from the market, Arthur's Seat offers a stunning view of the surrounding gorges. Visible from here as well as from Elphinstone Point are the ruins of Chandragad and Mangalgad. Just below Arthur's Seat is a place called the Window. Trekkers can make the extremely arduous trek to the Konkan from here. From this point you can look down at the 4,000-foot deep valley. Both these points are very popular with tourists. If you look carefully through your binoculars you will spot Pratapgad in the distance.

Between Elphinstone Point and Arthur's Seat is a small pond said to be used as a watering hole by tigers. The water here is very cold and sweet, similar to that found at the Devtanki on Sinhagad.

Kate's Point is probably the most picturesque spot in Mahabaleshwar, overlooking the blue waters of the Dhom Dam in the Krishna Valley, the bell-shaped Kamalgad towards the left and Panchgani's tabletop in the front. Kate's Point can be reached through a thick undergrowth of trees. From the edge of Kate's Point you will be able to see a formation of rocks known as Needle's Hole.

Clearly visible from Lodwick Point is Pratapgad. Also visible from here is the two-headed peak known as Saddleback Point. To the west of Mahabaleshwar is the popular Bombay Point, also known as Sunset Point. 3 kilometres from the market place are found Helen's Point and Robber's Cave. Closest to the marketplace is Wilson Point.

30 kilometres from Mahabaleshwar, along a very scenic route, lies Tapola, on the banks of the Shivsagar Lake. The scenic road winds through the mountains, with the Koyna Valley to one side and the river to the other. Speed boats are an attraction at Tapola.

Local produce:

Mahabaleshwar is famous for its strawberries, raspberries and mulberries. At the edge of the Venna Lake locals sell huge quantities of these fruits, in addition to fresh carrots and radish. The local apiary produces excellent honey. On a guided tour, you can witness how honey is collected here.

The surrounding forests are lush and full of an interesting variety of flora and fauna. It is not possible to spot too many wild animals as they are frightened away by the large crowds always present in the hill station.

Accommodation to suit all budgets is available in Mahabaleshwar. Among the established hotels are Dina, Savoy, Paradise, Shreyas, Blue Heavens and the MTDC holiday cottages. During the season rates can vary from Rs 400 to Rs 1,500 per head.

Good bus and taxi services are available from Mumbai, Pune and Satara. The travelling time from Mumbai is about seven hours. You will need at least four days to see Mahabaleshwar properly.

Matheran

From the time I was a child, I have spent a lot of time exploring the different regions of Maharashtra. Roaming the mountains and

Fact File

Best time- All year

Location -- Toy train from Neral or by road upto Dasturi Point (Elevation: 2600 feet)

Getting there - One and a half hours by road or train to Neral. 20 minutes by road from Neral. The scenic narrow gauge train journey from Neral (2 hrs.) is recommended

Where to stay -- MTDC, Private hotels

Where to eat -- Plenty of eateries

dense forests has brought me much joy. The Ratangad to Harishchandragad area in the Western ghats, the forests near Vasota and the area from Jawhar to Gambhirgad have especially fascinated me. The forests near Bhimashankar are very popular with tribals and serious trekkers. Other people are put off by the amount of walking and physical discomfort involved in visiting places like these that are off the beaten track. The ordinary tourist prefers well-known places like Mahabaleshwar and Matheran even though they can prove to be an expensive proposition.

Matheran is my favourite getaway. I visit it at least twice a year. My first introduction to Matheran was with my parents. In addition to the cool climate and the dense forests, the major attraction was the toy train running from Neral to Matheran. My father also enjoyed exploring so we would get up early in the morning to take long walks to Panorama Point. On one such walk I remember switching on the transistor to hear Rag Todi being played on the santoor by Pandit Shivkumar Sharma. That exhilarating experience remains with me even today. I never understood anything about classical music then but I had the intuitive feeling that what I was listening to was unique and special. I give Matheran the credit for awakening my interest in classical music.

I have trekked through the various hills around Matheran at different times of the day and despite visiting each of the points several times I still derive the same pleasure from every new visit. My favourite spots are Garbut Point and Alexander Point. I also enjoy spending the evening at Madhavji Point.

Fortunately Matheran still has a heavy forest cover. As you walk through the forests in the morning you will hear the chirping of birds greeting the sun and without realizing it you will have wandered deeper into the forest than you might have wanted to. In the morning hordes of people make for Panorama (Sunrise) Point. Evening sees them all converging at Sunset Point. The sunrise is equally beautiful from Garbut Point. For sunsets head for Panorama Point or near Charlotte Lake.

Matheran in the monsoon has a different charm even though it is difficult to really see anything. Just sipping a cup of hot tea, wrapped up cosily in a shawl, with the clouds gathering around you, makes up for the disappointment of not being able to visit the points. I still make the time to take two days off from my hectic schedule in Mumbai to re-energize myself in my favourite hill station.

Matheran is most conveniently located for visitors from Mumbai and Pune. At a height of 803 metres (2,600 feet) Matheran has the thickest forest cover after Chandrapur. The green cover and the red earth add to its quaint charm. Several parts of the mountains have eroded, creating good lookout points all named after the British who discovered them. Matheran lies slightly apart from the main Sahyadri range. This range of mountains begins from Haji Malang at Kalyan; followed by the Badlapur hills and the Navra-navari hill. Further ahead is the Chanderi peak which stands out like a comb, followed by Mahismaal hill, Nakhind hill and Peb, and finally, Matheran.

The toy train to Matheran traverses between the Peb hill and Panorama point in Matheran. The ruins of a fort can be seen on the Peb hill.

In 1850, an Englishman named Mallet, then Collector of Thane, spotted this hill from Chowk village. An avid trekker, he and a local villager climbed up to the spot that is now known as One Tree Point. He is said to have climbed down via Rambagh Point.

Mesmerized by the place, he later built a house there. Several of his friends and other Britishers followed his example. Since then of course, Matheran has become a very popular hill station.

At the foothills of Matheran on the Mumbai-Pune railway line is the village of Neral. The toy train starts from here and takes two hours to cover a distance of 21 kilometres! The experience however is one that all tourists look forward to. It is said that this train began running in 1907 as a result of the inspiration of a gentleman named Adamji Peerbhoy.

The secret of Matheran's beauty lies in the fact that no motorized vehicles are allowed in the town. People travelling by car can climb the hill from Neral but have to halt their vehicles at the Dasturi Junction just below Mountberry point. By limiting vehicles the town has remained pollution-free. A 25-minute walk from Dasturi junction and you are in the Matheran market. Most of the hotels are situated near the marketplace.

There are several ways of getting to Matheran:

- The toy train from Neral.
- The path leading to Little Chowk point.
- The 8-kilometre tar road from Neral.
- The 13-kilometre path from Karjat to Garbut Point.
- The 19-kilometre route from Gadeshwar Lake via Panvel, Ner, Waghachi Wadi, emerging at Porcupine Point.

The climate is mostly moderate. The temperature in summer averages 20 to 30 degrees centigrade. In winter it fluctuates between 15 to 25 degrees centigrade. In May the evenings are very pleasant. The best time for picnics is between September and March. Waterfalls are visible at several places at this time. Heavy rainfall is experienced between June to August; and clouds rule over Matheran. For days on end there is no sunlight and villagers are confined to their homes.

Though tourists usually stay away from Matheran during the monsoon, serious trekkers have changed that. A few hotels are now functional during the rains. According to me the real beauty of Matheran can be experienced during the rainy season. Anyone who enjoys walking through the mist-filled forests will love the place in the monsoon. There are over 150 types of trees and several medicinal plants to be found in these evergreen forests. The biggest advantage of the green cover is the shade it provides so that you can wander around without discomfort.

Places of interest:

Charlotte Lake : One kilometre from the market, this is Matheran's main source of water.

Panorama Point : Known as the 'King' of all points, it is at the northernmost tip of Matheran, approximately 5.5 kilometres from the marketplace. Neral lies to the east while from the west you have a view of the Gadeshwar Lake and the area up to Panvel. If you look carefully you will spot the sea in the distance. Most people come here to see the sunrise but you can witness the sunset here as well. Monkey Point, Porcupine Point, Maldunga Point, Heart Point, etc, are all towards the west of this point. The Peb fort is visible from here.

Sunset Point (Porcupine Point) : The mountain facing this point is known as Prabalgad. The sun sets behind Prabalgad. 3.5 kilometres from the post office, it is possible to reach this point from Waghachi Wadi.

Louisa Point : Located 3.5 kilometres from the market, towards the western side of Matheran. The view from Rustomji, Chinoy, Malang, Honeymoon and Louisa Points is similar. On the road from Charlotte Lake to Louisa Point is Echo Point. Many tourists come armed with crackers to hear the resounding echo. The Edward and King George Points are also on this route.

Chowk Point : Situated towards the southernmost tip of Matheran. From here you can see the village of Chowk below. One Tree Hill Point is located close by. In front of One Tree Hill is one of the most intimidating valleys in the region. If you look carefully you will see a small path winding up to the peak of the hill. This peak is separated from the main mountain range. For many years it had only one solitary tree on it, hence the name; today there are several other bushes growing around it. A small pathway named Shivaji's Ladder was the route taken by Mallet when he first discovered Matheran. Khandala, Rajmachi, Nagphani as well as Manikgad, Karnala and Irsalgad can be seen from here. Chowk Point is 4 kilometres from the market while One Tree Point is 3.5 kilometres away. Charlotte Lake is on the route from One Tree Hill to the market. Alexander Point and Rambag Point are also on this route.

Garbut Point : 5 kilometres from the market, this is a large but generally ignored point. The road leading to it is very beautiful. One side plunges down into the valley while on the other stands the forest. The road from Karjat to Matheran is via Garbut Point.

Dasturi or Mountberry Point : The point after which motorized vehicles are banned. There are 2 gardens in Matheran, Paymaster Park and Nowrojee Lord Garden. There is a memorial to Hutatma Kotwal in the Nowrojee Lord Garden.

In addition to Charlotte Lake, Mallet's Spring and Walker's Tank are the other watering holes. Mallet's Spring does not dry up even in the summer. It is just 1.5 kilometres from the market. Walker's Tank is on the road to Louisa Point.

The most commonly found animal in Matheran is the monkey. They are totally unafraid of humans and will snatch a packet of biscuits out of your hand if you are not careful. Their favourite pastime is to create a racket on the tin roof of the hotels! Wild cats, spotted deer and hares also abound here. At times leopards from the forests below can be spotted, but they have never been known to attack humans in the area. A large variety of birds, including larks, kingfishers, robins etc. can be found. The Paradise Flycatcher, a pure white bird with a long tail can also be spotted in the area.

Local produce:

The locals depend mainly on tourism for a livelihood. There are several handicraft stores catering to the large tourist population. Deerskin shoes and chappals are a speciality. Miniature chappals and sandals are sold on the roadside. The honey and chikki from Matheran is also famous, and so are the white walking sticks.

Accommodation:

The timings of the toy train have been synchronized with the Mumbai-Pune trains. During the rainy season this service is suspended. A taxi service between Neral and Matheran is also available. For those who don't want to brave the curves up to Dasturi Point in their own cars, parking space at Neral is available with Dr. Shitut. Plenty of accommodation is available to suit all budgets. The MTDC guesthouse is close to Dasturi Point, bookings for which can be made at the MTDC office in Mumbai. Other hotels include the Kumar Plaza, Maneklal Terrace, Royal, Premdeep, Central, Shireen and Woodlands. Among the older hotels are Diwadkar, Laxmi, Girivihar, Regal and Lords. Rates vary from Rs 700-1,500 per head in the better hotels while the slightly less expensive range from Rs 200-300 per head. Private residences also take in boarders and their rates are much cheaper. For trekkers, Diwadkar's Hotel is the best bet for food. Three days is ideal for a break at Matheran.

Khandala

On one of the busiest roads in the country, the Mumbai-Pune highway, lies the hill station of Khandala, 92 kilometres from Mumbai. Although the ghat leading to it is actually called Bhor ghat, it is more popularly known as the Khandala ghat. Its height from mean sea level is 622 metres, approximately, 1800 feet.

Fact File

Best time- All year

Location -- On the Mumbai Pune highway, one and a half hour drive on the Expressway. 92 kms. from Mumbai (Elevation: 1800 feet)

Getting there - By Road, train or bus

Where to stay -- MTDC, Private hotels

Where to eat -- Plenty of eateries

Since the main Mumbai-Pune road cuts through this tiny town, tourists seeking a relaxed idyll with nature, often find that their sojourn is disturbed by the noise of the heavy truck traffic on the highway. Yet for those really wanting to make the most of this hill station, there are several places away from the highway where it is possible to enjoy nature's solitude. Situated as it is on the main plateau of the Sahyadris, the hill station is spread over a vast area.

If you are travelling from Mumbai, a tunnel is the first sign that you are nearing Khandala. On emerging from the tunnel you will be struck by the stupendous view of the valley on the left, making your difficult journey through the ghats more than worthwhile. If you arrive during the rainy season, you'll see the clouds hanging so low you can almost touch them. And then a ray of sunlight gently pushes aside the clouds, giving you a tantalizing glimpse of a sparkling waterfall crashing into the valley below. Tourists throng the short parapet wall here, while indulging in a cup of hot tea and roasted corncobs. Khandala is just around the corner.

Places of interest:

Rajmachi Point: Just before descending the ghat to Khopoli from Lonavala, on the right is Rajmachi point. From here the ruins of Rajmachi castle, Srivardhan, Manrajan and the Ulhas river valley are clearly visible

The Duke's Nose: Known in Marathi as Nagphani Point. As you climb the Bhor ghat you cannot miss a mountain to the right, noticeable for its sharp peak. The local people call it Nagphani point, due to its resemblance to a cobra's hood. From a particular point in Khandala this peak resembles the nose of a sleeping man, therefore the British named it The Duke's Nose. Slightly behind this is a smaller peak called the Duchess's Nose which must be reached first before you can climb to the Duke's Nose. To get there you have to walk for 10 minutes from Khandala station, leaving the town behind you. Left of the railway line is a tarred road going up the hill. A 10-minute walk up this road leads to a pump house, beyond which a path leads up the hill. This path winds around the hill. From here it is a short and relatively easy climb up to the Duke's Nose.

There is another route via the Tiger's Leap Point. This is a narrow path between INS Shivaji on the one side and Tiger Valley on the other. However, access to tourists via this route has now been closed.

On the top of the Duke's Nose is a small temple. The height of this peak is 3,200 feet from sea level and the height from the ghats is around 800 feet. Clearly visible from here are Karnala to the west, the Matheran range to the north-west, the Rajmachi to Kalsubai range to the north, Tung, Tikona, Koraigad to the south and Lohagad and Visapur forts to the east. This trek is very popular during the monsoon season.

Lonavala

Just down the road from Khandala is Lonavala, 96 kilometres from Mumbai, and probably the most popular getaway for many in the metropolis.

Places of interest:

Tata Lake (Lonavala Lake): After crossing the bridge over the railway line take the road to INS Shivaji. Ryewood Forest lies to the left. This is protected forest land and there are some very old trees here dating back over 75 years. It is also home to a Shiva temple and a small park for children. A few minutes away from Ryewood forest on the INS Shivaji road is the Tata Lake. A large variety of trees can be found on the many islands in the lake.

Bushi Lake: Another 4 kilometres ahead on the same road is Bushi Lake. This is the property of the Central Railway. During and after the rains this area is especially captivating. In summer however, this lake is completely dry.

Sakur Pathar: From the Bushi Lake you can see at a height, a flat plateau known as Sakur Pathar. There is a path leading to this from Bushi Lake. There were plans to make a hill station here but this did not materialize due to the acute shortage of water. Near the gate of INS Shivaji is a dusty road that leads to the plateau. In my opinion the plateau affords the best view in Lonavala - the Konkan on the one side and the Deccan expanse on the other.

Walwan Lake : As you leave Lonavala for Pune either by train or road it is impossible to miss the long Walvan Dam. About 2.5 kilometres from Lonavala, this is a popular tourist spot. At the foot of the dam is an exquisite garden.

Tungarli Lake : In the direction of Pune, a small 2-km approach road branches off to Tungarli, just before Walvan. The little reservoir here is quite picturesque and forms the chief source of water for the municipal area.

Shirota Lake : To reach this particular lake one has to follow the private rail line of the Tatas from Kamshet. One and a half times larger than the Walvan, this lake has the Rajmachi fort at its westernmost point. It is possible to begin a trek to Rajmachi fort from this spot.

There is plenty of transport to Lonavala and Khandala from both Mumbai and Pune. Any bus or train going to Pune from Mumbai will take a halt at Lonavala. Khandala is about two and a half hours from Mumbai. Other than several private hotels there is an MTDC rest house here.

Tadgaon, Uddhar, Unhere

Fact File

Tadgaon, Uddhar, Unhere

Best time- All year

Location -- Off Pali on the Mumbai Pune highway, About 110 kms from Sion, Mumbai

Elevation 1600 feet

Getting there - By Road, ST buses

Where to stay -- Unhere Zilla Parishad rest house, Tadgaon private hotel, at Pali

Where to eat -- At Pali

For those visiting Pali as part of the Ashtavinayak tour, there are several spots nearby worth seeing. 8 kilometres from Pali on the Mumbai-Goa highway is the village of Wakan. About a kilometre before Wakan there is a road to the right that takes you to Unhere and Uddhar. Unhere is 1.5 kilometres from here, while Uddhar is 7 kilometres.

Near the Vitthal Rakhumai temple at Unhere there are three hot springs. Surrounded by numerous trees, this is a pleasant spot to relax in or take a dip. The Zilla Parishad has a rest house here and food is available at the Chavan Hotel next door. After this interlude, it is possible to drive down to Uddhar. A right turn at the Uddhar village takes you to the ancient Rameshwar Temple.

There is a tank near the temple called Asthikund where people from the surrounding villages immerse the ashes of their dead. Clearly visible, straight ahead of the temple is the Tadgaon hill. On this hill too, is a temple dedicated to Rameshwar. To drive to this temple on the hill, however, one has to return to the main Pali-Khopoli road. On the road to Khopoli from Pali is a signpost that says 'Rameshwar Vaibhav-8 kms'. This is called the Kuravala junction and there is a 12-kilometre stretch of tarred road from this point to Tadgaon. Presently, the Rameshwar Vaibhav

Development Co. Pvt. Ltd. has developed this 1,600-foot high hill as a hill station. The road leading up the hill is a pleasure to traverse during the rainy season and is of special delight to birdwatchers who can spot Golden Orioles, Paradise Flycatchers and Bulbuls flitting between the trees. The forest abounds with hares, foxes and wild boar. At the foot of the hill is the Kawela Dam, which adds to the beautiful surroundings.

The Rameshwar temple is on the eastern side of the hill. From the path leading to the temple, the forts of Sudhagad and Sarasgad on the Sahyadri ranges can be easily spotted. To the west of the hill is a small village, and a short climb from here takes you to Sunset Point. From this point, the Meers hill range near Pen appears to be very close. During the monsoon, a short climb down will take you to a marvellous waterfall.

The height of Tadgaon is similar to Khandala and therefore, it has a pleasant climate. It is possible to spend an entire day here and return to Pali in the evening. An overnight stay is possible at the Shangri-La Hotel, where you can get a good meal as well. State Transport buses ply from Pali and Khopoli. The average distance from Sion to Tadgaon is 110 kilometres, Pune to Tadgaon - 110 kilometres, Khopoli to Tadgaon-40 kilometres and Pali to Tadgaon-20 kilometres.

Khodala, Jawhar, Mokhada, Devbandh, Suryamal

The Sahyadri range is like a divider separating the Konkan region from the Deccan region. While this is very apparent in southern Maharashtra, to the north this divide is not so clear, especially in the region of Khodala, Jawhar and Mokhada. The terrain here is composed of several small hills and therefore, various small hill stations like the ones named above have developed. Since the average height of the hills here is merely 1,500 feet, there are no deep valleys or breathtaking cliffs. The entire region is far softer and more serene. Blessed with a high rainfall, this is an extremely verdant region. After the rains the roadside is dotted with small waterfalls. Several bridges cross the small rivers which flow along the winding roads, creating several picnic spots.

Fact File

Khodala, Jawahar, Mokhada, Devbandh, Suryamal

Best time- All year

Location -- Off Mumbai-Nashik highway, at Thal Ghat.180 kms. from Mumbai (Elevation: 1500 feet)

Getting there - By Road, ST buses

Where to stay -- MTDC , government rest house

Where to eat -- same

Khodla, Mokhada and Jawhar lie off the Mumbai-Nashik road, near Thal Ghat. About 2 kilometres after the commencement of the ghat is a small road to the left. Twenty kilometres along this road is Khodala, another 20 to 22 kilometres ahead lies Mokhada, and further down the road is Jawhar. The distance between Mumbai and Jawhar is 180 kilometres. All three places have government rest houses.

Khodala is the first village you touch. There are plenty of places to see here beginning with the huge waterfall just before you enter the village. The Vaitarna lake and the Shrighata are among the other spots worth checking out. 12 kilometres down the Khodala-Wada road is Suryamal. From here several peaks such as Utwad, Harihar Trimbak and Kulang can be seen. There is a rest house here for those who wish to stay. Four kilometres from Khodala on the Khodala-Mokhada road, is Devbandh with its lovely Ganesh temple. Built on the banks of the river, this pink-coloured temple makes an alluring picture against the lush green. Another place worth visiting here is the centre started by a city-based NGO (non-government organization) Sahyadri Adivasi Bahuvidh Seva Sangh, for the betterment of the tribal people who live in this region. Well-to-do, city-based doctors, architects, bank officers drive down here every Sunday to do their bit to help the adivasis, the local tribals who have been deprived of basic medication and education for years and suffer from malnourishment because of the consumption of poisonous, locally-brewed alcohol. The above organisation has undertaken the task of providing them with basic first aid, helping them find hostels for their school-going children, teaching them co-operative farming and social forestry programmes. This NGO is doing some really commendable work.

After Devbandha, 18 kilometres further down the road is Mokhada. Several peaks like Utwad, Busgad and Phani are close by. Another 13 kilometres down the road is Jawhar. At a height of 1,600 feet it has earned itself the name of 'Mahabaleshwar of Thane district'! There are several spots worth visiting here. The MTDC runs a rest-house; on the opposite side can be seen the remains of the Jayvilas Palace. Other places of interest include the Dadar Kopra waterfall, Hanuman point, and Shirpamal, the place where Shivaji camped with his troops before proceeding to Surat. Sixteen kilometres from here is Bhupatgad, which is of special interest to avid trekkers. It is a mere one-hour climb from the village of Zaap nestling in the foothills.

Bhimashankar

Some of the thickest forest cover on the Sahyadri range can be found at Bhimashanker. It is the source of the Bhima River. Close to the source of the river is an ancient temple complex that is visited by hundreds of devout worshippers every Mahashivratri and Tripuri Purnima. Bhimashanker is not only a place of religious significance but an enchanting tourist spot as well.

Nearly 3200 feet high, the evergreen forest-filled Bhimashanker has a cool climate and affords a wonderful view of the surrounding region, thus becoming a favourite with tourists. The temple here is believed to date back to the Peshwas. Outside the temple are two large pillars between which a large bell dating back to the Portuguese period has been placed. A short walk behind the temple takes you to the river. When the water level here is low you can see a naturally-formed shivling in the river bed with a Nandi Bull alongside. The Bhimashanker forest is a major attraction. A large variety of trees including the jamoon, hirda, mango trees, bay leaf trees, etc., are found in abundance. Animals such as the leopard, sambar (deer), wild boar, foxes and mongoose inhabit the dense verdure.

The giant squirrel, which is otherwise rarely seen in Maharashtra is also known to reside here. During the night some trees appear to be luminous. The glow of light from the trees is apparently due to a particular kind of fungus which grows on them.

Fact File

Best time- June to March

Location -- Via Mumbai-Pune highway, from Talegaon or via Mumbai Kalyan via Malshej ghat.180 kms from Mumbai (Elevation: 3200 feet)

Getting there - By Road, ST buses

Where to stay -- MTDC , temple dharmashala

Where to eat -- same

A short walk to the west of the temple brings you to the highest point on the Bhimashanker hill. From here you can see the Konkan region approximately 2,500 to 2,750 feet below. Several forts including the Padar fort and the Peth fort can be spotted from here. The Matheran range of hills and Ghonemal and Siddhgad can also be seen. The view of the valley from Bhimashanker village is also seen. It is breathtaking. There are two small lakes, the Hanuman Lake and the Devi Lake, atop the hill.

The MTDC has cottages here which can be booked from Mumbai. There are also dharmashalas near the temple where one can spend the night. The food you get over here is strictly vegetarian.

There is a direct road from Mumbai to Bhimashanker. There are two main routes which can be taken. One is via the Mumbai-Pune highway. Just 35 kilometres short of Pune, you take the turning at Talegaon and proceed to Rajgurunagar and Manchar and from there to Bhimashanker. The other, more scenic route, is from Mumbai-Kalyan, Murbad, Junnar and then Bhimashanker via the Malshej ghat. The distance to Bhimashanker by both routes is around 265 kilometres. There is another alternative shortcut for trekkers, and that is to catch a State Transport bus heading to Kashela and Khandas at Karjat. The distance between Karjat and Khandas is 14 kilometres. From Khandas you have to walk around the Padar fort to reach Bhimashanker. This is about 11 kilometres through thick forest and a steep but exhilarating climb.

Bhimashanker experiences a slight water shortage during the summer but it is during the rains and the four months after the rains that this place should really be visited.

JUNGLES, SANCTUARIES & NATURE PARKS

JUNGLES, SANCTUARIES & NATURE PARKS

The state of Maharashtra is best known for its rugged terrain, yet between the mountain ranges and at the base of the numerous hills, lush green vegetation abounds. A large variety of flora and fauna can be found in the forests and sanctuaries, offering a fabulous experience.

Dajipur Sanctuary

> **Fact File**
>
> *Best time- June to March*
>
> *Location -- 75 kms. from Kolhapur at Phonda Ghat, 2300 feet*
>
> *Getting there - By Road,*
>
> *Where to stay -- MTDC ,*
>
> *Where to eat -- same*

One of the well-known ghats rising into the Konkan region from the Deccan plain is the Phonda ghat which connects Kolhapur to Rajapur. Just before the commencement of the ghat, is the village of Dajipur; on the way from Dajipur to Kolhapur, you will come across the Radhanagri dam project. On the drive from Radhanagari to Dajipur you will see that the waters of the dam run parallel to the road. The MTDC rest house at Dajipur is also located at the far end of the dam. The road winds through the forest and as you drive you get tantalizing glimpses of the Radhanagri waters. The distance from Kolhapur to Dajipur is 75 kilometres. The MTDC camp leads into the forest. The main attraction of this 20-square kilometre forest is bison, but you have to go really deep into the forest to actually see them. Leopards and boar are sometimes visible. The forts of Shivgad and Gaganbavda are close by.

Dajipur, at the head of the Phonda ghat, is located at a height of 2,300 feet, and therefore has a pleasant climate. The actual ghat is barely two furlongs from the main village, so spending an evening watching the sunset in the ghat is both convenient and truly rewarding.

Sagareshwar

Fact File

Best time- August and February

Location -- 4 kms. from Takari rail station, 25 kms. from Karad by road, 9 hours by ST bus, 1000 feet

Getting there - By Road,

Where to stay -- Forest rest-house

Where to eat -- same

Sitting among the valleys of the rivers Krishna and Sonhari near Karad and in the man-made sanctuary there, is the 750-year old temple complex of Sagareshwar. The South Central railway station of Takari is just 4 kilometres from Sagareshwar. By road, Takari is 25 kilometres on the Karad-Tasgaon road and is connected by bus to Karad.

In actuality this place is far removed from the sea, though local lore has an explanation of how this temple complex came by its name, which means 'the sea'. The son of Sagar, Jalinder, was a bad ruler and his people were tired of his atrocities. The gods decided to kill this king who so terrorized his people. The grief-stricken father came to this place to meditate. He had a revelation - Lord Shanker appeared before him and granted him a wish. Soon a few drops of the Ganga fell from Shanker's head. Sagar then asked that the Ganga should permanently reside in that spot and the place was duly named Sagareshwar.

This temple complex has 51 temples and 108 shivalings. There is water under the main Sagareshwar shivling. On closer inspection, you will notice that the temples are built in many different styles. Besides Sagareshwar, other temples include those dedicated to Kaileshwar, Trimbakeshwar, Bhimashanker, Panchmukhi Ganpati, Rameshwar, Nageshwar, Kuber, Veerbhadra, Karmeshwar and Aditya. There is also a samadhi of Kurkotak Rishi. The devout flock here in great numbers every Monday in the month of shravan.

A 1.5 kilometre walk from the temple through the Yeshwant ghat brings you to the main gate of the sanctuary. The efforts of D.M. Mohite, a well-known freedom fighter from this area, led to the development of this sanctuary.

The man-made forest of Sagareshwar

From the village of Takari is visible a mountain about 800 to 1,000 feet high. Behind this mountain, spread over an area of 5 square kilometres is the Sagareshwar sanctuary. It is difficult to believe that just 20 years ago, this was barren land. While the vegetation here may not be very dense, it houses a large variety of trees and plants. Teak, dhavda, jamoon, lime, acacia and banyan are among the 37 varieties of trees planted here. A lot of birds are attracted to the trees and you will find the crow pheasant, the warbler, the parrot and the peacock in large numbers.

In 1980, many animals were brought into this sanctuary, among them about 45 sambar deer, black buck and antelopes. Today their number has doubled. In addition, wolves, foxes, hares and jungle cats can also be spotted. An almost-tame baby black buck lives near the rest house, the staff call it their receptionist because it greets visitors and accompanies them from the gate to the rest house. A 5-kilometre stretch of kuchcha road has been constructed from the rest house into the middle of the forest. To the left of this road, a small pagoda-like structure has been built as a look-out. This is a fantastic point from which to watch the sunrise. From here, you can also spot the Lingareshwar temple in the valley. This could also be an echo point, as sound reverberates here. Further down the kuchcha road you come across the Van Vinayak Temple. An idol of Ganesh was found here while the road was being constructed. To the right of this temple is a small pond while, to the left is the Ambika ghat, from where you climb up to the top of the hill. Ranshool Point, at 2,762 feet from mean sea level, is the tallest point. Visible from here in clear weather are the Jyotiba temple near Kolhapur, and Machhindragad to the right. The river Krishna and its valley and Takari station are also visible.

To the left of Ranshool Point is Kirloskar Point. The view from both points is more or less similar. Near the Kirloskar Point is the

Kolhebil Cave. If you walk through it you can reach the Bhairav temple. There is a path from this temple straight to Takari station. To the right of Ranshool Point, at a place known as Mahangund Point, is a large round stone, balanced at the very edge of the hill. Villagers say that this stone has been like this ever since the Koyna earthquake in 1967.

It takes at least 2 days to visit the temple complex, the sanctuary, indulge in bird watching and visit the various points of interest at Sagareshwar. The best time to visit is between the months of August and February, when the weather is very pleasant Arrangements to stay can be made at the forest rest house. The journey from Mumbai to Karad and then Karad to Takari takes about 9 hours by State Transport bus.

Nandur Madhyameshwar

Fact File

Best time- All year around

Location -- 50 kms. from Nashik

Getting there - By Road, by private transport

Where to stay -- Irrigation Department's Guest House

Where to eat -- same

In Maharashtra there are some places very popular with birdwatchers hoping to sight migratory birds. While most of these places are known only to regular birdwatchers, they have the potential to attract even regular tourists. The Nandur Madhyameshwar bird sanctuary is one such place.

The sanctuary is named after the ancient temple located there. Thanks to the dam built on the confluence of the Godavari and Kadva rivers, there is a large reservoir. With dense forests and rich bird life, this is an ideal place to visit.

It is possible to sit on the wall of the dam when the water level is low. Storks, sandpipers, kingfishers and red-wattled lapwings can be seen in large numbers. While local villagers floating on rubber tyres struggle to catch fish, the kingfisher quietly sitting close by, suddenly swoops down on to the still water emerging triumphantly with his catch. Not even the local fishermen put him off and this drama is enacted daily, allowing you to see the brightly-plumed bird up close.

It is also possible to see many birds while sitting in the Irrigation Department's picturesquely-set guesthouse, hidden amongst the trees. The loud chattering of parrots and the sound of the crow pheasant provide slightly raucous background music. Drongos, hornbills and robins can be easily spotted. At sunset this scene is picture-perfect. The red-orange rays of the sun spread across the sky create a glorious backdrop for the numerous birds flying across the skies, and all this is reflected in the placid waters of the lake.

This place has not been developed commercially for the tourist, because although it is only 50 kilometres from Nashik it is difficult to get there unless you have your own vehicle. The State Transport bus service between Nashik and Nandur is skeletal, restricted to a couple of buses. If you miss them you have to make your way in short breaks - first Nashik to Pimpalgaon (29 kilometres), then Pimpalgaon to Niphad (18 kilometres) and finally Niphad to Nandur (13 kilometres). It is possible to hire jeeps from Niphad to Nandur. There is another road from Nashik to Nandur via Sinnar.

At Nandur there is a rest house belonging to the PWD. The British built this well-equipped rest house in 1907. You can book this rest house through the Nashik Public Works Department (PWD). This place is a treat for birdwatchers, and once you visit it you realize why it has been called a mini-Bharatpur.

Vikramgad

Vikramgad is off the Mumbai-Ahmedabad highway on the Manor-Jawahar road. About 21 kilometres from Manor and 106 kilometres from Mumbai is the small village of Vikramgad. The name is actually a misnomer as there is no fort here. There are, however, several other interesting spots in the vicinity worth seeing. Just 6 kilometres from here is a small waterfall called Pilucha Dhabdhaba, which becomes quite grand during the monsoon season. The dam on the Deheraja River near here is also worth seeing, offering quite a spectacular view.

The distance between Vikramgad and Jawahar is only 25 kilometres, so many people make Vikramgad a base for picnics to both places. The Dabosa Waterfall, the Jambhaparsi Waterfall and the Jaysagar Lake, all close to Jawhar, are quite close to Vikramgad as well.

Fact File

Best time- All year around

Location -- Off Mumbai-Ahmedabad highway on the Manor Jawahar road, 106 kms. from Mumbai

Getting there - By Road, by private transport

Where to stay -- Government Guest House at Vikramgad, farmhouse

Where to eat -- same

For trekkers there is an ideal trek from Vikramgad to Bhupatgad through the Pinjal river valley. After spending a night here, it is also easy to access the Kohoj Fort on the Wada-Manor road. Just 7 kilometres from Vikramgad on the Manor road is the Bilya Mountain. The Kavdas and Dhamani Lake on the Surya River are 17 kilometres from here while the Mahalaxmi mountain near Charoti is 30 kilometres.

There is a government guest house at Vikramgad where arrangements to stay can be made. In addition, there is a farmhouse called Nature Trails belonging to Harikrishna Divekar. A long time associate of Dr Salim Ali at the Bombay Natural History Society, Divekar has planted over 350 varieties of trees and plants on five acres of land. The tourist shacks built by him boast all modern conveniences. Because of the vegetation, birds of all types flock here. Divekar runs this entire project with the help of local adivasis.

Nearly all buses from Manor or Jawhar to Nashik halt at Vikramgad. This is a pleasant place to visit either in the monsoon or during the winter season.

Bilya Mountain

The 40-kilometre stretch from Gambhirgad to Vikramgad is located in hilly terrain with dense forest. The result of this lush vegetation is that animals abound within the forests. In addition to foxes, boar and hares, this forest is also home to leopards.

Fact File

Best time- June to March

Location -- Near Vikramgad

Height:1,000 feet

Getting there - By Road, by private transport

Where to stay -- Government Guest House at Vikramgad, farmhouse

Where to eat -- same

Observers say that once, even a tiger was seen in the Kirmira mountain region near Gambhirgad.

On the Bilya Mountain located near Vikramgad, 7 kilometres down the Vikramgad-Manor road, there are several marks to show that leopards inhabit this area. The Bilya Mountain is not very high - just about 800 to 1,000 feet from mean sea level. The weirdly-shaped pinnacles of this mountain make it quite easy to recognize. A path about 7 kilometres from the main tarred road from Vikramgad leads you to the mountain.

Once you see the vegetation here it is clear why leopards inhabit this area. Tall trees line the path on both sides and at the base of these trees are several kinds of bushes, ideal for leopards to ambush their prey. Teak, sheesam, hirda and ficus trees can be seen. Once you leave the main road a 1-kilometre path takes you through dense forest and suddenly you find yourself walking through shoulder high bushes. There is a slight incline but it is not at all difficult to traverse. The eroded edges of the mountain are clearly visible to the left. Deep cavities formed by massive stones falling on each other can be seen. While you rarely see a leopard, the remains of its meal are often clearly visible in the caves. A short climb above these caves and you can see the splendour of Vikramgad. In addition to the animals, several varieties of birds like the crow pheasant, bulbul, kite, cuckoo and robin can also be spotted.

This is a very pleasurable trek during the rainy season. It is convenient to spend the night at Vikramgad.

Pal-Yaval Sanctuary

The Satpura range spreads over the border of Maharashtra and Madhya Pradesh. Most of this mountain range is covered by lush foliage. A part of this forest near the Tapi River has been declared a sanctuary, and is known as the Pal-Yaval sanctuary. Spread over 177 square kilometres, this sanctuary has a wide variety of fauna and flora. There is an excellent government rest house at Pal which can serve as your base.

Fact File

Best time- June to March

Location -- On the Maharashtra-Madhya Pradesh border, 80 kms. from Bhusaval, 25 kms. from Raver

Getting there - By Road, by private transport

Where to stay -- Government Guest House at Pal

Where to eat -- same

The well-equipped rest house has a beautifully laid-out garden. Enhancing the beauty of the garden is a specially-built log hut. The sweet smell of the flowers in the garden make your stay here really pleasurable. The fact that there is such a well-planned rest house in this remote part of the jungle is one of the best things about this sanctuary. The actual sanctuary begins once you cross the river opposite the rest house. Pictures and names of birds have been put up on the barks of the trees, making it easy for one to identify them. Some nilgai (blue bull) and stags have been kept in cages. Trees found here include various kinds of acacia. Tigers, leopards, blue bulls, stag, spotted deer and hyenas inhabit this forest. There is ample opportunity for bird watching near the riverside. Robins, crow pheasant, drongo, bulbul, peacocks and partridges are among the birds you can see. Numerous wagtails and hoopoes can be seen foraging for food. There are also numerous kingfishers and herons. The best part is that some very rare birds can be spotted very easily here.

The nearest bus stand is the one at Raver. There are regular buses from Bhusaval and Jalgaon to Raver. The distance from Bhusaval to Pal is 80 kilometres while Raver to Pal is about 25 kilometres. Thanks to the abundant trees and the elevation, the weather here is quite cool. Accommodation can be obtained at the rest house. You need at least a couple of days to soak in the beauty of this place.

Tansa Sanctuary

Fact File

Best time- June to March

Location -- Off the Mumbai-Nashik highway, 109 kms. from Mumbai

Getting there - By Road, by private transport

Where to stay -- Rest House at Tansa

Where to eat -- same

Most people are familiar with the fact that Mumbai gets its water supply from the lakes of Tansa, Vaitarna and Bhatsa. The area around Tansa and between Vaitarna and Tansa has been declared a sanctuary and makes a pleasant getaway from the city.

On the Mumbai-Nashik highway is Shahpur; about 6 kilometres further is the road leading to Tansa, running parallel to the railway line. About 14 kilometres from here is Tansa Lake. During the monsoon this is a very pleasant drive, running through the lush green forest, seeing only glimpses of the blue waters of the lake before it suddenly appears before you. Most of the 216 square kilometres of forest is full of teak trees. Mango, iron wood and ficus are the other trees seen. Monkeys, spotted deer, stag, boar and the occasional leopard live within this forest. Peacocks, hornbills, crow pheasants, bulbul, kingfishers, skylarks and coppersmiths can be spotted if you are lucky. A beautiful 22-kilometre long road runs through the jungle and around the whole of Tansa Lake before it reaches Vaitarna Lake. On the one side you can see the small island on Tansa and on the other, the Mahuli fort. To use this road, however, prior permission from the Mumbai Municipal Corporation is necessary. No photography is allowed here. The Forest Department as well as the Mumbai Municipal Corporation have rest houses at Tansa which have to be booked in advance. For all enquiries contact the office of the BMC or the Forest Department at Shahpur. There is also a rest house at Vaitarna. To get to Vaitarna you have to take the road to Khardi from the highway or take the left turn at the Khardi railway station, the distance being about 16 kilometres.

A stay at Tansa will also give you the opportunity to explore the Mahuli fort. There is a direct road from Asangaon village up to the fort. A regular bus service connects Shahpur and Tansa.

Khanvel

> **Fact File**
>
> *Best time- August to November*
>
> *Location -- On the Maharashtra-Gujarat border in Dadra-Nagar Haveli, Off the Mumbai Ahmedabad Highway from Kasoti via Kasa-Sayvan and Udhwa.138 kms. from Borivili, Mumbai*
>
> *Getting there - By Road, by private transport*
>
> *Where to stay -- Silvassa Rest houses*
>
> *Where to eat -- same*

A relatively unknown place within easy reach of Mumbai is Khanvel, on the border of Maharashtra and Gujarat in the union territory of Dadra-Nagar Haveli. Here in the midst of the forest, the Silvassa Forest department has built excellent rest houses, special ones for VIPs and others for the ordinary tourist. These well-maintained rest houses are atop a hill near the river Sakhaltod. A residential cook is available. Bookings for these small cottages can be made at the Forest Department, Silvassa. The scene here is extremely soothing to the eye. In front flows the river, while Gambhirgad stands proudly in the background. Deer and blue bull graze near the rest house in a fenced-off area. There are also two small greenhouses with a variety of plants.

About 17 kilometres from Khanvel is Dudhani, the Damanganga catchment area where the Forest Department has boating facilities for tourists. Australian acacia trees border both sides, leaving a carpet of yellow flowers for you to walk on. The road to Khanvel from the Mumbai-Ahmedabad highway is from Charoti via Kasa-Sayvan and Udhwa. The distance between Borivali and Charoti is 90 kilometres and from Charoti to Khanvel, 48 kilometres. It is also possible to reach Khanvel via the Jawhar-Silvassa road. The distance between Mumbai to Jawhar is 130 kilometres and Jawhar to Khanvel is 43 kilometres. There is a regular State Transport bus service from Udhwa and Talasseri on the Mumbai-Ahmedabad highway. The best time to visit is between August and November.

Nagzira

> **Fact File**
>
> *Best time- All year around*
>
> *Location -- 122 kms. from Nagpur*
>
> *Getting there - By Road, by private transport*
>
> *Where to stay -- Forest Rest houses*
>
> *Where to eat -- same*

Nature has been specially bounteous to the Chanda and Bhandara districts of Maharashtra. Nowhere else in the state can you see such thick forests (mostly full of teak). The Bhandara area is also known for its bauxite mines and has several small lakes. The lush vegetation is home to a large number of animals and birds.

A part of this forest has been declared a protected area by the government and converted into a sanctuary, with the result that the animal population here is steadily increasing. The sanctuaries of Nagzira and the Navegaon Bund are fast gaining popularity among nature lovers.

In the middle of the 53 square kilometres of forest, the Forest Department has built small cottages around the lake with poetic names like Madhukunj, Latakunj and Nilay. There is no electricity; living in the midst of illumination from petromax lamps and lanterns, and the background music of animal sounds, is a new and exciting experience. In summer the sound of the animals is really loud, as most other watering holes dry up and the animals begin gathering around the lake as dusk approaches. While the experience can occasionally be scary, if a forest officer accompanies you, he will accurately identify the sound of each animal.

Sambar deer (stag), blue bulls, antelope, bison, bears, leopards, tigers, bonnet monkeys, hares and jungle dogs inhabit the forest. Teak, dhavda, tembhrni, moha, halai palas and in some places bamboo can be seen. Birds such as kingfishers, partridge, woodpeckers, peacocks, kites, herons and even flamingoes can be seen here. There are however some rules to be observed while birdwatching here. Entry into the sanctuary is allowed only during the day, between 7 a.m. and 7 p.m. No noisy tourists here, radio and tape recorders are prohibited. Smoking is not allowed.

For reservations contact: Deputy Conservator of Forests, Wildlife Division, Near Government Press, Nagpur.

The nearest railway station is Gondia. The distance between Gondia and Nagzira is 45 kilometres. The nearest bus stop is Sakoli. The distance between Sakoli and Nagzira is 22 kilometres and Nagpur to Sakoli is 100 kilometres.

Tadoba Sanctuary

Fact File

Best time- All year around

Location -- 45 kms. from Chandrapur and 195 kms. from Nagpur in eastern Maharashtra

Getting there - By ST bus; Road

Where to stay -- Forest Rest houses

Where to eat -- same

Located near Chandrapur in eastern Maharashtra, Tadoba is the oldest sanctuary in the state. First opened in 1955, the sanctuary covers an area of 116 square kilometres in the 509 square kilometres area of forest. In the middle of the sanctuary is a lake which has water all the year round. The lake is encircled by small hills full of dense green forest. This sanctuary is known for the large number of bison and crocodiles which inhabit it. The number of bison in Tadoba today is 143. In the summer season when the temperature here reaches 40 to 45 degrees Celsius, and most of the water holes spread through the forest dry up, all the animals converge at the main lake. During this season, at dawn or late in the evening, you can see large herds of bison near the lake. Tigers, leopards, jungle cats, jackals, bears, mongoose, boar, spotted deer, antelope, stags, nilgai, hares, bonnet monkeys, civets and Indian porcupines are the other animals which can be seen here. Several high machans have been constructed at strategic spots within the forest to enable people to sit silently and observe the animals. Seagulls, kites, herons, hornbills, robins, golden oriole, peacocks and bhardwaj are among the nearly 181 varieties of birds seen in the forest. The Tree-pie bird can always be seen at the banks of the lake near the rest house.

The Tadoba jungle is a tropical deciduous forest having teak, bamboo, dhavda, bibla, tendu, moha and khair. The name Tadoba is derived from a local tribal chief named Taru, who died in a fight with a tiger. There is a temple dedicated to him near the edge of the lake. A crocodile-breeding farm located near the rest house is also worth visiting. Hyena, mongoose and jackals prey on crocodile eggs in the area, resulting in a noticeable decrease in the crocodile population, hence this breeding centre was started.

The Tadoba sanctuary is 45 kilometres from Chandrapur while from Nagpur via Chandrapur it is 195 kilometres away. There is a special State Transport bus to Tadoba from both places. From Nagpur via Umrer and Khadshingi, Tadoba is 140 kilometres away.

There is a picturesque rest house near the lake. For reservations, you have to contact the Deputy Conservator of Forests, Tadoba National Park, Chandrapur.

Melghat (Semadoh and Kolkas)

Fact File

Best time- All year around

Location -- 51 kms. from Amravati to Semadoh

Getting there - By ST bus; Road

Where to stay -- Forest Rest houses at Dhakna, Kolkas, Belkund, Tarubandha and Semadoh

Where to eat -- same

The area of Semadoh and Kolkas, near Chikhaldara in the Satpura range of mountain is known as the Melghat Tiger Project area. The dense deciduous forests cover an area of 1,571 square kilometres of which 308 square kilometres have been declared the core area, called Gugamal. Here, preservation of flora and fauna is a priority. This is the only forest in Maharashtra where you can be sure to see a tiger. Leopards, bison, spotted deer, antelope, bears, wild dogs, boar, nilgai, hyenas and bison can be seen here in large numbers, and their population within this sanctuary is steadily growing.

The forest has developed in the river valleys of the Sipna and Dolar and mostly comprises teak, sheesum, niwas, haldu, Arjun bahava, dhava, ironwood, hirda and ficus trees. There are tourist rest houses at Dhakna, Kolkas, Belkund, Tarubandha and Semadoh. Shacks and tents are also available at Semadoh. A State Transport bus service runs from Paratwada to Semadoh. Paratwada is 51 kilometres from Amravati. The distance between Semadoh and Paratwada is 42 kilometres. From Semadoh the forest department has special mini buses to take you into the sanctuary. The buses take you up to the Kolkas rest house, by the River Sipna and through the dense forest. Just 6 kilometres from Kolkas is a helipad. The late Prime Minister Mrs. Indira Gandhi, is known to have come and relaxed at the rest house in Kolkas. From the rest house is a wonderful view of the semicircular-shaped River Sipna. Close by is a machan which has been built as a look-out point.

If you take a walk with a forest guard along the pathway which runs through this area you are sure to spot some deer and bison. Near the river you will spot kingfishers and Karkoche nar, while inside the forest, golden oriole, hornbills, paradise flycatchers, skylarks and neelkanth abound. This area is mainly inhabited by the Korku adivasis who live in hamlets in the area between Ghatang and Semadoh. There is a road from Chikhaldara to Semadoh. The nature museum at Semadoh is also worth seeing. For bookings at the rest house here you should contact the Divisional Forest Officer, Melghat Tiger Project, Parvatwada, Dist: Amravati.

Navegaon

Another sanctuary located in the Bhandara district of Maharashtra is Navegaon, though the lake here is much larger than that of Nagzira. The lake has been developed by Mr Kolu Patel, who built a bund here. The local villagers regard him very highly and call him 'Kolasur dev'.

The Navegaon sanctuary is spread over 133 square kilometres and has a variety of trees including dhavda, halia, teak, moh, teiwa, palas and Indian laburnum. Stags, antelopes, nilgai, hares, grey jungle fowl, monkeys, wild dogs, leopards, tigers and bison are animals which can be spotted here. Several migratory birds stop at the large lake. Black ibis, cormorants, cranes, water fowl,

Fact File

Best time- All year around

Location -- 135 kms. from Nagpur

Getting there - Nearest railhead Gondia 65 kms. away, nearest bus halt is at Sakoli, 35 kms. away

Where to stay -- Forest Rest houses at Dhakna, Kolkas, Belkund, Tarubandha and Semadoh

Where to eat -- same

kingfishers, flamingos and seagulls can be seen here. A rough path goes right into the lake enabling bird watchers to get really close to the birds. There are some dormitories and a garden near the lake, while to one side is a beautiful log hut from where you can see the entire lake, the mountain range called Nishani and the Zenda Pahad which stands in the background. Several watch towers have also been built in the forest.

This area is 1,500 feet above sea level and since it is close to water, gets extremely cold in winter.

The nearest rail head is Gondia. The distance between Navegaon and Gondia is 65 kilometres. The nearest bus halt is at Sakoli, 35 kilometres from Navegaon. The distance between Nagpur and Sakoli is 100 kilometres.

For reservations contact The Regional Manager, MTDC, Seetabaldi, Nagpur, or the Deputy Conservator of Forests, Wildlife Divison, Near Government Press, Nagpur.

The Murud Forests

If you are visiting Padmadurg and the Janjira castle near Murud on the Konkan coast, it is worthwhile to spend a few extra days to see the other tourist places in the area. About 10 kilometres down the Murud-Rev Danda road at Nandgaon is a huge Siddhi Vinayak temple. The entire area is covered with coconut palms, mango and pophali trees. After spending some time here, take the road to Roha just outside Nandgaon village. This deserted road takes you up a hill and as you climb higher the beautiful Nandgaon-Kashid coast is visible to the left. After about 5 kilometres down this road you will enter a dense forest. The village of Supegaon is 7 kilometres

Fact File

Best time- All year around

Location -- Off Kashid - Revadanda road at Nandgaon on the Konkan coast

Getting there - By road

Where to stay -- At Murud

What to eat: Carry food and water for a day trip

from Nandgaon on this road. Just one furlong short of Supegaon village, you will see a small red earth *kuchcha* road leading into the forest, known as Kesoli-Phansad. While it is possible to drive through this forest in a jeep or on a motorcycle, the best way to explore it is on foot, with a local villager acting as your guide. The forest is limitless; endless varieties of trees can be seen here including ironwood, teak, kinjal, sheesam, bibla, dhaman, sutav, mango, jackfruit, kokum, hirda, jamoon, cashew, bamboo and kevda. The presence of kevda obviously means that several kinds of snakes are also found here including the cobra, the krait and the python. On the Nandgaon-Roha road you will often see these reptiles crossing from one side of the road to the other. There is also a range of animals including porcupines, barking deer, stags, leopard, spotted deer, boar, hares and monkeys. Peacocks, parrots, bhardwaj, skylarks, and bulbuls are some of the birds seen here. About 4 kilometres down the *kuchcha* road you reach Kesoli where the ruins of the Wada (residence) of the Murud Nawab, and the remains of a well and a mango plantation are visible. There is a wonderful view of the Nandgaon-Kashid beach from here. It is a rare treat to get a view of the beach from a tall forest-filled hill. The stretch of forest continues for about 8 kilometres to Phansad. On the way you come across open grounds called Dhunyacha Maal, Bhandwacha Maal, and Chakacha Maal. This entire ghat road which begins about 4 kilometres after you leave Nandgaon and continues up to 6 kilometres after Supegaon, and the forests that stretch between Supegaon and Kesoli, are comparable to the forests of Mahabaleshwar-Matheran and Bhimashanker. This is, however, a relatively unknown area and therefore, the tourist will not find any conveniences here. The best way to see this place is to stay at Murud and make a day trip.

Pench - Pandit Jawaharlal Nehru National Park

Fact File

Best time- All year around

Location -- 60 kms. northeast of Nagpur

Getting there - On the Nagpur Jabalpur highway

Where to stay -- Forest Rest houses at Sillari, Ranidoh and Totaladoh

Where to eat -- Same

North-east of Nagpur City in the Nagpur district is the Pandit Jawaharlal Nehru National Park. Spread over an area of 258 square kilometres, this park has good tarred roads and well-equipped rest houses set amidst dense forests, where it is quite easy to see various animals and plants and trees, making it a very popular spot with tourists. The park is split into the eastern and western sides by the river Pench. This park adjoins the Pench Sanctuary in Madhya Pradesh and the total area covering both sanctuaries is about 1,000 square kilometres. The animal population is very large considering the vast area of forest which is open to them. There are 5 forest rest houses here at Totaladoh, Ranidoh, Sillari, Koleetmara and Gharpendhari.

About 60 kilometres from Nagpur on the Nagpur-Jabalpur highway is the village of Jungli Pakshi. The road into the forest begins from the left of this village. About 9 kilometres down this road is Sillari, one of the rest houses located at the farthest end of the park. Near here, close to the Pimpariya village, is the 2,250 feet high Goliya Pahad in the Satpura mountain range. The Sillari rest house is on the road from Jungli Parvat to Totaladoh. Totaladoh is 12 kilometres from the Sillari rest house. One kilometre down this road is a turning to the left; the *kuchcha* road here takes you straight to Ranidoh, 8 kilometres away. Tall teak trees border both sides of the road and from a curve in the road you can see an unforgettable view of the outfall of the Pench river, 1.5 kilometres ahead of Ranidoh.

Of all the rest houses here, the Ranidoh rest house is the most ideally located, and with the best view. Surrounded by teak, ironwood and moha trees, the garden in front of the rest house is filled with several colourful flowers. Just ahead of this garden is a view of the Ranidoh Mountain and the Pench river. On the mountain opposite are the ruins of the Ghuggusgad, belonging to the Raja of Gond. Across the river Pench; further ahead from Ranidoh, are the ruins of the ancient village of Nanpur. It is said that the natives of the present city of Nagpur originally hailed from this village.

Dotted throughout this forest are several water holes like the Phephadi Kund. You can reach these spots with the help of the forest rangers and at dusk you can see animals gathering here. Tigers, leopard, antelopes, bison and deer visit these water holes at twilight.

Twelve kilometres down the tar road from Sillari is the Totaladoh rest house, built on a hill in surroundings that are very similar to Ranidoh. To the right you can see the wall of the Meghdoot reservoir on the Pench river. The reservoir is in Madhya Pradesh. There is a one kilometre long road from Totaladoh to the wall of the dam. This entire reservoir is encircled by the forest. A kuchcha road going around the reservoir has been specially constructed to watch animals. If you wait along this 15-kilometre stretch of road you will see herds of deer and bison. Nilgai, gazelles and peacocks also make an appearance. As this road goes deep into the forest, it is better to be accompanied by a forest officer.

Ambakhori

About 4 kilometres from Totaladoh is Ambakhori, another place worth visiting. On the way you will see a small temple dedicated to Sai Baba, built by the villagers. The road to Ambakhori goes slightly downhill. Straight ahead a waterfall rushes down a cliff wall. In the midst of this dense vegetation is a small temple dedicated to the Cobra god. If you walk alongside this flowing water you will reach the main river. This waterfall flows on to merge into River Pench. From December to May there is not much water in the river and you will be able to see the

Fact File

Best time- All year around

Location -- 60 kms. northeast of Nagpur

Getting there - By rail from Nagpur to Jungli Pawan 64 kms., ST bus service,50 kms. by Nagpur - Ghatpendhari road

Where to stay -- Forest Rest houses at Ranodoh and Totladoh

Where to eat -- Same

large whitish, ash-coloured rocks in the river bed. The funnily-shaped rocks and the grooves formed on them due to the erosion of the water make a very interesting sight.

To the south of Ranidoh on the other side of the Pench river are the Kolitmara and Ghat Pendhari rest houses.

The forest here is best described as a tropical, dry, deciduous forest. Teak, saja, vija, tiwas dhavda, moha, tendu, palas, sheesam, halad, tembhurni and bamboo are the trees seen here. Tigers, leopards, stags, spotted deer, antelopes, nilgai, boar, bears, gazelles and jackals are found in the forest. Colourful peacocks, woodpeckers, hornbills, golden orioles, drongos, wagtails, owls, mynahs and bulbuls flit through the trees. The best time for bird watching is just before sunrise or sunset. It is quite cold here in winter. Nature is at its best between the months of September and March. However, the best time to see animals is summer, although the heat can be quite unbearable at that time.

The distance between Nagpur railway station and Jungli Pawan is 64 kilometres. There is a regular State Transport bus service from the Nagpur State Transport stand. The Nagpur-Ghatpendhari road is a stretch of 50 kilometres. There is also a bus service from Khaykya.

The best way to wander around the forest is by jeep. The alternative is to go on foot.

For reservations at the Ranidoh or Totaladoh rest houses, contact the Deputy Conservator of Forests, Wildlife Divison, near Government Press, Nagpur.

You will need a minimum of two days to see the entire sanctuary. Those travelling from the Mumbai-Pune region will need at least four to five days, taking into account travel time.

Nannaj Bird Sanctuary

> **Fact File**
> *Best time- All year around*
> *Location -- Sholapur District*
> *Getting there -*
> *Where to stay - Forest Rest house in Nannaj*
> *Where to eat - On the highway dhabas*

In 1987, an area of 7,818 square kilometres of grassland in the Sholapur district were declared a protected area in order to protect the rare bird called the Great Indian Bustard. This area covers the talukas of Mohol, Karjat, Shri Gonda, Nevasa and Madha.

The buff-and-black-coloured bustard lives on the plains, among bushes and scrub plain, and is not easily visible. A full-grown male bird is three and half feet tall. The neck and stomach of the bird are white and it has a conspicuous black crested crown and gorget. The bustard has a prominent large whitish patch near the tip of its wing. Its call is like a bark or a bellow, something which sounds like 'hook'. While mating the male bustard utters a deep, far-reaching moaning call while strutting before the female. The mating season is between August and December. The female bird is shorter, about 2.5 feet tall. A good runner, the bustard, by spreading its broad wings, takes off like an aeroplane, but does not fly at a great height. A sanctuary official showed me the egg of a bustard. The egg was pale brown and lay in a shallow dish-like depression at the base of a bush. Within a month the baby bird will emerge. It grows to full size within a year.

The bustard had nearly become exrtinct; now thanks to the sanctuary and the protection it offers, there are a hundred Great Indian Bustards today. In addition to these birds there are herds of deer and black buck in the sanctuary, and hares, jackals, foxes, hyenas, porcupines and mongoose. Golden orioles, hornbills and plovers are the other birds here, while pythons, chameleons and iguanas form the area's reptile life.

Tall watch towers have been constructed in the sanctuary and binoculars are available with the forest officals. If you want to spot a bustard it is best to take an official along.

The Borivali National Park

> **Fact File**
>
> *Best time- June to March*
>
> *Location -- I km east of Borivali station, off the Mumbai Ahemadabad highway*
>
> *Getting there - By suburban train, by road*
>
> *Where to stay -- Mumbai or Forest Rest house*
>
> *Where to eat - Small eateries near the entrance or carry your own food*

Living in a metropolis like Mumbai can be really stressful and many Mumbaikars seek solace in nature, taking short breaks to nearby hill stations or beaches.

One of the nearby getaways that I like to visit is the Borivali National Park. Of course, I make sure that it is not a public holiday or else the crowds there can be off-putting! Spread over 90 square kilometres, once in the Borivali National Park or the Sanjay Gandhi Udyan, it is easy to forget that you are in one of the busiest cities in the world. To the north of the Park is the Vasai creek, to its south is the Aarey colony, Goregaon, while to the west, stretching out till Thane, is a large expanse of forest.

I shot here for Sai Paranjape's film *Papiha*. The film is about forests and I play the role of a forest officer. The shooting schedule took us to several forests in Maharashtra including Nagzira, Navegaon, Ballarsha and Mahabaleshwar. The remaining parts of the film, what is known as patchwork in film making, was shot in the Borivali National Park. Shots of the Borivali National Park were used alongside shots of the Nagzira forest, but it is virtually impossible to distinguish where one ends and the other begins. The point I am trying to make is that certain parts of the Borivali National Park have such dense vegetation that it is like any other forest in the state.

On the banks of the Tulsi Lake within the Park is a picturesque log hut, used only by forest officials. It is easy to forget everything while sitting at the edge of this lake. The only sounds are of the kingfisher skimming the water to catch his prey and the fluttering of the heron's wings. The shrill sound of the barbet and the sweet tones of the skylark provide the background music. If you sit here quietly you will see various birds including the bhardwaj, papiha (Hawk cuckoo), bulbul, drongo and the golden oriole. At the end of the road in the forest are the Kanheri caves dating back to the second and third century.

There is a lion safari within the park. A closed vehicle will take you around a protected area where lions are allowed to roam freely. Several leopards also roam the forests here. Occasionally we see reports in the newspaper about residents who live near the Park being harassed by a leopard. The forest officials have the task of hunting the leopards out and confining them to the forest area. A few animals which have been caught can be seen in a cage outside the bungalow of the chief forest officer here. Monkeys, boar and deer also inhabit the park.

Teak, ironwood, bamboo, mango, sheesam and pangara are among the large variety of trees found here. A visit to the park during the monsoon season is a pleasant experience. About one kilometre to the east of Borivali station and just off the Mumbai-Ahmedabad highway, this forest is a wonderful place to spend a day away from the bustling metropolis.

Nature Parks

Nature in all its wild glory is something that fills us with awe and reverence. However, many of today's nature conservation projects are a synthesis of natural beauty and human efforts at preserving the wealth of flora and fauna that our land possesses. Maharashtra is a state blessed by Mother Nature's bounty. Each wildlife sanctuary here has its own flavour and character.

The blackbuck reserve at Rehkuri is known as the Rehkuri Kalveet reserve, owing to these graceful animals that abound here. A mention of Koyna is hardly complete without an appreciation of the vast Shivsagar lake. The fort of Prachitgad is an enduring companion to the Chandoli nature reserve. The firsthand experience that one gets while trekking through such wilderness and sylvan surroundings, is something that I have tried to recreate in this book. I hope I succeed in transporting you through these black and white pages, to the lush wonderland of these reserves.

The Gautala Forest Reserve

> **Fact File**
>
> *Best time- June to March*
>
> *Location -- Kannad Taluka, Aurangabad District*
>
> *Getting there - By road to Chalisgaon,*
>
> *Where to stay -- Forest Rest house*
>
> *Where to eat - Same*

This forest sanctuary includes a total of 17 villages in the Kannad Taluka of Aurangabad district. It was set up in 1986. With an area covering around 250 square kilometers, it is 15 kilometres from Kannad village and 20 kilometres from Chalisgaon. Kannad is 60 kilometres from the district headquarters, Aurangabad. The same road continues to Chalisgaon. Two kilometres after you leave Kannad, there is a turning to the right. Follow this turn, and it will lead you right to the entrance of the Gautala Sanctuary. Once you enter your name and other details, you can take your vehicle inside.

The entry into the reserve immediately makes one aware of the rich variety of flowering shrubs, gigantic trees and other flora. A little ahead, a small rivulet makes its way amid a sandalwood grove called Chandan Nala. Its banks are noted for the presence of peacock, parrots, and a number of colourful birds. The satbhai, weaver bird, dayal, bulbul, kotwal, and chandol are also seen. The end of this nallah marks the beginning of a thickly-wooded portion, the Gahir Jungle. There is a temple to Lord Hanuman here. The reserve owes its name to a lake in front of this temple, called Gautala. The entire landscape around the lake is a grassy plain, and until a few years ago, cowherds would bring their cattle to graze in these sweet pastures. The name Gautala, meaning grazing pasture, thus stuck.

The lake is edged by bamboo, palas, raanpimpal, ranshevga, lime, and tamarind, and is populated by water fowl and other water birds. For the convenience of nature lovers, there is an observation platform near the lake. The raised stage serves its purpose exceedingly well, for there is no better place to catch a ringside view of entire Gautala. To the left rises the Satmala hill, with Manjarmal behind it. The Nagad river has its origins in the Satmala hills. The Nagad river, and two other sources of water - the Garada and Nirbhor—are important watering holes, because in summer, all the other water catchment areas dry up. Only these three provide water to the animals that come here.

There is a steep hillock on the opposite side of the Gautala lake. The hillock is thickly forested with trees of many different types. Many of them are almost full-grown and the hill is visible from a distance wearing its green cap. The hillock has a cave within which is a water tank. There is a stone idol of the Sage Gautam, who is believed to have undertaken many years of penance here. The hill, is therefore, called Gautam hill in his memory.

Beyond Gautam hill, the road continues amidst thick forest. This green avenue leads for about 5 kilometres to a clearing where the path branches out in four directions. The fork to the left passes through the Mhais Ghat before heading for Chalisgaon. The Autram Ghat lies between the Kannad-Chalisgaon road. The thickly wooden tracts of this ghat have been included in the reserve boundaries, and the pass, is therefore, also referred to as Gautala Autram Ghat.

The Gautala forest reserve supports a large ecosystem containing many species of plants, trees, and flowers. The animals that have been sighted here include leopard, jackals, chital, hyenas, wolves, blackbuck, wild boar, the sambhar, bison, and smaller animals. The Gautala is thus, an important preserve of plant and animal life on the Kannad-Chalisgaon belt.

Guest houses can be booked at Puranwadi and Patnadevi.

For inquiries, contact-

Deputy Conservator of Forests, Aurangabad Forest Division, Station Road, Aurangabad.

OR

Forest Officer, Gautala - Autram Ghat Forest Reserve, Kannad, Dist. Aurangabad.

Chandoli

Fact File

Best time- January and May

Location -- Battis Shirala taluka, Sangli District

Getting there - By ST bus from Karad via Dhebewadi and Julewadi

Where to stay -- Irrigation Department Rest houses at Chandoli and Varna

Where to eat - Same

The Chandoli Sanctuary is most well-known, among other reasons for being the protected habitat of many varieties of butterflies. A few of the species that have been recorded here are not found anywhere else. Apart from this, the proximity to the fort of Prachitgad, and the sanctuary's sylvan beauty, makes this a favourite haunt of the wildlife photographer and nature lover.

Chandoli is a dam constructed across the Varna river in the Battis Shirala taluka of Sangli district. The Chandoli backwaters contain the Chandoli sanctuary. There are three routes leading here. Either you can start from Karad and travel via Dhebewadi and Julewadi. The second is from Malkapur, but one has to get down at the Lavale turning and continue on foot. The third route is from Ratnagiri. Till Sangameshwar, you come by intra-state transport. From here, till you reach Nayri village, you are on foot. One side of the Prachitgad fort lies in the reserve, and from Nayri, if you climb the fort and descend on the other side, you are in Chandoli. Established formally in 1985, the forest area measures 309 square kilometres. It encompasses within its expanse, the forested areas of Sangli, Satara, Kolhapur, and Ratnagiri.

The forest here is semi-evergreen. The area receives an annual rainfall of 2500 milli-metres. The Chandoli lake passes through a delightful section of thick greenery, and a boat ride through a tunnel of bent trees touching the water is a tranquil experience. The jungles around the village of Durgwadi are ideal for a well-equipped trekker. The hills of Durgwadi give a complete view of the lake.

The forest reserve abounds in flora and fauna. Trees like the ain, behda, jambhul, hirda, pangara, jackfruit, coconut, umbar, avla, mango and apta make up the ecosystem which sustains hundreds of insects, birds, and smaller creatures. The animal life too is rich. The tiger, leopard, bison, bear, wild boar, sambhar, monkeys, sayal, frogs, hares and wild dogs are often sighted here. Eagles, falcon, kites and owls are some of the predatory birds who make the ecosystem complete, while the nightingale, myna, satbhai, hole, khandya, sutar, bharadwaj, and peacock add beauty to the environment. The lake and the backwaters of the dam are home to many water birds like cranes and storks, while reptiles such as lizards, snakes and pythons, are found here. Besides, animals of the smaller kind, like some remarkable butterflies, make for a perfectly-maintained food chain. Within the jungles, there is a place called Siddheshwar, which is surrounded on one side by a rocky depression. Bears have made this their home.

The ideal time to visit Chandoli would be sometime between January and May. It is wise to take along a guide, or a local official of the Chandoli reserve. The forests are thick and abound with wild animals, so getting lost is quite easy and frightening. Vehicles are permitted inside, but one feels one is trespassing. When you are on foot you can be one with the forest. The sights and sounds of a real, live jungle, the surprises in store, all make a trip around Chandoli a thrilling and delightful experience. Of course, you are far removed from all traces of human settlement, for this is the real thing—so, make sure you are well-equipped with a good supply of water, eatables and other essentials.

At Chandoli and Varna, the Irrigation department has made arrangements to put visitors up at guest houses. Food is also provided here.

For inquiries, contact,

Sub divisional Forest officer, Sangli Forest Division, Sangli.

Koyna Forest Reserve

The Koyna lake, which nestles in the Sahyadri mountains, is the region around which the Koyna Reserve is now a protected wildlife sanctuary. It was set up in 1985 with the motive of preserving the rich natural beauty which characterizes the Sahyadri foothills. Spread over the talukas of Javli and Patan, the reserve covers over 422 square kilometres, extending up to Ratnagiri.

Fact File

Best time- February to May

Location -- Near Mahabaleshwar and Satara

Getting there - By ferry from Bamnoli to Koyna

Where to stay -- Irrigation Department Rest houses at Chandoli and Varna

Where to eat - Same

Koyna is accessible from Mahabaleshwar and Satara. Bamnoli is the nearest town to Koyna. From Mahabaleshwar, a 25-kilometre drive will take you to Tapola. From Tapola, however, you will have to take a ferry to come to Bamnoli. There is a frequent bus service to and from Satara and Bamnoli. The boat ride from Bamnoli to Koyna is an experience of sheer beauty. This is the Shivsagar lake, which one has to cross to reach the foothills of Vasota fort. The distant peaks of the Sahyadris seem to be watching you and wishing you a good journey. The lake is encircled by a ring of thick green, and your eyes will wander over the soothing scene till your soul is completely at peace.

One tongue of the Shivsagar lake touches the foothills of Vasota fort. This is where the boat will dock. Alight from the boat, and you will see a narrow nala or canal, traversing through fronds of trees. If you walk along the edges of this canal, you could startle a bison, a bear, or some other animal, behind any bush.

If you cross the nala, you can walk up to the Indal checkpoint at Vasota fort. There are remnants of ancient buildings here. The karvand abounds. A short brisk walk will help you catch up with the nala, which again makes an appearance. There is a dilapidated stone temple of Lord Maruti some distance ahead. The evergreen forests of Koyna now begin to envelop you.

The jungles of Koyna are so thickly wooded, that at times you are cocooned in a dark green tunnel with barely any sunlight filtering through. The sky too is not visible. Whenever the sun touches the ground, it is in the form of a shaft of light that looks magical. A wide variety of trees, both common and rare, are found here. The anjan, savar, ihrda, behda, ain, Mango and others have made the Koyna reserve a very important natural park. The trees support many shade-loving medicinal plants like the karvy, kadipatta, shikakai, tamalpatra, vavding and others.

The Koyna reserve has been divided into three sections - Vasota, Maharkhor, and Indavli Met. All the major forest areas of Indavli, Kusavli, Sindhi, Balvan, Morvi, Mhalung, Vaghavle, Kusapur, Tapola, and the Kandatki valley have been included in this park. The natural protection which the boundaries of the Shivsagar lake have been blessed with, has made the Koyna reserve an excellent example of a forest that can endure anything. The presence of this massive lake supports a large variety of animal life. Tigers, leopards, bears, bison, wild cats, wild boars, saayal, hyenas, wild dogs, monkeys, hares, and many smaller species, all add to the magnificent variety of this park. Hunting is not allowed and there are strict instructions against disturbing the environment.

The Vasota fort is located centrally. The rivers of Koyna, Kaandatki and Solshi are visible from the reserve. The area receives an annual precipitation of 200 inches, and thus forms a breeding ground for various birds and insects. If you visit Koyna, do so between February to May.

For inquiries , contact:

Deputy Conservator of Forests, Satar Forest Division, Satara.

Rehkuri Kalveet Wildlife Park

The Rehkuri plains were once home to hundreds of blackbuck who moved around the gentle grasslands in herds. Around 1950, a census alarmingly revealed, that there were barely 10-12 of these in the entire area. The Government swung into action, and the Rehkuri Kalveet forest reserve was set up. Hunting of the animal was made punishable, and a law to that effect was laid down by the Forest Department. The numbers of this graceful animal are now on the rise, and the last recorded strength exceeded 300.

The forest reserve of Rehkuri Kalveet lies in the Karjat taluka of Ahmednagar district. Around 160 kilometres from Pune, it lies on the Shrigonda-Karjat road. One can go to Rehkuri from Pune, via Bhigwan. Buses going from Pune to Jamkhed also stop at Rehkuri. The area measures 550 acres.

Fact File

Best time- All year

Location -- Karjat Taluka, Ahmednagar District

Getting there - 160 kms. from Pune on the Shirgonda-Karjat road

Where to stay -- Forest rest house

Where to eat - Same

The Forest officers at Rehkuri have spared no efforts to ensure that the present population of the deer is maintained in as natural a way as possible. Many species of grasses have been planted here for the animals. Apart from this, neem, babul, khair and nilgiri have been planted in large tracts. This has resulted in a marked rise in the population of blackbuck. The entire plains are a lush green and herds of the herbivores now wander around grazing in their favourite pastures as they did earlier. It is important to state here that India is the only existing habitat for the blackbuck, and against this fact, Rehkuri's upkeep is of paramount importance.

Roughing it out in these grasslands is a unique experience. From time to time, one comes across herds of deer quietly grazing. The males and females are generally in separate groups. The crown of the male is adorned with a magnificent pair of antlers that is sometimes almost two feet high. The animal is jet black except for a small patch on the stomach. This stag is also called Krishnamrug. The female is slightly smaller in stature, and minus the horns. She is reddish pink in colour. The hierarchy amongst the herds is very marked, and the dominant males and females protect their respective herds.

The Rehkuri plains give the nature lover a unique insight into these majestic athletes of the grasslands. If you're lucky, you will be witness to a fight between two males competing for a territory or for a particular herd. Both the participants charge at each other with a ferocity that has to be seen to be believed. The fight is dramatic and fierce, but the opponents rarely, if ever, injure each other. The defeated male retreats and the supremacy of the winner is in no doubt. The horns, glorious ornaments which the male carries, are often damaged in such tussles.

The blackbuck is one of the fastest in the animal kingdom. Its speed has been recorded at an impressive 60 kilometres per hour. When a predator hunts for a kill, its presence is usually announced to the deer thanks to the warning cry of birds. The blackbuck cocks its ears, pounds its hoofs in the ground, and is off in a fraction of a second, leaping over obstacles in its way with the agility and grace of a world-class hurdler. The sight is sheer poetry in motion. Every movement of the animal is fluid, the muscles working with raw energy.

Though Rehkuri was set up primarily to ensure the restoration of the Kalveet, the reserve is home to wolves, hyenas, jackals, sayal, and the mongoose. Besides, the plains resound with the cries and songs of birds like the satbhai, parrot, chitoor, khandya, khatik, sutar and bharadwaj. Birds of prey like the eagle and falcon feed on these. The reserve also has a lake where most animals come to drink water. There is a beautiful nursery on the banks of this lake. The lake reverberates with the calls of water birds. The white throated stork, vanchak, cranes, water crows, water fowls and ducks are common here. The reserve is also home to the peacock-the Maldhok Mor.

A fifty-feet high observation tower has been erected right in the centre of the grassy plain of Rehkuri. All through the day, the entire area of the reserve can be scanned. In the morning and evenings, herds of black buck can be sighted at various locations. Afternoons are siesta time, as the entire region acquires a lazy calm. All the animals retreat to their places of rest, usually under a tree. Earlier, these deer, would often ransack the farms and fields that touch the reserve in search of food. Every night, herds of them would enter a field and destroy standing crops of groundnut, hulga, bajra, jowari, moong, til, and mustard. The forest department, therefore, has begun to cultivate these crops within the confines of the sanctuary itself.

Apart from the lake that is a natural watering hole, the forest dept has constructed a number of reservoirs. The blackbuck naturally loses the salt content from its body. You will find heaps of strategically placed salt licks so the animals can restore their body salts. The areas in and around Shrigonda, Jamkhed, and Nevasa have a recorded strength of 3,000 blackbuck. This remarkable change is due to the efforts of the Forest Dept and the officials who actually run the Rekhuri Kalveet Wildlife Park. The Government of India has prohibited hunting and trading of the protected animal, and an offence is punishable with a fine of Rs. 2,000 and 7 years imprisonment. These measures may not put a complete end to the poaching, but it has definitely done much to restore the grassy plains of Rehekuri, the tranquil and rightful home of the graceful Blackbuck.

Melghat Tiger Project

Melghat is the only Project Tiger enclave in Maharashtra. The forested areas of Chikhaldar and Dhaarni talukas fall within this reserve. The headquarters of the project is situated in the Parvatwada taluka of Amravati district. Melghat is 60 kilometres from Parvatwada, and 100 kilometres from the district of Amravati. Semadoh, a little closer to Melghat, can be reached by State Transport buses from both these towns.

The vast Melghat reserve can be toured in a minibus provided by the Forest Department. There are specially-marked forest tracks on which one can go on foot. Private vehicles are also allowed. The minibus leaves from Semadoh every evening at 7.00 sharp, and completes a tour of 30 kilometres through the Melghat forests.

From Parvatwad, the first stop is at the Bihali entrance gates. The Melghat forest reserve is what you are now entering. There is a ghat ahead, the road along it going to Semadoh. There is a bridge across the river Sipna, and on the other side is the forest rest house at Semadoh. The entire drive is amid lush green forests. Huts belonging to the Korku adivasi tribe dot the

Fact File

Best time- January and June

Location -- Parvatwada Taluka, 100 kms. from Amravati

Getting there - By mini bus from Semadoh

Where to stay -- Forest rest houses at Kokaj, Semadoh, Raipur, Jarinda, Tarubandi, Dhargad, Hatru, Maklu, Dhakna, holiday homes and tourist lodges at Semadoh

Where to eat - Same

landscape. Semadoh has a museum of natural history. Most of the exhibits here, of course, relate to the Melghat territory and there is lot of information about Project Tiger. The flora and fauna have special sections along with interesting nuggets about the Adivasi community who have been living here for decades. A huge map of the entire Melghat tiger reserve shows you the park at a glance. The museum also has a small theatre where films on wildlife are screened and slide shows with informative commentary are held.

To travel through Melghat, you can either mount an elephant, which lumbers around in daytime; a bus too is available, starting at 7 pm in the evening. The forest reserve is full of surprises and thrills. In the ghat of Raipur, you could be deafened by the loud chattering and racket created by a group of excited monkeys. These animals are completely at home up high on the tallest branches of trees, and they swing from branch to branch with ease. The ghat ends at the lake of Pimpalwada. The thick undergrowth seems to ease a little. The lake sustains water fowl and peacocks, whose harsh cry punctuates the silence.

The Kuapati nallah gives way to the Raipur woods. A timber doorway leads to the protected forest area of Melghat. The road continues into the Chatpatti nallah. In the gloom, we switch on our searchlight and many pairs of eyes are glowing in the dark. We are being watched by the denizens of the jungle, and the feeling is eerie. This part of Melghat is full of flying squirrels. Like a parasail, these squirrels literally fly from one tree to another with the help of webbed skin under their forelegs. The nallah ahead is a home for bears. These furry animals are black and have a strip of white on their back and head. They burrow in the soft ground and lie in wait to sip honey from the honeycombs deep underground, beneath the roots of trees.

Yet another nallah awaits you - this is the Bhondha nallah. We now come back from Bhoplya Pad, to rejoin the Raipur road. We are now entering even deeper forest. The path is rocky and a nallah tinkles between the stones. This rivulet has a depression. Water buffalo are aplenty here so the nallah is called Mahishasur.. Sambhar traverse this entire area. Sightings of the great predators - the tiger and the leopard, are extremely rare, and one needs the patience of a real wildlife enthusiast to be able to actually see these majestic creatures.

The ideal time to visit Melghat is sometime between January and June. Hunting or any other kind of wild sport is strictly prohibited here. Leopard, tiger, wild buffalo, sambhar, wild boar, monkeys, chital, nilgai, chausingha, bears, wild cats, stag, flying squirrels, hyenas, wolves and hares are some of the animals flourishing under the forest department's protection. Around the water sources, peacocks, water fowls, cranes, storks, ducks, and many other water birds have given life to these wet spots. There are ample treats in store for the avid birdwatcher, for vaplors like the eagle, falcon and kite live here in perfect harmony with nature. Parrots, the weaver bird, doves, bulbul, Sutar, myna also abound.

The Melghat reserve has around 250 species of trees. Bamboo groves too are planted in large clusters. Medicinal plants grow in the shade of these larger trees. The entire forest is deciduous. For the tourist, there are forest rest houses at Kolkaj, Semadoh, Raipur, Jarinda, Tarubandi, Dhargad, Hatru, Makhlu, and Dhakna. Semadoh even has holiday homes and a tourist lodge. For the adventurous who want to rough it out there are tents on hire.

For inquiries, contact

Regional manager, Melghat Tiger Reserve, Paratwada, Dist.Amravati, Maharashtra - 4441005.

Navegaon National Park

> **Fact File**
>
> *Best time- November to May*
>
> *Location -- Arjuni Morgaon taluka, Bhandara District*
>
> *Getting there - By road or by narrow gauge train 137 kms. from Nagpur on the Nagpur-Raipur highway*
>
> *Where to stay -- Forest rest house on prior booking*
>
> *Where to eat - Same*

This nature park is extremely well-known for being an important destination for migratory birds who come from as far away as Siberia. The area also has a rich history of nature awareness amongst its surrounding human settlements. Navegaon is approximately 35 kilometres from the village of Sakoli, which lies on the Nagpur-Raipur national highway. Sakoli is about 102 kilometres from Nagpur. You can also travel by a narrow gauge train on the Gondiya-Nagbheed rail route: this train stops at Navegaon. The nature park is just 2 kilometres from the railway station. It is a part of the Arjuni Morgaon taluka of Bhandara district. State Transport buses plying between Gondiya and Nagpur also halt at Sakoli. From Sakoli, you can take another bus to Navegaon. Set up officially in 1975, the park is huge and has tracks for vehicles. Trekkers too will find convenient signs and pathways.

The entry to Navegaon nature reserve has a wonderful surprise for the visitor - a marvellous view of the Navegaon lake. The lake is a manmade one, and the ancestors of Mr. Madhavrao Patil were the enterprising pioneers who took the first step in converting the dense forest areas here into a haven for bird and animal life. The mammoth task of transforming this lake into a sanctuary has been acknowledged by India's most famous authority on birds, the ornithologist Dr. Salim Ali. Mr. Patil not only achieved the task of giving a source of water to the region, he actually set about populating the area around the lake. Since it was a Nave gaon, (new village, in Marathi), the name stuck and the national park, when established, took on the name. This lake is also sometimes referred to as the Navegaon dam. The forest department maintains an excellent rest house on the banks of the lake. You can either stay here, or just use the restaurant/mess facilities of this lodge. Dense forest cover borders the lake. In such surroundings, a full moon night at the forest rest house is a journey into paradise. In soundless calm, the placid waters of the lake reflect all the glory of the moon, and you will value this experience more than any luxury resort you have been to.

Every morning and evening, the lake throngs with water fowl, ducks, cranes and migratory birds. Their cackle and cries carry far into the jungles beyond. The fish-eating eagle too makes a rare appearance. Winter brings out the full beauty of Navegaon. Thousands of migratory birds flock the lake and there are birds as far as the eye can see. These visitors make Navegaon their home for six months, and then return to their own homes. Migratory birds from Rann of Kutch, Ladakh and Tibet, Europe and Siberia have been coming here for many years. Many Himalayan birds also visit to escape the falling temperatures of the north.

To watch this congregation the banks of the lake have a convenient observation post. Even the casual tourist can catch sight of about a dozen different birds at any given time. Boating in the lake is permitted, and a ride on the clean waters is extremely invigorating. There is a small islet in the lake, on which a cottage stands. There is also a memorial dedicated to the father of the man who began this mission of creating this oasis. Both these have been erected by the same family.

Navegaon boasts of over 350 kinds of birds. Of these, at least 100 are guests who come here to escape winter at home. Several hills and peaks of the Satpura range are covered in the Navegaon nature reserve. One can see the Kolasur Pahad, Satbahini (seven sisters), Kala Pahad, Gidhad Pahad, and Vadbagha Pahad from any part of the reserve. The summit of Satbahini hills, at 750 metres, is the highest point in Bhandara.

A village called Kholi lies ahead. You can see the official entry point of the park here. Thick forest leads to a spring - the Kamkazari. The spring is perennial and is an important watering hole for animals. An observation post has been discreetly placed close to the rivulet. It is a perfect view from up here. Animals of all kinds head towards the spring, and much of the area around the Kamkazari too is easily visible from here. The Kamkazari hillock is a stone's throw away. The hill of Agezari, in the same vicinity, has a grassy plain on top. These grasslands support various herbivores like the chital, sambhar, and up the food chain, predators like the leopard and bear. The tableland has a similar observation post from where the entire area is seen. There is also a bracing breeze here at all times.

Navegaon is one of the forests in Maharashtra where the natives of this land still live and earn their livelihood by carrying out age old activities like hunting, gathering forest produce and ancient methods of farming. Beyond the Kamkazari lake is the Dhaavalghat, which is home to adivasis. They also have a temple here, the shrine of Lord Waghdev. The road you are following branches off near this temple. The path straight ahead goes to the Badbagha canal. You now come upon a very wild, very sylvan part of the park. The forest is not only dense, it is full of a rich variety of trees - the ain, moh, saavar, avli, behda, anjan, and medicinal plants that shelter in the shadow of these trees. The leopard, sambhar, and bears come to this nallah for water. Here also, there is an observation tower.

As you leave the nallah behind, the Mamabhasha road stretches ahead. Before this road was made, there were two massive ain trees. One of them was 95 feet tall, and the other just 10 feet shorter. These gigantic trees had trunks with a 12-foot diameter! Unfortunately, the trees had to be cut down, probably to accommodate the road. The jungles of Baderai lie to the left. There is a temple of Lord Baderai, the deity of the local adivasi folk. There are quite a few buffalo here. They come to drink water at a very picturesque stream nestling amidst bamboo trees. The Baderai hillock rises just behind the temple. Kala Pahad is opposite this hillock. Every monsoon, as the rains lash the forests, peacocks can be seen pirouetting atop this hill. It is a romantic sight, and somewhat akin to velvet curtains parting to reveal the sensuous magic of a lightfooted dancer. No wonder, then, that the hill is often referred to as Mornachi Hill, the hill of dancing peacocks.

The thick undergrowth of Chutiya woods leads to the Jambhul Jhari. There is a pond here, surrounded by bamboo. Leopards and buffalo are frequent visitors. The Navegaon reserve is rich in water supply, and there are actually 200 natural reservoirs here! There is a pretty little museum here with stuffed birds and pugmarks of animals preserved in plaster of Paris.

The ideal time to visit the Navegaon reserve is from November to May, when this deciduous forest is green and not too hot.

For inquiries, contact

Deputy Conservator of Forests, Wildlife Division, Nagpur Forest Dept., Govt. Printing press, Nagpur.

LAKES, RESERVOIRS, HOT SPRINGS, WATERFALLS, CAVES

LAKES, RESERVOIRS, HOT SPRINGS, WATERFALLS, CAVES

A rugged terrain is characteristic of Maharashtra, but there is much more on offer for the nature lover. Lakes abound, in addition to several dam projects, stretching from the Konkan into the dry hinterland of Marathawada and Khandesh. In the rainy season abundant waterfalls spring up, adding to the magic. Hot springs are found in the area between north and south Konkan.

Lakes

There are several lakes near Mumbai, Pune and Satara which are ideal one-day picnic spots. Shrouded by abundant trees, the lakes attract a variety of birds, much to the delight of birdwatchers. Among these lakes are the Bhoj lake near Badlapur, the Kakuli lake near Ambernath, the Kaas lake near Satara, the Sakhre lake near Boisar and the Devkop lake near Palghar.

A number of attractive, though unknown smaller lakes are found in the mountain range between Haji Malang and Matheran in the Mumbai-Karjat region.

Tapola Lake : A Mini Kashmir

While traversing the Poladpur-Mahabaleshwar ghat road you will come across many signs exhorting you to visit Mini Kashmir. One of the roads south of Mahabaleshwar leads to Tapola village, a distance of 26 kilometres. The road runs between the Koyna and Solshi river valleys. The rivers empty into the Shivsagar lake. Motorboats skim across the surface sending up a spray of water across the lake. The large lake is surrounded by thick forests and there is no sign of human habitation for miles. The forts of Jungli

Fact File

Best time- Avoid monsoons

Location -- Tapola village, 26 kms. from Mahabaleshwar

Getting there - By road

Where to stay - Mahabaleshwar

Where to eat - Good eateries near lake

Jaigad and Vasota as well as Parvatgad and Chakdev can be seen from here. The first two forts can be reached via Khirkundi while Parvatgad and Chakdev can be reached via Parvat village. Motor launches from Tapola will take you to Bamnoli and Kaas lake. You can see the entire area by launch for a nominal charge. Travelling through the mountainous forests is an entirely novel experience for city-dwellers. Tourists from Mahabaleshwar now also visit Tapola, resulting in large crowds. It is certainly a place worth seeing.

Gadeshwar Lake

From the Panorama Point at Matheran you will see a lake in the valley below. This is Gadeshwar or Panvel Lake, located on the Panvel-Waghachiwadi village road. Trekkers are familiar with this route as they take it to climb to Matheran via Sunset Point and Monkey Point. Just before the Panvel State Transport bus stand on the Mumbai-Panvel road is a road leading to Nere village, the first 7 kilometres of which are tarred. Thereafter the road becomes *kuchcha*. Two kilometres down this road, to the left, is Shantivan, a colony developed for lepers. If you continue straight down the road you will reach Gadeshwar Lake. The 9-kilometre distance from Nere can be covered by jeep or motorcycle in the summer; during the rains there is no alternative to walking. The lake is especially beautiful in the rains. The mountains of Matheran, Peb, Nakhind, Chanderi, Navra-Navri (meaning groom and bride) and to the extreme left, Haji Malang, are all visible from here.

The trees provide shade even in the mid-afternoon sun. The evenings are an enchanting time; sitting at the edge of the lake will make you want to meditate to the accompaniment of the soft strains of a flute on your Walkman. Lots of birds including storks and egrets visit the edge of the lake. Only very rarely will you spot a fox or hare; there are no other animals to be found here. It is possible to return to Mumbai after a day spent here, but I think one should climb up to Matheran via Waghachiwadi instead. The climb provides an excellent opportunity for photographers to capture the lake from different angles. The rainy season is the ideal time to do this. Recently, a good motoring road has been built till Maldunga village which encircles the lake.

Kalote Lake

Fact File

Best time- Avoid summer

Location --Karjat - Khopoli

Getting there - By road 73 kms. on the old Mumbai Pune road 2 kms. from the Kalote junction

Where to stay - Khopoli or Mumbai

Where to eat - Many eateries on the highway

Wherever the road network exists in the Karjat-Khopoli belt, the villages in the surrounding areas have developed. The Neral-Matheran belt and the Chowk-Karjat belt exemplify this. A lot of city-dwellers have built farmhouses in the area, especially around Bhilawle lake. However just 10 kilometres from here is the beautifully unspoilt Kalote Lake. About 73 kilometres from Mumbai on the Mumbai-Pune road is the Kalote junction. From here, 2 kilometres down a *kuchcha* road will lead you straight to the lake. Hemmed in by mountains on three s sides and bordered by trees through which you can glimpse small huts, it is hard to believe that the lake is so close to the highway. Fatigue seeps away as you soak in the refreshing surroundings. In the distance, buffaloes graze quietly while village children frolic nearby.

Not very close to Karjat station, it is still a good walk for trekking enthusiasts. If you cross the hill near the lake you will be on a straight path to Karjat station. Palasdhari and Bhilawle lakes are nearby, Manikgad fort is to the west. Khandala is just 18 kilometres from Kalote junction. If you have your own car, you can be in

Khandala within 45 minutes of visiting the lake. The Madhganesh temple is 8 kilometres from here. During the rainy season it is very picturesque. Summer is very hot though there are many trees near the lake providing shade.

Kaas Lake

> **Fact File**
>
> *Best time- September to March*
>
> *Location --West of Satara*
>
> *Getting there - 26 kms. from Satara on the Satara - Yavateshwar road*
>
> *Where to stay - Satara*
>
> *Where to eat - Carry food if you want to spend a day near the lake*

There are several places of interest near Satara: among these are Ajinkyatara Fort, Sajjangad (10 kilometres), Pateshwar, Kanher Dam, Yavateshwar and last but not the least, Kaas. The lake is 26 kilometres west of Satara on the Satara-Yavateshwar road. The road leading to the lake is a treat for nature-lovers, especially after the rains in September. Everything is a fresh new green. Visible to the left is the Sajjangad fort while to the right is the Kanher Dam. The road suddenly curves around the mountain and you come to a plateau where, encircled by dense trees, is the Kas Lake. To one side you will notice a range of flat-topped mountains, similar to Panchgani's tabletop. Several boulders can be seen on the side of the road, upon which black-faced monkeys sit watching you. Kaas is very similar to the Venna lake in Mahabaleshwar. A road leads around the lake into the Kaas village. The Kasaidevi temple is just outside this village. From here you will get an excellent view of the lake and the green-coloured guest house on its banks. A *kuchcha* road from the village takes you to this guest house. This lake is 3,500 feet from mean sea level and in the monsoon it plays host to big, black clouds. The red mud, cool climate and lush greenery is conducive to a wonderful holiday except for one jarring factor - the empty beer bottles littering the place, a nuisance which ought to be checked immediately.

Kakuli Lake

> **Fact File**
>
> *Best time- September to March*
>
> *Location -- Kakuli village*
>
> *Getting there - off Sheel Phata on the Thane-Pune highway towards Kalyan*
>
> *Where to stay -- Railways bungalow, Day's outing from Mumbai*
>
> *Where to eat - Carry your own food*

For those wishing to take a break from the hectic life-style of Mumbai, there is the little-known spot of Kakuli just an hour and a half away. To get here you have to go via the Sheel Phata on the Thane-Pune highway. Take the road towards Kalyan and then the Badlapur MIDC road. 10 kilometres to the right is a pipeline from which a 2-kilometre *kuchcha* road leads to Kakuli village. Close by is the Kakuli lake, popularly known by villagers as the GP tank. If you walk along the wall of the dam you will reach a dense forest within which is a small bungalow belonging to the Railways. You can spend a day here with prior permission from Thane. The Badlapur hill is on the other side of the lake, and close to that is the Haji Malang range. The reflection of the the Badlapur hill in the placid waters of the lake makes a pretty sight. Lots of birds, especially cranes and parrots, can be seen. The brightly-plumed kingfisher swoops down on to the water looking for a good meal while larks and bulbuls flutter around. Those who enjoy trekking can climb the nearby hill on which, at a height of 2,500 feet is the Tawli Guha. A path leads up to this cave from the lake. Excellent for a day's outing from Mumbai.

Bhandardara

On the road from Mumbai to Nashik and Igatpuri you will notice to the right the Baleshwar range of mountains including Alang, Kulang, Madan and Kalsubai. On the Konkan side of this range of mountains is the Ratangad fort. The source of the Pravara

River lies in a cave on this hill. A dam has been erected across this river near the village of Shendi, resulting in the grand reservoir of Bhandardara. Located in a very hilly region, this reservoir is at a height of 2,400 feet from mean sea level and among the few in India at such a height.

Fact File

Best time- June to March

Location -- 180 kms. from Mumbai off the Mumbai-Nashik highway

Getting there - Turn off right at Ghoti after Igatpuri

Where to stay -- MTDC resort

Where to eat - Same

The hills, which encircle Bhandardara, have an average height above 4,500 feet The reservoir set against this magnificent backdrop of mountains makes an enchanting sight. To the right of the reservoir are the Alang, Kulang, Madan and Kalsubai peaks while to the left, the peak of Ratangad fort is clearly visible.

The village of Bari is 6 kilometres from Bhandardara. Anyone wishing to climb Kalsubai, the highest peak in Maharashtra, has to pass through this village. From here the climb to Kalsubai is about 3,000 feet and can be completed in about 3 hours. It is possible to take in Kalsubai in a day if you spend the night at Bhandardara. The MTDC guest house overlooks the lake, affording a spectacular view of the calm waters.

Sunset at Bhandardara is an unforgettable experience. The sun goes down just beyond the Ratangad fort disappearing into a gap in the mountain, creating the illusion of a sparkling diamond ring. To watch this beautiful scene all you have to do is take a walk down the Bhandardara-Randha road. A small park has been created at the foot of the dam wall. After the rainy season, water is let down into the garden somewhat like a waterfall, under which visitors are allowed to revel.

About 12 kilometres further down from Bhandardara is the spot where the overflow from the Bhandardara dam falls into a deep gorge This waterfall is known as the Randha falls and is one of the major tourist attractions here. Nestled among the rocks at the top of the waterfall is a temple dedicated to Ghorpadai Devi.

The peak of the Chomdev mountain is also visible from near the waterfall. There is a good tarred road from Bhandardara to Randha and a regular State Transport bus service as well.

On the western banks of Bhandardara in the village of Ratanwadi and at the foot of the Ratangad hill is situated an ancient Shiva temple. Built on difficult terrain, this rock-cut temple is nearly 30 to 32 feet high and has beautiful carvings on it. Near the temple is a small pond named Vishnutirth. Formerly, to get here, villagers from Shendi village would take a launch from the village of Murshet. Today there is a track where a jeep can take you straight to the temple. This road is an offshoot of the Bhandardara-Randha road, skirting the entire lake before climbing upward. Taking this *kuchcha* road is like visiting another world; the bumps are forgotten as you wind through dense forest, with the mountains on the one side and the lake on the other.

Those who enjoy climbing can reach the Ratangad fort in just two hours from Ratanwadi. A small iron ladder takes you to the topi a few steps later you can see the door of the fort, on which there is a statue of Ganpati. There are several water tanks and scattered ruins of the fort on the plateau. The river Pravara springs from its source in Ratnabai's cave. From a height of 4,500 feet there is a grand view of the Konkan and the surrounding mountain peaks. To the south is the imposing Aajoba mountain while, to the north is the mountain range from Kulang to Kalsubai. If you leave Bhandardara in the early hours of the morning, it is quite possible to visit both the Ratangad fort and the Ratanwadi temple before returning for the night.

Bhandardara is 180 kilometres from Mumbai via Igatpuri and Ghoti. There is a regular bus service from Igatpuri and Ghoti. The MTDC guesthouse at Bhandardara is built at a perfect spot and offers an excellent view of the lake. Bookings should be made in Mumbai, at least a week in advance. There is also a Hotel Roopmanohar just behind the MTDC guesthouse. To really enjoy a holiday here you need at least four to five days.

Upper Vaitarna

> **Fact File**
>
> *Best time- June to March*
>
> *Location -- Off the Mumbai-Nashik highway*
>
> *Getting there - Turn off left at Ghoti after Igatpuri*
>
> *Where to stay -- Government Rest House*
>
> *Where to eat - Same*

When asked to draw a landscape most kids invariably draw the same thing—a blue river, a small hut besides the river, the sun rising from behind a mountain and birds flying in the sky. Surprisingly there is a spot which is just as picture perfect. Most people know that Mumbai is supplied water by five main reservoirs on the outskirts of the city, namely Tansa, Bhatsa, Tulsi, Vihar and Vaitarna. This last, Vaitarna Lake, is near Shahpur village, built on the Vaitarna River in the Konkan. On this same river just beyond the Kasara ghats at a height of 1,500 feet is yet another lake called the Upper Vaitarna.

After you have crossed the Kasara Ghat, leaving Igatpuri behind, you will come upon the important market town of Ghoti at a distance of around 145 kilometres from Mumbai. On the Mumbai-Nashik highway the road which turns right from here takes us to Bhandardara, Kalsubai and so forth. The road to the left takes you to Upper Vaitarna. About 16 kilometres from here is the large lake. At a height of 3,000 feet on a nearby hill is a small temple located just 3 kilometres from the lake.

In summer this terrain is dry and dull, but after the rains it metamorphoses into a fascinating green carpet from which small yellow flowers peep out. The government rest house on the banks of the lake is built at an enviable spot, sitting pretty amidst various flowering plants and tall eucalyptus trees. The blue water of the lake, and the mountain ranges in the background complete this perfect picture. Trimbakeshwar, Harihar, Utvad and the Fani Mountains are easily recognizable. Rising to 1500 feet from mean sea level, the climate here is always pleasant. In September, after the rains, the fluffy clouds atop the tree-lined hills look wonderful.

A further 13 kilometres ahead, on the Ghoti-Upper Vaitarna

road, is the Shri Ghat. The view of the sunset from this point is truly wonderful. This same road goes ahead towards the smaller hill stations of Khodala and Suryamal. Just before you reach Shri Ghat there is a road to the right which takes you straight to Trimbakeshwar.

It is possible to make arrangements to spend the night at the rest house at Upper Vaitarna at very reasonable rates, with good quality food. A perfect place for a weekend break for people from Mumbai and Nashik.

Manikdoh

Fact File

Best time- June to March

Location -- Pune District, 6kms. from Junnar

Getting there - On the Bhimashankar-Malshej road

Where to stay -- Manikdoh Project Rest Houses

Where to eat - Same

The Name ghat is an old ghat road in the Sahyadri mountain range in Pune district on the Bhimashanker-Malshej road. Near here is the source of the River Kukadi. To one side are the forts of Jeevdhan, Chavand and Shivneri while to the other are the Hadsar Fort and Lenyadri, famous for its Ganesh temple. The river flows between these two mountain ranges. A dam has been constructed across this river near the Hadsar fort, creating the Manikdoh reservoir.

The important trading centre of Junnar is just 6 kilometres from the Manikdoh dam. There are regular State Transport buses plying from Mumbai, Thane and Kalyan to Junnar. The distance between Mumbai and Junnar is 175 kilometres and it takes about five and a half hours to cover. There is a State Transport bus service from Junnar to Manikdoh. At a considerable height from the dam are the Manikdoh project rest houses, from which there is a breathtaking view of the lake. The small, partially submerged temple of Muktai is clearly visible from here. It is also easy to spot the forts of Shivneri and Chavand from this point. The glass frontage of the rest house enables one to see the sun setting in all its glory, its colours spilling over into the water. The Manikdoh reservoir is approximately 1,750 feet from mean sea level, therefore the climate here is always cool. While it is possible to get a meal at the rest house, to stay here, you need to book in advance with the Chief Executive Engineer, Manikdoh Project, Narayangaon, Pune district.

Other places in the area that you can visit at the same time are Shivneri, Hadsar, Jeevdhan and Chavand forts, Naneghat, the ancient temple of Kukdeshwar and the Ganesh temples at Lenyadri and Ozar. The Kukdeshwar temple, about 16 kilometres from Junnar, though almost forgotten, is located at a very beautiful spot. State Transport buses run from Junnar to this place. Before reaching it the bus goes through Chavandwadi, the village at the foothills of the Chavand fort atop Kathalmath hill. This hill has steep slopes on all sides as high as 150 feet. On the side where the waterline comes down, there are very steep steps that will leave you short of breath. After a short walk you can see the entrance to the fort. An ancient ruined temple of Chawandibai with a statue of the goddess still exists. On the plateau there is a tank and an arch. The most impressive item on this 3,500 feet high fort are the seven circular water tanks which have been dug here.

The Shivneri fort which is nearby is 3,350 feet from mean sea level. From Junnar it is a 900 feet climb. The massive wall-like side of the fort is dotted with innumerable caves which can be seen quite clearly from the village. The dome of the mosque as well as several parts of the fort are also easily recognizable from afar. Steps carved into the hillside dating from the Satavahana period, take you up to the fort. On this route you pass through seven doors; after the fifth, is the Shiva temple. After the last two doorways, you can see the ruins of a building which was formerly the granary. Further ahead is a water tank called the Ganga - Jamuna. North of this is the building where the great Mavla king, Shivaji, was born.

Another place that can be visited easily from here is the Lenyadri Ganesh temple, part of the Ashtavinayak (eight-Ganesh temples) tour. This is just 5 kilometres from Junnar and 11 kilometres from Manikdoh. There is a regular bus service from

Junnar to Lenyadri. Ozar, also an Ashtavinayak pilgrimage centre, is just 8 kilometres from Junnar.

Bhoj Lake and Kundeshwar Lake

Fact File

Best time- June to March

Location -- 74 kms. from Mumbai

Getting there - 6kms. from Sheel Phata

Where to stay -- Day's trip from Mumbai

Where to eat - Carry your own food

In the mountain ranges between Mumbai and Karjat, that is, between the Haji Malang mountain and Matheran, there are several small, beautiful but unknown lakes. One among these is the Bhoj Lake. Situated against the backdrop of the Badlapur hill, the Navranavari hill and the Chanderi and Mhaismal peaks, few people are aware that such a delightful picnic spot exists only 74 kilometres from Mumbai. Six kilometres after the turn at Sheel Phata (Junction) is the MIDC pipeline road which takes you to Badlapur. The road from Badalpur station also joins this road. Another 3 kilometres ahead is the Jyuweli village. Two kilometres later, take a right turn at Dahivali village. This road takes you straight to the Boj dam and the lake. There are proper steps enabling you to climb on to the wall and survey the awesome beauty of blue water garlanded by green trees set against imposing hills in the background.

A further 4 kilometres down the same road is another wonderful spot - Kundeshwar which can be reached by crossing a tiny ghat after Bhoj Lake. Actually Kundeshwar is at the northernmost tip of the Bhoj Lake. Clamber down a short distance from where the road ends, edge past a small waterfall and you stumble on to this glorious spot of nature. The flow of water from the Badlapur hill and the Navranavari hill has formed a deep valley in which lies the ancient temple of Girishanker. The whole view is fascinating. At the foot of the mountains is an ancient cave, with waterfalls on either side and dense trees enveloping the area, reminding one of scenes from an African jungle. The temple was probably built in former times as an ideal spot for meditation. The abundant water and the several lakes in the area ensure the presence of a variety of birds. Kingfishers, egrets, hornbills, drongo, robins, larks and cuckoos are among the birds which can be seen.

Several people from neighbouring villages converge on the lakes for day picnics and to bathe under the waterfalls. Since it is just an hour and a half away from Mumbai, carry your lunch and make the most of this spot. For the more adventurous, trekking down the many paths in the surrounding forests can be great fun.

Panshet

Fact File

Best time- August and September

Location -- 38 kms. from Kanhoji Jedhe Chowk, Parvati in Pune

Getting there - One hour drive from Pune, ST and private buses and taxis available

Where to stay -- MTDC guest house

Where to eat - Many eateries

It was the great flood of 1961 in Pune that focused attention on the Panshet dam. But that is history. Today Panshet and its neighbouring lake of Varasgaon have developed into excellent tourist spots and a full-fledged water sports centre has been started here.

To get to Panshet you take the road from near the Parvati hill to Sinhagad. Panshet is 38 kilometres from the Kanhoji Jedhe Chowk, near Parvati in Pune. The road to Sinhagad branches off about 20 kilometres before Panshet. The road to Panshet thereafter runs alongside the Khadakvasala dam and the Mula river right up to Panshet. Sinhagad is to the left, remaining in sight for quite a while. During the rainy season this is a lovely drive. Built on the Ambi and Mose Rivers, to the right is Varasgaon dam and to the left is the Panshet dam. Speed boats, water scooters and other water sports facilities are available in the Varasgaon dam. By the month of May the water here is very low. It is in the months of August and September that this place is really worth a visit. Between the two lakes the MTDC has built a guest house, for which bookings can be done either in Mumbai or Pune. It is possible to visit Sinhagad during the day and then spend the evening at Panshet. There are regular buses from Swargate, Pune, to Panshet.

Shivsagar Lake, Bamnoli and its Periphery

Fact File

Best time- September to December

Location -- South of Mahabaleshwar

Getting there - To Tapola and from Tapola by launch or one hour's drive on the Tapoli-Bamnoli road

Where to stay -- Santaji Hotel, Bamnoli

Where to eat - Same

To the south of the Mahabaleshwar range of mountains, the Koyna River and its tributaries the Solishi and Kandati merge to create the almost 51 kilometre-long Shivsagar lake. Heavy rainfall causes the lake to be surrounded by a forest so dense that you need a sickle to clear a path through. Villagers living in the small hamlets near the lake will tell you that except for elephants, camels and lions, all other animals can be seen in the forest. While this may be an exaggeration, it is true that bears, tigers and deer have been spotted. Nature lovers will enjoy trekking through the forest and must start at Bamnoli village. There are launches from Tapola (26 kilometres from Mahabaleshwar) which take you straight to Bamnoli in half an hour. The alternative is the hour-long drive down the Tapoli-Bamnoli road. The best route is the road from Satara to Kaas Lake and then on to Bamnoli. The distance from Satara to Kaas is 26 kilometres while Kaas to Bamnoli is another 12 kilometres. The ghat road begins once you leave Kaas and about 1,500 feet below the blue waters of the Shivsagar shimmer invitingly. You have to see the place for yourself to really understand its beauty. About 4 to 5 kilometres short of Bamnoli village you can see the lake with colourful launches bobbing up and down on its waters. It is possible to hire launches to take you round the entire area. The distance to Vastoa and back is about 36 kilometres. It takes about an hour to get to the village of Met

Indavali at the foothills of Vasota. It is a day's trip from Bamnoli. The Santaji hotel at Bamnoli offers boarding and lodging facilities.

The confluence of the rivers Koyna and Kandati is near Met Indavali. You can get to the Chakdeo fort from here. The launches to Vasota are quite expensive, so it is to your advantage if you have more people in your group. Large groups are also preferable because the rest of the journey is through dense forest.

The best season to visit this place is the four months after the monsoon. The launch service is closed during the monsoon and in the months of May and June the water level in the lakes is quite low. During the months of December and January the weather is very pleasant and it is an enjoyable trip.

The Pelhar Lake

Fact File

Best time- June to March

Location -- Off the Mumbai - Ahmedabad highway before Vajreshwari

Getting there - Pelhar village, 3 kms. before Vajreshwari

Where to stay -- Vajreshwari, Virar or Vasai

Where to eat - Same

Many tourists are familiar with the tourist spots of Vajreshwari and Ganeshpuri, famous for their hot springs and for the ashram of Nityanand Maharaj. State Transport buses ply from Virar and Vasai to Vajreshwari, 57 kilometres from Mumbai on the Mumbai-Ahmedabad highway. Just 3 kilometres short of Vajreshwari is the village of Pelhar. If you alight here, the road through the village takes you to the Pehlar Lake. A good tarred road enables you to take your vehicle right up to the lake. Two cowsheds mark the end of the 1.5-kilometre road; a dusty pathway from here leads to the dam wall. During the rains the water falls over this wall, creating an extremely attractive sight. Although not large, this reservoir is very eye-catching, ringed by the Tungareshwar range on all sides. The lush green surrounding this beautiful lake makes it look like a sapphire set among emeralds. Hares, foxes, wild boar are aplenty in these forests. Villagers claim that an occasional leopard can be spotted. Not very *well-known*, the lake is not crowded, and affords a wonderful place for a picnic.

Trekkers spending the night at Vajreshwari, Virar or Vasai can combine this trip with a visit to the Takmak fort. About 14 kilometres further down from the Vajreshwari junction on the Mumbai Ahmedabad highway is a road that leads to the fort. Take the right turn near the Ramkrishna Mission building till you get to Sakwar village from where a path leads to the fort. This 200 foot-high fort has some ruins including a water tank and a couple of cannons lying around. From the fort, the Tansa river can be seen to the south and the valley of the Vaitarna to the north. The road from the other side of the fort goes down to Thakurpada and Vandri Lake and to the Dhekale village on the Mumbai-Ahmedabad highway.

Vandri Lake and the Hot Springs at Sativali

Fact File

Best time- June to March

Location -- Off the Mumbai - Ahmedabad highway in Dekhale near Manor village

Getting there - By road or by train to Palghar

Where to stay -- Vajreshwari, Virar or Vasai

Where to eat - Same

Slightly to the north of Mumbai near Manor village are several places worth a visit. Take the train to Palghar (Western Railway) from where you can get a direct State Transport bus to Manor, 18 kilometres away. You can drive down from Mumbai on the Mumbai-Ahmedabad highway and take the turning to Manor (85 kilometres from Bandra, Mumbai). Just 16 kilometres short of Manor village you come to Dhekale village. Turn right here and 3 kilometres further is the Vandri Lake.

To the east are the Kondra hills while to the south is the Takmak range and nestling in between is the large Vandri Lake. There are not many trees around the lake, yet it is very pleasant and makes an ideal picnic spot. A pathway from the lake takes you to Takmak fort via Thakurpada.

Another 2 kilometres further down towards Manor village is the Satoleshwar Mahadev temple. It is special because of the hot springs located here. There are three such hot springs in the northern Konkan region - the Vajreshwari springs on the river Tansa, the Sativali hot springs on the river Vaitarna and the Kokner hot springs on the river Surya. There are three large and three small tanks opposite the temple here at Sativali. The small tank to the left has hot water and you can see the steam rising from it. The other tanks have relatively lukewarm water. Some of these tanks have been maintained purely for bathing. There are two more tanks to the left of the temple. The tanks are watched over by the many herons and drongos in the vicinity.

Trekkers will find several forts in this area. Just behind Sativali is the Tandukwadi fort, which can be reached through Tandukwadi village. There is an easy route to the Kohoj Fort via Waghote. To get there you go to Charoti about 10 kilometres ahead of the Manor junction on the Mumbai-Ahmedabad highway. Take the road via Khadkone village till you get to Asherigad. The slope here is steep and not as easy as it looks. Around 21 kilometres right of Manor is Vikramgad, which is a trekker's haven, with plenty of interesting spots. This entire area is packed with delightful surprises both for the ordinary tourist and for the more intrepid trekker.

HOT SPRINGS

Hot Springs at Sav

The River Savitri runs parallel to the Mumbai-Goa highway about 18 kilometres after you leave the village of Mangaon en route to Mahad. About 11 kilometres short of Mahad, a road to the right takes you to the riverbank, where you can take a small boat to cross the river for just Rs 1.50 per head. A short walk through a tree-flanked path takes you to the Sav hot springs. The whole experience is quite invigorating. There are seven tanks in all and the main tank has water which is as hot as 50 degrees Celsius. The water is not so warm in the other tanks, which are also smaller in size. Like other hot springs in Maharashtra the water here too smells of sulphur. Close to these tanks is the dargah of a Muslim fakir, Shah Sailani. On holidays, tourists flock to the place to pay respects at the dargah and then partake of the waters here which are said to have healing properties. However, the crowds here are nothing compared to the crowds at Vajreshwari. Sitting in nature's lap, this spot is lovely for a day's outing. It is worth taking a break here en route to Goa. However, the place is not commercialized so you should carry your own food and drinking water.

Fact File

Best time- June to March

Location -- Off the Mumbai - Goa highway, 18 kms. after Mangaon

Getting There - By boat to Sav

Where to stay -- A day's outing

Where to eat - Carry your own food and water

Nadhal Lake

Just before the Chowk junction on the road from Mumbai to Pune are the tall hills of Prabalgad to the left, behind which are the even taller hills of Matheran. Between these two hills is another smaller hill, easily distinguishable because of its peculiar shape. The boat-shaped peak is known as Irsalgad. At the foothills of Irsalgad is the small but beautiful Nadhal lake. About 59 kilometres from Mumbai, just 2 kilometres short of the Chowk junction, is a tarred road to the left. At the start of the road is a sign that says Kalpataru; just half a kilometre from here lies the lake. The steep slopes of Irsalgad are reflected in the placid waters of the lake. In the rainy season, a large part of the hill is enveloped in misty clouds, and the lush green surroundings are especially beautiful. While there are plenty of trees towards the hillside, the other side is quite bereft of greenery. Bullbuls, drongo, robins, orioles and mynas abound and their voices are the only sound in the otherwise silent surroundings. It's hard to believe that you are just a stone's throw away from the busy Mumbai-Pune highway!

Fact File

Best time- June to March

Location -- 59 kms. from Mumbai, Off the old Mumbai-Pune highway

Getting there - 2kms. before Chowk junction at Kalpataru

Where to stay -- A day's outing

Where to eat - Carry your own food and water

Trekkers can find their way into the small hamlet of Vishalwadi just after Chowk village, which is 2 kilometres from here. Vishalwadi is at the foot of the Irsalgad hill. Prabalgad is also close by. The distance from Chowk to Vishalwadi is 3 kilometres. There is also a road from Chowk to Matheran's Chowk Point.

Anyone driving from Mumbai to Pune should take an hour's break here, or better still, carry a picnic lunch and enjoy it at this lovely spot.

Mulshi Lake

Following the unbearable heat of April and May, the month of June is much-awaited, especially by the people of Maharashtra, for with it comes the monsoon. The rains wash away not only the hot weather but also the heat-induced lethargy and suddenly you are raring to explore the rejuvenated landscape. Everywhere the dry yellow is turning into a healthy lush green and nowhere is it more apparent than in the Sahyadri ranges.

South-west of Lonavala and west of Pune lies one such place which is at its best during the monsoon season - the Mulshi Lake. Lying to one side of the mountain, the Mulshi Lake covers a large area. The Mulshi dam provides water for one of the largest hydroelectric power stations and there is naturally, tight security near the dam and photography is prohibited. About 5 to 6 kilometres down the road, after the Mulshi village, is Walne ghat and the village of Walnewadi. From here onwards you can literally soak in the beauty of Mulshi at leisure. The ghat road is narrow and full of curves and the State Transport bus often has to reverse before it can inch forward! A short way down from Walnewadi, and Mulshi Lake stretches before you in all its

Fact File

Best time- June to March

Location -- Southwest of Lonavala , 45 kms. from Pune

Getting there - 5-6 kms. from Mulshi dam, Walnewadi village, ST buses

Where to stay -- A day's outing

Where to eat - Carry your own food and water

magnificence. Part of the Ratnagiri Mountain protrudes into the waters of the lake up ahead, and to the left is the wall of the dam. To the right are visible the tall peaks of Hattidand and Pagota. The height of Pagota is nearly 4,000 feet from mean sea level. On top is visible the plateau locally called Lavmal. It takes about two hours to get to this plateau from Walnewadi. From the top you get a view of the entire Mulshi Lake and the Konkan area.

Those who enjoy trekking can go to Dhangad or Koraigad on the western banks of the lake. To get to Dhangad you have to go to Tiskari village at its foothills, while to reach Koraigad you have to go to Ambavane village. There are Statae Transport buses to both these villages from Lonavala. Formerly there was a launch service from Mulshi dam to Tiskari. This used to be a three to four hour journey. Nowadays, since roads to almost all villages have been constructed and State Transport buses ply regularly, the launch service has become irregular. Mulshi is about 45 kilometres from Pune. Buses to Mulshi from Pune's Swargate bus station leave every one hour, the first leaving at 6 a.m. There is also a bus service from Lonavala to Mulshi via Ambawana-Shedani. Mulshi is a day trip from either Pune or Lonavala. If approaching Mulshi from Pune, arrangements for food can be made at Paud village, but after that it is best to carry your own food and water.

Bhilawale Lake

Most tourists, both young and old are aware of only one picnic spot near Mumbai and that is Matheran. But very close to Matheran is another ideally situated picnic spot—Bhilawale Lake. About 67 kilometres from Mumbai on the Mumbai-Pune highway is the Chowk junction. The left turn here takes you to Matheran. Just 2 kilometres down this same road is a signpost that leads to the Bhilawale Irrigation project. From here, 1.5 kilometres down a *kuchcha* road, is the Bhilawale Lake.

Fact File

Best time- June to March

Location -- 67 kms. on Mumbai Pune highway near Chowk junction

Getting there - on the way to Matheran Bhiwale Irrigation Project

Where to stay -- A day's outing

Where to eat - Carry your own food and water

The fertile land and pleasant surroundings have made this area very popular among the rich and famous who have built several private farmhouses here. The result is that on either side of the road are a series of well-planted trees! The *kuchcha* road ends at the lake which is skirted by a small path. The blue water, red mud and green trees in the background remind you that you are in the Konkan. To one side of the lake is visible a bungalow with a red-tiled roof, while to the other side there is a white bungalow. Both these houses add to the splendour of colours making the lake picture-perfect; a photographer's delight in fact. Several hills and forts are visible from here including Matheran, Karnala, Manikgad, Irsalgad, Prabalgad and Shivpuri hill.

An amusement park called Wonderland is close by, where it is possible to indulge in some boating.

Devkop Lake

There are several relatively unknown lakes in the Thane district of the northern Konkan region. Among these are Tansa, Vaitarna, Vandri, Pelhar and Devkop. Devkop is perhaps the most easily accessible of all these lakes. The very location of this lake is what mesmerizes you at first sight. Just after the ghat, on the Manor-Palghar road lies the Devkop lake. The Devkop junction is about 4 kilometres from Palghar on the Palghar-Manor road. Turn left here and the road leads up to the hill beside the lake. The lake is

Fact File

Best time- June to March

Location -- Off the Manor - Palghar road

Getting there - By road

Where to stay -- A day's outing, Palghar

Where to eat - Carry your own food and water

surrounded by high hills on three sides, while on the fourth, the long wall of the dam stretches from one mountain to the other. The Asava fort, Palghar fort and the Tandulwadi fort are part of the mountain range which rings this reservoir. The mountainside is covered with green trees and complemented by the still blue waters of the reservoir, so this makes for a stunning effect. Near the lake is the Waghoba Devacha mandir (temple). Walking along the wall of the dam is a delightful experience, providing the photographer with myriad angles to capture on film. Trekkers can climb easily to Palghar fort from here.

Despite being very close to Palghar town, this lake is virtually deserted. On the other side of the mountain beside the lake is the Surya river where the Kokner hot springs are located. If you have a vehicle it is possible to see this place and then return to Palghar. Many tourists visit Palghar to see the beaches here, but just a short diversion will allow them a glimpse of another paradise.

The Surya River Area

The northern Konkan region has three main rivers, Tansa, Vaitarna and Surya. There are several interesting tourist spots and picnic places in these three river valleys, and of these Vaitarna and the Upper Vaitarna Lake on Vaitarna River and the Tansa Lake on Tansa River are quite popular among picnickers from Mumbai.

Surya River also has two lakes, the larger one is called Dhamani, and the smaller one, which has formed as a result of the overflow from this lake, is known as Kavdas.

Fact File

Best time- June to March

Location -- Off the Mumbai Ahmedabad highway, 109 kms. from Mumbai

Getting there - Charoti Junction towards Javhar by road

Where to stay -- Day outing, Palghar

Where to eat - Carry your own food and water

To get here you take the Mumbai-Ahmedabad highway up to the Charoti Junction, 109 kilometres from Mumbai, and 24 kilometres ahead of Manor. A right turn here takes you to the hill station of Javhar. About 6 kilometres down this road is the Kavdas Lake. A small park has been developed along the side and the predominant sound here is of chattering birds. On the far side of the lake the tall Gambhirgad Mountain is visible. To really appreciate the beauty of this lake you should drive down the Charoti-Javhar road ignoring the Kavdas turning. Two kilometres from here the road winds through a ghat, skirts the lake and continues. Here, from a height, you can see the entire lake in all its glory.

This same road takes you to Dhamani Lake. Dhamani is the major dam on the river Surya, and the lake here is quite deep. From here the water goes on to Kavdas. The distance between Kavdas and Dhamani is about seven kilometres. No photography is permitted here. Javhar hill station is three kilometres from Dhamani. Vikramgad is also quite close by and just 17 kilometres from the Talawada junction is Dhamani and Kavdas. It is therefore convenient to make a trip to these two lakes while staying at Javhar or Vikramgad.

Another place in this vicinity is Mahalaxmi hill. The tapering slim peak of Mahalaxmi is visible from quite a distance as one approaches Charoti. About 1,600 ft. high, the hill has a Mahalaxmi temple on it. There is also a cave near the peak. The distance from Charoti to the temple is about 4 kilometres.

Gambhirgad is another attractive destination for trekkers, and from here it is possible to take the route from Charoti via Sion. The Sakhare Lake on the Charoti-Vangaon road is 18 kilometres from

Charoti junction and is also worth a visit. Charoti is 24 kilometres from Dahanu, so it is possible to get here by rail. Make Dahanu your base and visit all the places in this area.

Savne Lake at the Foothills of Manikgad

> **Fact File**
>
> *Best time- June to March*
>
> *Location -- Off the Mumbai-Goa highway, 71 kms. from Sion, Mumbai*
>
> *Getting there - 17 kms. From Savroli junction to Chavne village*
>
> *Where to stay -- Karnala, A day's outing*
>
> *Where to eat - Carry your own food and water*

The dome-shaped peak of Manikgad is easily identifiable from both the Mumbai-Goa and the Mumbai-Pune highway. Just west of this fort and slightly below its summit is a very beautiful lake known as Savne Lake. There is a *kuchcha* road from Savne village to the lake. The other road is through the Adivasi settlement of Jambivali. In spite of being so close to two major highways, the atmosphere near the lake is completely serene. Dense forest can be seen to the western end of the lake. The reflection of the imposing Manikgad (1,900 ft.) and the green jungle background is clearly visible in the clear waters of the lake. In the distance, to one side you can see the majestic Karnala hill while to the other side are the mountain ranges edged with the green farmlands of the Adivasis. The dense forest cover near the lake houses plenty of birds and the chirping of birds like the skylark and sandpiper echo through the hillside.

The edge of the lake has several varieties of ducks nestling in its water, while on the other side countless herons walk through the fields adjoining the lake. After a short while you realize that you are sitting amidst nature at its best. Along with the sounds of birds, animals sounds too can be discerned. Hares, foxes, wild boar and even leopards are known to inhabit these forests. Several types of water birds and water snakes can also be seen in the lake.

To get here, you take the State Transport bus to Savne village. From the village to the lake is a *kuchcha* road. The alternative is to take a jeep or a motorcycle and drive down to the edge of the lake from the Mumbai-Goa highway. About 55 kilometres from Sion (Mumbai) on the Mumbai-Goa highway you cross a small bridge and come to a railway crossing. Here to the left is the Saroli junction. About 7.5 kilometres down this road, you will see the signboard for Chavne village. Follow the same road for a further 3 kilometres till you come upon a tarred road to the right which goes via the villages of Karade and Jambivali to the lake. This stretch is about 5.5 kilometres long, of which the latter half is a *kuchcha* road. Thus the distance from Savroli junction to the lake is approximately 16 kilometres, while from Sion it is 71 kilometres.

It is also possible to get here from the Mumbai-Pune highway via the Patalganga-Reliance project road. The time taken from both highways to Savne is around an hour and a half. No food or snacks are available near the lake, so you would be well-advised to carry your own. Trekking in the rainy season to Manikgad or to the fort of Sankshi Baddrudin from here is great fun. If you stay at Karnala you can cover Savne, Manikgad and Baddrudin in 2 days.

Sakhare Lake

North of Mumbai right up to Talasseri is typical Konkan countryside with its rugged mountain slopes, green trees and red earth. There are several lakes in this region, large ones like Tansa, Vaitarna, Dhamani and smaller ones like Devkop, Pelhar and Sakhare. It is the last-mentioned Sakhare that is ideal for birdwatchers and photographers. The Dhamani and Kavdas lakes are to the right of the Charoti junction on the Mumbai-Ahmedabad highway. Exactly in the opposite direction to the left is this small and serene Sakhare Lake. On the Charoti-Vangaon road the Mahalaxmi hill is in view to the right for quite a while. Cross Sarni village, turn left and travel another 15 to 16 kilometres and you will see the Sakhare Lake. The road skirts the entire lake and approximately 18 kilometres from Charoti you will come to the wall of the dam. The water here is quite shallow and kingfishers

Fact File

Best time- June to March

Location -- Off the Mumbai-Ahmedabad highway,

Getting there - Turn left from Charoti junction on the Charoti-Vangaon road: By rail to Boisar and take Boisar-Charoti ST bus

Where to stay -- Javhar or Vikramgad

Where to eat - Carry your own food and water

have a virtual feast of fish. The lake is circled by lush greenery and it is possible to walk quietly along the perimeter of the lake and watch the birds. At the slightest sound the ducks and water fowl start flapping their wings, and in seconds the lake is desolate with not a single bird visible. The best thing to do then is to sit quietly at the side, in the shade of a tree and wait for the birds to return. If you blend in with the surroundings, the birds will ignore you and you can enjoy their company for a longer time. Brahminy ducks, snake birds and grey herons are among the varieties of birds you can see here. Because of the adjoining forests, bulbuls, cuckoos, barbets and robins are also visible. Since the lake is quite shallow you can spot several kinds of fish as well.

If you have a vehicle, getting here is no problem. Just take the Mumbai-Ahmedabad highway and go via the Charoti junction. By rail you can alight at Boisar and take the Boisar-Charoti State Transport bus. It is possible to take a tour of all three lakes here - Sakhare, Dhamni and Kavdas - by alighting at either Boisar or Vangaon station, and staying the night at Javhar or Vikramgad.

WATERFALLS

Dabhosa Waterfall

On the Javhar-Silvassa road, about 18 kilometres from Javhar, is the Dabhosa waterfall. No obstacle blocks your view of this waterfall and you can see it spilling over right from the top of the peak to the bottom. About a kilometre and a half off the main road, a small *kuchcha* road takes you to Dabhosa village. Thereafter, there

Fact File

Best time- June to September (350 foot fall)

Location -- 18 kms. from Javhar on the Javhar-Silvassa road, Javhar is 130 kms. from Mumbai

Getting there - ST bus from Javhar to Dhabosa village

Where to stay -- Javhar, Vikramgad, Karnala, A day's outing

Where to eat - Carry your own food and water

is a rather difficult patch of uneven road that takes you close to the 350 foot-waterfall. Even from this point it is not possible to actually see the depth of the fall. It is only after you come to a flat summit that you can see the entire waterfall in all its glory. Ringed by trees, the foam of the water falls into what looks like a circular-shaped lake. It is a breathtaking view and there is no doubt that this waterfall must rank among the most beautiful in Maharashtra. It is convenient to stay at Javhar and visit this waterfall. The distance between Mumbai and Javhar via Vikramgad is 130 kilometres. There is a regular State Transport service between Javhar and Dabhosa. The waterfall is at its peak capacity during the rainy season or just after the rains.

Waterfall near Vihigaon Village

Fact File

Best time- June to September

Location -- Off the Mumbai-Nashik highway, 6 kms. from Kasara

Getting there - By road, private vehicles

Where to stay -- Igatpuri or rest house at Khodala

Where to eat - Carry your own food and water

About 7 kilometres along the road from Javhar is a small lake near Jatsar village. Full of white and pink lotus flowers, this small lake is the habitat of several varieties of birds. Between the months of November and April, snake birds, Brahminy ducks, cormorants, egrets and other such migratory birds can be spotted here, just before you hit the Mumbai-Nashik highway on the road to Javhar, about 36 kilometres. About 18 kilometres short of Vihigaon, just after crossing a small culvert on the Vaitarna River, you hear the sound of water falling, and then to your right you see this strikingly impressive waterfall. Park your vehicle at the side of the road and you can enjoy its full impact. The distance between Kasara and Vihigaon is just 6 kilometres, so it is quite easy to get here from Kasara. Trekkers should check out the nearby Balwantgad. This waterfall can be seen all year round, but is in full form during the rainy season.

Pallu Waterfall

Fact File

Best time- June to September (50 foot fall)

Location -- Off the Mumbai-Javhar road,near Vikramgad, 105 kms. from Mumbai

Getting there - By road, private vehicle

Where to stay -- Vikramgad resthouse, Nature Trails Farmhouse

Where to eat - Carry your own food and water

This waterfall is about 105 kilometres from Mumbai on the Mumbai-Javhar road near Vikramgad. While travelling from Vikramgad to Javhar, you reach the signpost for Jambha. A one-kilometre *kuchcha* road leads to the river Dehraja. Cross the river and a short five-minute walk later you will reach the waterfall which, though much smaller compared to the Dabhosa or Vihigaon falls, is still very attractive. It falls from a height of about 50 feet from a semi-circular formation. On both sides of the waterfall are dense forests and birds can be heard singing. Perfect for a day's picnic especially if you stay in the nearby Vikramgad rest house or the Nature Trails Farmhouse.

Pandavgad

> **Fact File**
>
> *Best time- June to September (350 foot fall)*
>
> *Location -- 46 kms. from Mumbai; Off the Mumbai-Pune Highway on the Thane-Belapur road*
>
> *Getting there - By ST bus from Konkan Bhavan to CBD, or from Kopra rail junction to Kharghar by private vehicle, or by new road from CBD*
>
> *Where to stay -- A day's trip*
>
> *Where to eat - Altoona or carry your own food and water*

Some time ago, a small locality called Ove camp was in the news because a plane crashed here. This small place is located in the hills near the Thane-Belapur road, an area dotted with small industries. Running almost parallel to the road is a mountain range clearly in sight of anyone travelling on the Mumbai-Pune Highway. Tucked way inside these 1,200 feet high mountains is the CBD locality. Right next to Ove camp is Pandavgad, a place worth visiting in the month of October or just after the rains. Ove camp is 3 kilometres from Taloja on the Thane-Pune road.

Take the *kuchcha* road from the camp, cross a canal and you reach Pandavgad. Despite its name there is no fort here. Instead in a deep (350 feet) gorge is a foaming white waterfall which tumbles down a sharp-edged mountain. Halfway down the waterfall is a cave, which can be easily reached by a dusty path. Near the main waterfall is a smaller waterfall popularly called Nangrya. Folk tales recounted by villagers here say that the Pandavas stayed in this cave during their period of exile, and hence the name. There are several caves like this scattered throughout Maharashtra and all are called the Pandava Caves!

To get here, take the State Transport bus to the CBD quarters near the Konkan Bhavan on the Pune-Mumbai highway (the distance from Mumbai to CBD is 31 kilometres), or alight at the Kopra junction, about 4 kilometres further down. A signpost here reads 'Pune-120 kms'. To the left of this signpost is a road leading to the village of Kharghar. There is a path from Kharghar straight to the waterfall, a distance of about 4 kilometres. If you have a vehicle you can take the road to Taloja, 8 kilometres from Kopra junction and then down to Ove camp, a further 3 kilometres. The waterfall is about 10 to 15 minutes from here.

Situated 46 kilometres from Mumbai, it is just right for a day trip. Carrying your own food is the ideal thing to do, although you can get a decent meal at Altoona. Its proximity to the city does have drawbacks: it is best avoided on Saturday and Sundays when the place gets quite crowded. A new road takes you from CBD to the waterfall, a distance of 5 kilometres.

Thoseghar

Fact File

Best time- All year round (1000 foot fall)

Location -- Near Sajjangad in Satara

Getting there - ST bus from Satara, By road to Sajjangad junction 13 kms., Thoseghar village 11 kms.

Where to stay -- Thoseghar village

Where to eat - Carry your own food and water

There are large areas around the city of Satara worth exploring. Ajinkyatara and Yavteshwar are the most popular. If you look to the south-east from these hills, you will see a range of mountains stretching for miles. Standing slightly apart from the main range is Sajjangad. A road from Satara takes you to the base of Sajjangad; continue along this road till you reach a steep ghat road that will take you to the flat plateau of the mountain next to Sajjangad. As you drive to the khind (pass) you will see Sajjangad just below. The distance between Satara and Sajjangad junction is 13 kilometres. Thoseghar is 11 kilometres after this junction. It is like any other small village on the Sahyadris and has approximately 250 houses. There is a good tarred road from Satara right up to the village, but if you really want to see the best parts of Thoseghar, you will have to travel on a *kuchcha* road. While a jeep or motorcycle is the preferred mode of transport on this road, the other alternative is to proceed on foot. About 5 kilometres from Thoseghar village is a small lake formed by the bund built on the Tarli River. The blue waters of the lake stand out against the red earth of the mountain and the green trees, making this place an extremely attractive sight.

There is a small outhouse near the dam where arrangements can be made to spend the night. Since there is no electricity here it would be more convenient to spend the night at Thoseghar village. Just before the lake, a dense forest near Maldev village attracts attention. Here you can see birds like the shrike, crested lark, sasana, owls and animals such as the mongoose and jackals. One kilometre down the road from Thoseghar village to Thoseghar lake is the Chalkewadi junction. Take a left turn here and about 1.25 kilometres further down you have to leave the road to enter the forest. Walk downhill for a little while and you will come to a 1,750 foot-high pinnacle. From 100 feet below you can see a waterfall hurtling right down to the base. The best view is obtained by going to Chalkewadi and then walking down on a *kuchcha* road, for 5 minutes. You get a full view of this waterfall. The height of this waterfall from top to bottom is about 1,000 feet. Both sides of the valley have straight, clean-cut edges. Dense vegetation on the pinnacle, hanging creepers, dark overhanging rocky cliffs and the waterfall falling in all its glory makes for a wonderful, awe-inspiring sight. Time flies by as you watch the strong wind wafting the flocks of birds hovering around the waterfall, up into the air. If this area is ever developed as a proper tourist resort, undoubtedly this waterfall will be a major attraction. Water is plentiful here even in the summer.

Since this place has not been developed commercially, there are no restaurants or hotels. In Thoseghar village you will find only a small tea stall. The village sarpanch and other villagers are always ready to extend their hospitality however, and will make arrangements for your stay. There is a State Transport bus service between Thoseghar and Satara. Thoseghar is about 3,500 feet above mean sea level, therefore the weather is always cool.

CAVES

Maharashtra has a venerable legacy of caves. Tourists from all over the world flock to Maharashtra to see the Ajanta caves, famous for their beautiful paintings; or the Verul caves with their rock-cut sculptures. In addition to these well-known ones, there are several other caves in Maharashtra, some small, some large, lying scattered among the hills in the region. Each cave has a charm of its own and provides historical interest on a trek.

Many of the caves are found within the hill forts, or in the hills surrounding the forts. Some fine examples of these are the caves near Shivneri or Rajmachi. Very often, groups of 4 to 5 caves can be located on the outskirts of small villages. Enquiries regarding the names of the caves will always elicit the same response from the villagers. "The caves are called 'Pandavleni', because the Pandavas once stayed here!" The caves were probably cut out to provide shelter to the Buddhist bhikshus who would travel from place to place spreading the word of the Buddha, or maybe as a shelter for the ordinary traveller. Proximity to the fort probably ensured safety for the travellers. There is no doubt however, that the caves form an interesting part of history and visiting the caves is a pleasure in itself.

I had mentioned earlier that the Ajanta caves and the Verul caves came into limelight because of the paintings and sculptures found there. The Kanheri caves too have an important place in archaeology. The caves near Nashik, and the Karla caves are also now *well-known* to tourists. In addition to these, there is a small village near Indapur named Tale, at the foot of the Tale hill. Further ahead from Tale, is a small village called Kuda in which is a Buddhist cave worth seeing. Located in the hill just behind the village, the cave is clearly visible from the village. A small path leads you to the cave at a height of approximately 200 to 250 feet. Two huge stone elephants flank the entrance to the cave which has some attractive pillars. As the village is not on the tourist map, there are no hotels or restaurants in the vicinity.

On the Thane-Pune highway near Taloja is the Pandavgad village. The mountains nearby are huge and from a scraggy peak a waterfall drops on to the rocks below. Halfway up this peak is a cave. Legend says that the Pandavas spent their years of exile here, thus the name Pandavgad. The enticing setting has made this cave a popular tourist spot. Numerous caves like this are found all over Maharashtra, many of them named after the Pandavas.

To the north of Wai and south of Bhor, lies another Pandavgad. This fort dates back to the Stone Age. At the foot of this fort is the village of Dhavadi. Here too are some interesting caves. Similarly the caves near Lohare village are also worth seeing, but there is little information about these.

Kuda Caves

Fact File

Best time- June to September

Location -- Off the Mumbai-Goa highway, 19 kms. from Roha and 15 kms. from Idnapur in Raigad District

Getting there - Tale- Mandad road to Kuda village

Where to stay -- In Roha

Where to eat - Carry your own food and water

The village Tale is at the foot of Talgad around 19 kilometres from Roha and 15 kilometres from Indapur. Tourists who visit Talgad should spare time to travel a little further to see the Buddhist caves near Kuda village. The entire stretch from Talgad to the Kuda caves is a very interesting site.

To reach this spot, you have to take the Tale-Mandad road to the south of Tale village. Mandad is around 14 kilometres from Tale. About a kilometre before Mandad a *kuchcha* road turns to the left. About 1 to 1.5 kilometres down this road is the tiny village of Kuda.

The hill behind which the cave is located is clearly visible from the village. A small path leads up to the cave, situated at a height of approximately 250 feet. There is a direct motorable road to the caves, but it is in poor condition. About 4 kilometres before Mandad, a small road towards the left leads to the hill. About a kilometre down this road is a bend, beyond which are the caves.

From the bend in this road you can see the Murud creek and in the midst of it, the Ghosalgad fort. During full tide, especially in the monsoon, the view here is most picturesque. There are a total of 13 caves in Kuda. Within the first cave, the walls of which are covered by ancient writing, is a stupa. This cave is much larger than the others. The sixth cave towards the left also has a stupa within it. This is the cave whose walls are adorned by elephants outside. When you stand with your back towards the cave, Kuda village with the Murud creek in the backdrop is clearly visible Watching the sun set into the shimmering water is a spectacular sight. Although there are no restaurants or hotels nearby, anyone who visits Talgad should take time off to visit these caves. An extra hour is all that it takes to add some beautiful memories to your visit.

Ajanta Caves

Fact File

Best time- All round the year

Location -- 388 kms. from Mumbai, plus 19 kms. from Aurangabad

Getting there - ST buses, Tourist buses from Aurangabad

Where to stay -- MTDC Aurangabad, private hotels

Where to eat - Eateries at Ajanta and Aurangabad

The Ajanta caves are about 19 kilometres from Aurangabad. The distance between Mumbai and Aurangabad via Manmad is 375 kilometres, while via the Highway, it is about 388 kilometres. State Transport buses as well as tourist buses and private cars ply on this route.

The Ajanta caves date back to sometime between the second century BC to the fifth century AD and were created by Buddhist monks who lived there to preach Buddhism. Some British officials first discovered them in the nineteenth century.

There are a total of 30 caves dug into the Satmala range of mountains, and in them you will see countless sculptures of the Buddha, all of exquisite workmanship. The paintings (frescos) here are unique; the colours as beautiful today as they were centuries ago. Several of the caves have the stories from the Jatakas depicted upon the walls. Most of the caves have been built in such a way that daylight is available only for a few hours.

Cave No. I has the most famous of all Ajanta images, the Bodhisatva Padmapani, with lotus flower in hand. Another picture of Avalokiteshwara in shades of gold is outstanding. The pearl necklace around his neck looks absolutely lifelike. In Caves Nos. 1,2,16 and 17 the paintings on the ceilings are still in excellent condition. Cave No. 17 has the Apsaras (dancing), while in Cave No. 16 is the Buddhavihar. In this cave there is information about the king and his ministers who patronized the building of these caves. Cave Nos. 9 and 19 have several paintings of the Buddha including one of a standing Buddha and several colourful stupas. Cave No. 26 depicts the life of the Buddha. Almost all the caves have numerous pictures of the kings and queens of the time with their serving maids, giving us an idea of the elaborate dress and cosmetic rituals of the women of that time.

Cut into a horseshoe-shaped edge of the mountain, the caves are world-famous and the number of tourists, both domestic and international, visiting them is phenomenal. The Maharashtra Tourism Development Corporation offers accommodation here, booking for which can be made at Mumbai, Pune or Aurangabad.

Ellora Caves

These caves are 30 kilometres from Aurangabad. A total of 34 caves, the Verul caves were built from the fifth to the eight-century BC. Of these 16 are Hindu caves, 13 Buddhist and 5 Jain.

Fact File

Best time- All round the year

Location -- 388 kms. from Mumbai, plus 30 kms. from Aurangabad

Getting there - ST buses, Tourist buses from Aurangabad

Where to stay -- MTDC Aurangabad, private hotels

Where to eat - Eateries at Ellora and Aurangabad

Cave No. 10 contains a sculpture of the Buddha sitting under the Bodhi Tree. In Cave No. 11 there is a sculpture of Hiranyakashapu while in Cave No. 21 is a sculpture of Rameshwar. Cave No. 19 is said to resemble the caves at Elephanta, located off Mumbai coast. Cave No. 32 is dedicated to Jainism. The lotus flowers atop the ceiling and the sculpture of the Yaksha on the lions should not be missed.

The rock-cut temple of Kailash, carved out of a single piece of rock, is said to be an architectural marvel. The pillar within this complex and the numerous sculptured elephants are world famous. It is difficult to believe that this entire temple was sculpted with the use of a mere hammer and chisel.

Pitalkhora Caves

In the Satmala (Satpura) mountain range there is another set of caves, about 78 kilometres from Aurangabad. The 13 caves date back to the second century BC and are marked by huge chaityas and an eight-pillared hall (vihar). The sculptures here are of lions and horses and strange images of lion-headed women.

The MTDC runs a bus service to this spot. For further information about the buses and their timings contact the MTDC office at Mumbai or Aurangabad.

Fact File

Best time- All round the year

Location -- 388 kms. from Mumbai, plus 78 kms. from Aurangabad

Getting there - MTDC buses from Aurangabad

Where to stay -- MTDC Aurangabad, private hotels

Where to eat - A day's trip from Aurangabad

Lonad Caves

Lonad village is approximately 7 kilometres from Kalyan in Bhiwandi taluka. The Rameshwar temple in the village is quite *well-known*. The caves are dug into the hills about 4 kilometres outside the village.

The best way to get to Lonad is through the Bhiwandi bypass on the Mumbai-Nashik road via Thane. Once you leave the Kalyan-Bhiwandi crossing take the left turn at the Sonale junction. Around 2 to 3 kilometres from the Sonale junction, turn right. After travelling about a kilometre or so down this road, you will notice a hill about 250 feet high and several stone quarries; the road towards the right will take you to Lonad village. Currently, there is a small signpost pointing the way to the Gajanan Maharaj temple. The caves are located near the centre of the hill, towards the left and can be reached on foot within 20 minutes from the bottom of the hill.

Fact File

Best time- All round the year

Location -- 7 kms. from Kalyan in Bhiwandi Taluka

Getting there - Through Bhiwandi bypass on Mumbai-Nashik highway, 2-3 kms. from Sonale junction

Where to stay -- A day's trip from Mumbai

Where to eat - Eateries at Kalyan-Bhiwandi bypass

Towards the left of the main cave is a water tank. The right-hand side wall has sculptures of the king and queen and his council of ministers. The entrance to the cave is also covered with several engravings. Inside the cave there are two sculptures covered with vermilion powder (sindhoor) and a picture of Gajanan Maharaj. The view from this cave extends right from the Malang peak near Kalyan to Matheran.

In a field near the small settlement of Chaudharapada which is located just near this hill is Gaddegaal. Lonad village is one kilometre down the main road. In the village is an ancient sculpture-filled Ram Temple. Lonad is approximately 45 kilometres from Mumbai via the bypass. It is also possible to reach here by State Transport bus from either Kalyan or Bhiwandi. There are several small dhabas on the Kalyan-Bhiwandi road junction of the bypass where meals are available. No restaurants or dhabas can be found in Lonad. This could actually be a day's trip from Mumbai. Travelling in your own vehicle is a distinct advantage.

Karla, Bhaje, Bedse Caves

The Karla Caves : These are about 12 kilometres from Lonavala. These century-old caves have steps cut into the hill leading right up to them. There were several chaityas and viharas located here. The chaitya at Karla is regarded as the biggest in India. The chaitya hall measures 124 feet in length, 45 feet in breadth and 48 feet in

Fact File

Best time- All year but best during monsoons

Location -- Off the old Mumbai Pune highway, Karla is 12 kms. from Lonavala, Bhaje and Bedse are nearby

Getting there - By ST bus or vehicles from Lonavala

Where to stay -- MTDC Karla or Lonavala or a day's trip from Mumbai or Pune

Where to eat - Many eateries

height. The wooden arches used in the construction of this chaitya hall have remained intact without suffering any ill effects of the weather. Just outside the main cave is the Ekvira Devi temple. In addition to the caves, the MTDC rest house in Karla has also become a popular tourist spot.

Bhaje Caves : These caves too are off the Mumbai-Pune highway. While the Karla caves are located on the left-hand side, the Bhaje caves are towards the right of the road. Cross the railway tracks at Malavali station and the Bhaje village is about 3 kilometres down the road. The steps leading to the cave are visible from below. A climb of approximately 20 minutes and you are at the 250 feet high cave. From here you can see the massive Lohagad and Visapur fort. There is a road from Bhaje which goes directly to Lohagad and Visapur fort.

These caves are similar to the Karla caves but of a much smaller size. They are built in the same architectural style . Several stone stupas can also be seen here. Bhaje is 14 kilometres from Lonavala.

The Bedse caves : Towards one side of Visapur is Lohagad while towards the other side is the hill where the Bedse Caves are located. To reach these caves, you have to take the road via Kale Colony, Kamshet.

Other Caves

The Gandhaar-Pali Caves : Off the Mumbai-Goa highway, approximately 6 kilometres from Mahad junction. The caves are in the mountains seen on the left hand side while travelling to Goa.

There are 28 caves in all and they date back to the second or third century AD. Chaityas, Viharas, wall sculptures, images of

Fact File

Best time- All round the year

Location -- Off Mumbai -Goa highway, 6 kms. from Mahad junction

Getting there - By road

Where to stay -- A day's trip from Mumbai

Where to eat - Eateries on highway

Buddha and animal sculptures can be seen here. The caves are close to the hot springs on the River Savitri, and it is possible to take in both places during one trip.

The Thanale-Khadsamble caves : On the Ashthavinayak route you touch Pali village. From Pali the bus goes up to Nadsur. These caves are 8 kilometres from that point.

Fact File

Best time- All round the year

Location -- On the Ashtavinayak route near Pali village

Getting there - From Pali to Nadsur by ST bus, 8kms. from Nadsur, Khadsamble Caves are 13 kms. from Sudhagad and Dhangad

Where to stay --Pali

Where to eat - Eateries in Pali

Dating back to the second century BC, there are a total of 23 caves here. There are two chaityas, two stupas and several viharas. In recent history these caves are known to be the place where the revolutionary Vasudeo Balwant Phadke took shelter while fighting the British.

The Khadsamble Caves are 13 kilometres from Sudhagad and Dhangad. There are 21 caves in all and these also are said to date back to the second century BC.

Tilsa

As we have seen, there are several small hill stations in the Thane district like Javhar, Vikramgad, Khodala and Suryamal. Similarly, there are also some major lakes in the area, like Tansa, Vaitarna and Bhatsa. Dense forests are found in the district especially near Wada village in the region falling between the Tansa and Vaitarna lakes. The rivers of Vaitarna and Tansa take a meandering course through

Fact File

Best time- All round the year

Location -- 6 kms. from Wada village on the Wada-Khardi road

Getting there - By road

Where to stay --Khodala, Vikramgad or Javhar

Where to eat - Small eateries at Wada

these forests and finally merge into the Arabian Sea. Small tributaries like Deherja and Pinjal join the main Vaitarna River near Manor and Saprya villages, respectively. Tilsa is located at the place where the Pinjal River merges into the Vaitarna.

The village of Tilsa is on the banks of the Vaitarna river, 6 kilometres from Wada-village on the Wada-Khardi road. Not many know of the existence of this sleepy village, which comes to life twice a year, when villagers from surrounding hamlets converge here to celebrate Dassera and Holi. The fair takes place near the Shiv Mandir, built on the banks of the river. One of the peculiarities of this place is that no one kills the fish in this river. Several large-sized fish can be seen frolicking in the waters. The local people call them Devmase (God fish). The fish, which weigh anything between 5 to 100 kilos, jump up to eat pieces of dough or gram thrown into the river. They are particularly plentiful during Dassera and Holi.

There is a splendid view of the surrounding region from the Shiv Mandir. In the months of August-September, when the water in the river has receded slightly, small, tree-covered islands are visible in the river bed. Tourists proceeding to Khodala, Vikramgad or Javhar can visit Tilsa en route, for a short break, by taking the road from Wada. The distance between Mumbai and Wada is 95 kilometres; Tilsa is a further 6 kilometres ahead. There is another approach road from the Mumbai-Nashik highway via Khardi, but this road is often in poor condition especially during the rainy season.

Phaltan

Phaltan is a historical town 110 kilometres from Pune. Mention Phaltan and the first thing that comes to mind is the Naik-Nimabalkar family, originally a Rajput clan. Their real surname was Pawar and the original patriarch's name was Nimbraj. He was a well-known resident of the Dhar province in Northern India. Later he renounced everything and left to meditate in solitude. He died in the year 1291.

Fact File

Best time- All year

Location -- 110 kms. from Pune

Getting there - By ST buses

Where to stay -- Many hotels

Where to eat - Plenty of eateries

The seventeenth generation after Nimbraj was Mudhojirao II. His daughter Saibai married Raja Shivaji. Mudhojirao's third son Bajaji was the general-in-charge of Phaltan when he was captured as rebel by the Bijapur Sultan. A death sentence was awarded, but several rich and influential noblemen interceded on Bajaji's behalf so he was let free. The Bijapur Sultan had, however, laid down a condition that Bajaji should embrace Islam. Bajaji agreed on the condition that he be allowed to marry the Sultan's daughter, Shahjadi. The Sultan agreed and the wedding took place in some style. Bajaji thereafter stayed at the Bijapur court for five years before the Sultan returned his Jahagiri (lands) to him. The noblemen in Phaltan were, however, dismayed that Bajaji had embraced Islam. Bajaji himself was keen to revert to his original Hindu faith, so in the presence of Shivaji and his mother Jijabai, purification rites were conducted at the temple at Shikhar Shingnapur and he was welcomed back into the faith. Shivaji later gave his daughter Sakubai in marriage to Bajaji's second son Mahadji and presented him the deed of Valhe village. Bajaji died circa 1676. A memorial to him can be seen even today in the Naik-Nimbalkar crematorium at Phaltan.

There were several other well-known figures in the Naik-Nimbalkar dynasty; among them, the well-known Sagunabai. In the recent past it was Malojiraje Naik-Nimbalkar who did a lot to improve the conditions in the town of Phaltan, starting schools, colleges and a sugar co-operative. Malojiraje also served as a Minister in the Maharashtra cabinet for some time. He was very popular. His residence, the Manmohan Palace and the Shriram Temple are places of importance here. Phaltan is a temple town. Other than the Shriram Temple, there is another stone-carved temple to the right of the palace. Built by the Hemads, the temple dates back to the twelfth century. There is also a Math belonging to the Mahaanubhav sect in Phaltan. There is a grand Jain temple here, in addition to several smaller temples.

About 35 kilometres from Phaltan is the Shambu Mahadev temple at Shikhar Shingnapur and the samadhi of Gondavlekar Maharaj. Hundreds of tourist flock to visit these two places. During the months of November-December, the Ram Rath festival is celebrated here. The Sant Dnyaneshwar Palkhi also passes through Phaltan on its way to Pandharpur.

There are several good places to stay here. This quiet, historical town should be visited at least once.

Potholes of Nighoj

Fact File

Best time- April and May

Location -- Off the Mumbai-Malshej road, to Ale Phata (37 kms.) and to Nighoj (43 kms.)

Getting there - By private vehicle

Where to stay --A day's trip from Pune or Malshej

Where to eat - Eateries at Ale Phata or Shirur

Nighoj is located on the road to Shirur off the Mumbai-Malshej road via Ale Phata. The distance between Mumbai and Malshej is 145 kilometres, Malshej to Ale Phata is 37 kilometres, and Ale Phata to Nighoj is 43 kilometres. Just outside Nighoj village runs the Kukadi River. From here there is a road to Shirur via Haji Takli. This is close to the Pune-Ahmednagar Road.

The bed of the Kukadi River, visible in the months of April and May when the water here has dried up, has been termed one of nature's wonders. Due to the erosion of the rocks by the water, the riverbed is a fascinating sight. Deeply gouged gorges with giant potholes cover the entire bed of the river. On the banks of the river is a small white temple dedicated to Malganga Devi. Villagers here tell all kinds of folk tales about the river. Watch your step while walking alongside the riverbed as the banks of the river have a very uneven surface.

MUSEUMS AND UNUSUAL PLACES OF INTEREST

MUSEUMS AND UNUSUAL PLACES OF INTEREST

A museum informs and delights. It is also provokes serious thought and a sense of history. The museums of Maharashtra reverberate with the tradition of this land and its people.

The Lokmanya Tilak Museum

Fact File

Best time- All year

Location -- Kesari Wada, Pune

Getting there - City transport

Where to stay -- Pune city

Where to eat - Eateries at Pune

This is a place where the memories of Lokmanya Bal Gangadhar Tilak are kept alive. His name alone seems sufficient to ignite the spirit of freedom that once burned in the heart of one of the fathers of the Indian freedom movement, and the author of the fiery slogan ' Swaraj is my birthright and I shall have it'. Needless to say, the museum dedicated to this lion of the freedom struggle evokes more than a touch of national pride.

The museum is housed on the first floor of the Kesari Wada at Pune.

The Satara Museum

The Maratha empire's second front-Satara-is a city with a glorious past. Protected by the strongholds of seven forts, this picturesque place nestles amid the hardy sentinels of the mighty Sahyadris - namely, the bastions of Ajinkyatara, Sajjangad, Pandavgad, Vairatgad, Chandangad, Vandangad, and Sadashivgad. It was the brave Shahu Maharaj who proclaimed this town to be his capital. Ever since, Satara has been the capital

Fact File

Best time- All year

Location -- Satara town

Getting there - City transport

Where to stay --Satara

Where to eat - Eateries at Satara

of the Maratha rulers.

Opened in 1970, due to the efforts of people like Yashwant Rao Chauhan, the Shri Chhatrapati Shivaji Maharaj Sangrahalya, Satara, is a valuable storehouse of artefacts and ancient souvenirs. Other pioneering spirits included Dr M.G. Dixit, the first curator of the museum, his associate Madhukar Inamdar and the residents of Satara, who contributed money and artefacts.

The Karmarkar Museum

Fact File

Best time- All year

Location -- Sasavne village, 18 kms. from Alibaug

Getting there - By road

Where to stay -- Alibag

Where to eat - Eateries at Alibag

Sasavne village, about 18 kilometres from Alibag, is the home of Vinayak Pandurang Karmarkar, a highly-respected sculptor whose works through the years have gained wide acclaim in many parts of the world. Karmarkar set up a museum of his works in his own home at Sasavne. The ancestral house, more than 70 years old, contains a collection of statues, murals and sculptures.

Fact File

Best time- All year

Location -- 8 kms. from Roha on the Mumbai-Mahad road

Getting There - By road

The Wood Exhibits of Kolad

The obscure village of Kolad, 8 kilometers from Roha, on the Mumbai - Mahad road shot into prominence because of the unique woodwork of

Where to stay -- Roha

Where to eat - Eateries at Roha

Ramesh Ghone who was deeply inspired by the Kelkar museum of Pune. The museum is based in his workshop, which is a five-minute walk from his residence.

The Raja Dinkar Kelkar Museum

Fact File

Best time- All year

Location -- Shukrawar Peth, Pune

Getting there - City transport

Where to stay -- Pune

Where to eat - Eateries at Pune

This is the collection that one man has single-handedly put together.

Born in 1896, Dinkar Gangadhar Kelkar, alias Kakasaheb Kelkar, has been collecting artefacts ever since his childhood. The museum, located in the downtown Shukrawar Peth in Pune, is the biggest one of its kind in the world. After the untimely demise of his son Raja Kelkar, Kakasaheb devoted himself totally to the museum, and it became an all-consuming passion. The museum was named the Raja Dinkar Kelkar Museum in memory of his late son.

The romance and grandeur of this museum has earned the grand old man of India's cultural heritage a Padmashri and many other honours.

Kapuskar

The studio of Sharad Kapuskar is perched on a picturesque hill in the village of Bhugaon, close to Pune. Sculptor of the Kasturba and Mahatma Gandhi statues in the Aga Khan palace, he also made the statue of Shivaji Maharaj for the Shivaji Smarak at Juhu Chowpatty .

His workshop has busts of Pandit Bhimsen Joshi, Gangubai Hangal, Sonali Kulkarni and many others.

Joshi Miniature Railway Museum

Fact File

Best time- Open only on weekends, between 5.00 and 6.30 pm

Location -- Pune city near Karve road near Sangam Press

Getting there - City transport

Where to stay -- Pune

Where to eat - Eateries at Pune

Much before you reach the temple of Mrutyunjeshwar on Pune's busy Karve Road, there is a road that turns to the left, towards the Sangam press. The Joshi rail museum is close by, five minutes after you turn in to this lane. There is a prominent signboard that reads 'Joshi's museum of miniature railways'. Bhausaheb Joshi had always loved to collect scale models of trains, buses and automobiles, and this hobby slowly began to take the shape of a serious pursuit. In 1991, he added a hall to his existing bungalow and decided to make it the theatre for his Railway Museum. He wrote to companies asking for accessories, and those that he could not get, he made on his own. Painstaking effort went into making the electrical circuitry, the route that the trains would follow, and a control room. Visitors must remember, though, that the museum is open only at weekends. Every Saturday and Sunday, you are welcome between 5.00-6.30 p.m, to chug around a world of tracks and yards.

The Dr. Ambedkar Museum and Memorial

The Ambedkar memorial is built in the backyard of the Hanuman hill near Pune's Symbiosis College. It synchronizes perfectly with its rocky neighbour, and is designed like a Buddhist stupa. With its dome shape and landscaped surroundings, it is a serene place. A number of

Fact File

Best time- All year

Location -- Pune city near Simbiosis College on Hanuman Hill

Getting there - City transport

Where to stay -- Pune

Where to eat - Eateries at Pune

objects belonging to the architect of India's constitution are kept here.

UNUSUAL PLACES OF INTEREST

Gulanchwadi, Naney Ghat, Darya Ghat—these are names you must have heard somewhere, read somewhere. If you like traveling off the beaten path, places like these will enchant you with their pristine isolation. Maharashtra is full of such places that are waiting to be 'discovered'. For a person stricken by true wanderlust, these forays will give him an unforgettable high.

Naney Ghat

Fact File

Best time- All year

Location -- 34 kms. west of Junnar in Pune District

Getting there - By road

Where to stay -- Junnar

Where to eat - Eateries at Junnar

Naney Ghat lies 34 kilometres to the west of Junnar, in Pune district. The ruggedness of this mountain pass poses a never-ending challenge to rock climbers and mountaineers. One of the rock faces reveals a cavernous hollow. This historically important cave contains hieroglyphs and inscriptions of Maharashtra's earliest recorded royal family, the Satavahanas. In the words of Ashoka the Great, 'The timeless writings of history, when imbibed again and again, shall instill a sense of appreciation for their beauty and meaning.' The truth of this statement instantly becomes clear when you visit the caves of Naney Ghat.

The second century BC saw the decline of the empires to the north. It was sometime in 30 BC that the Satavahana clan began its ascendancy. The Matsyapuran mentions as many as 30 rulers of this dynasty. They are referred to in ancient texts, as Andhrabhrutya. King Simuk was the founder of this dynasty. The city of Pratisthan, now known as Paithan, was the capital from where the Satavahana Kings presided over their territory. The rock inscriptions at Naney Ghat tell you about these developments. Similar writings are found in the Buddhist caves at Karle, Bhaje, Kanheri, Junnar, and Kurde. The tablets at Naney Ghat are believed to be the oldest. Glorious tales of King Satavahana and Queen Naganika are carved into rock.

The entry to the Naney Ghat is marked by a single earthern jar, that was used to collect toll. The Naney Ghat was perhaps, an important octroi post, and hence, vital to Satavahana interests. The rock-hewn caves are a furlong from this spot. The entrance to the caves is flanked on both sides by inscriptions in the Bramhi script. The coins minted during the realm of King Kushaan, bear the embossed image of the deity - Nanaa. This currency became extremely popular throughout the land. The depiction of this deity is said to be the Indian incarnation of Goddess Parvati astride a lion. This picturization of Parvati appears on the coins of the Gupta kings. With the passage of time, Nanaa was corrupted to Naney. Since this ghat was a place where Naney (Marathi for coins) were collected, it became Naney Ghat.

The rock inscriptions give vivid details about the far-flung exploits of King Saatkarni. It is clear that he was a monarch with personal charisma and administrative skills. The cave had a statue of the father of the Sàtavahana dynasty, Simuk. There were also statues of King Saatkarni and his wife Naganika. The great Pranakarnayar, father of Queen Naganika, as well as her son Kumarabhaaya, also were represented here in the form of stone sculptures. Sadly, however, only the names of each individual, written in Bramhi script at the feet of each statue, now serve to identify these great men and women.

The tracts of Naney Ghat consist of 184 Buddhist caves. One of them also bears the wheel of King Saatkarni, an emperor who was benevolent and tolerant. These caves are historically very significant as they record the glory of one of the most shining eras of western India.

Darya Ghat

From Junnar, if you continue straight without turning at the Aptale fork, a 20 kilometre drive will take you to Amboli, which is a

Fact File

Best time- All year

Location -- 20 kms. to Amboli from Junnar

Getting there - By road

Where to stay -- Junnar

Where to eat - Eateries at Junnar

village nestling at the foot of the Darya Ghat. The tall shapes of Dhakoba can be seen. The source of the Meena river is also visible from here. The summit of this ghat is at the end of a gentle climb. Half an hour later, you pass through a thickly wooded area of Karvy, and you have reached the top. To the left, the rock face of Dhakoba makes a formidable wall. To the right, the road along Darya Ghat closely follows the edge of the cliff. A deep gorge separates the two. Deep down, at the bottom of the chasm, the Konkan spreads far, far, away.

The Darya Ghat was an important route for trade in cattle. Down below, there is an annual cattle fair in the village of Mhasa. This region, encompassing the hills of Meena Maval and Kukad Maval, are full of stories and legends. An oft-heard tale speaks of a man named Kondaji Navle. A rebel, he was some kind of a Robin Hood. Kondaji is said to have raised his voice against the atrocities of the dominant landlords. The years of 1939-44 saw his fame spread far and wide. Even today, villagers sing paeans in praise of this man who had the courage of a lion and the generosity of a saint. He was an expert at disguise and excelled in outwitting his pursuers time and again. Kondaji, idolized by the locals but a thorn in the flesh of the authorities, gave many a slip to the police, until he was finally arrested. In the end, it was betrayal by his own men that caused his arrest. Kondaji hailed from the little village of Ucchal at the base of the Darya Ghat. One can even visit the home of this legendary figure.

Mastani Lake

This is actually a man-made reservoir created by a dyke built by the Peshwas. During the monsoons, water from the surrounding hills collects here. The lake is located in the small settlement of Vadki, at the mouth of the Divey Ghat, about 18 kilometres from Pune, along the Pune-Saswad route.

Fact File

Best time- June to September

Location -- 18 kms. from Pune city on the Pune-Saswad road

Getting there - Vadki village near Divey ghat by road

Where to stay -- Pune

Where to eat - Eateries at Pune

The Mastani lake is spread over an area of 5.5 hectares. The dam is between three metres to seven metres high. A small Ganesh temple sits on the banks, with an idol of the Lord outside the shrine, as well as within. There seems to have been a palace close to this statue. There was an underground tunnel that led from this palace to a well on the periphery of the lake. You can still see one end of the well.

There is a temple of Lord Shiva as well as a statue of Lord Hanuman in the area around the lake. The lake is believed to have been dug under the instructions of Bajirao Peshwa I. In 1751, during the reign of Nanasaheb Peshwa, the lake was repaired and refurbished. Today, the lake is in a sad state of complete neglect. Moss and weeds have grown all over, and it is usually dry. The monsoons, however, bring out the natural beauty of this region in all its colours.

There is some confusion about exactly whom the lake belongs to. Some time back, one Brigadier Jenkins claimed to have owned it. Later, the lake was claimed by Sahjeevanwadi, at Urli Devaachi. The ownership of this lake is still uncertain. What is certain, though, is that if attempts are made to clean the lake and develop the surrounding landscape, this region has the potential to become an extremely popular tourist spot.

Doorshet

Eighty-five kilometres from Sion, along the Pali-Khopoli road, and 100 kilometres from Pune, is the scenic Doorshet. The Pali-Khopoli route is a dream drive.

As you go from Khopoli to Pali, there is a patch of 35 acres to the right, which comprises the main attraction of Doorshet. This part of the forest has been developed as a camping zone. There are numerous spots where a tourist can pitch a tent. Mr. Divekar, the enterprising wildlife enthusiast who has pioneered this effort, has also done much to enhance the natural wealth of these jungles. The main attraction is the huge waterfall here, dropping down one edge of the rock walls.

> **Fact File**
>
> *Best time- June to September*
>
> *Location -- 85 kms. from Sion, Mumbai on the Pali Khopoli road; 100 kms. from Pune*
>
> *Getting there - By road*
>
> *Where to stay -- Nature Trails,Doorshet*
>
> *Where to eat - Nature Trails*

The region in and around Doorshet is full of places of historical and natural wealth. The site of Umbarkhind, the Ganesh of Pali, hot water springs at Unheri, the shrine of Udhvar Rameshwar, the hillocks of Tadgaon, Sarasgad, Sudhagad, Thanavle, the caves of Khadsavli, all beckon the tourist. Make Doorshet your home for a few days, and you will be able to enjoy the multiple pleasures of this unique resort. To book reservations, contact:

Mr. Divekar,

'Nature Trails', Indravati Hall, Thane, Ph: 540 2308, 540 4553.

Manikdoha

Manikdoha is the name of a lake that was formed when a dam was constructed along the river Kukdi. The dam is close to the Hadsar fort. The Kukdi flows down the gorge created between two opposing, towering hill ranges. It originates somewhere near the Naney Ghat, in the heart of the Sahyadri strip that one encounters on the Bhimashankar–Malshej route.

Junnar is just 6 kilometres from the Manikdoha reservoir. Buses from Mumbai, Thane and Kalyan routinely go to Junnar, a distance of about 175 kilometres. The bus ride from Mumbai to Manikdoha takes about five and a half hours. The Manikdoha dam is 1750 feet above sea level. The weather here is pleasant throughout the year. The official guest house is constructed at a higher level. A clear

Fact File

Best time- All the year

Location -- 6 kms. from Junnar, Junnar is 175 kms. from Mumbai

Getting there - By ST buses

Where to stay -- Government guest house on prior booking

Where to eat - Food available on order at guest house

evening will give you a beautiful view of Manikdoha's vast expanse. The lake contains a temple of Muktai, partly submerged in water. The temple is visible from the guest house. Visible also are Shivneri, Jeevdhan and the fort of Chavand.

The guest house is built at a very good location. From here, every day a magnificent sunset is on offer. The orange flames of the sun lick the calm blue waters of the lake before slipping down beyond the hills. It is a hypnotizing sight and needless to say, an unforgettable experience. To book a room, it is necessary to correspond with the Chief Executive Engineer, Manikdoha project, Narayangaon, Pune. Dining and mess facilities, however, are available at short notice.

Manikdoha is a very good place to stay, even better as a base to visit other places like the nearby forts. The Naney Ghat and Darya Ghat, along with the ancient temple of Kukdeshwar and Lenyadri, are all just a few hours from Manikdoha.

Thebaw Palace

The Thebaw palace is one of the landmarks of Ratnagiri. As you enter this city and go around the Shivaji statue, the road to the left leads to this rambling, three-storeyed bungalow. This dwelling is a sad, but enduring symbol of India's ancient links with Myanmar, known as Burma many years ago.

In 1935, Burma separated from India. At the time, Emperor Thebaw was the ruler of this country. In 1878, King Thebaw ascended the throne of Burma - he was only 19 years old. He ruled for a short period of 7 years, after which the British conquered the entire land. The same fate suffered by many Indian sovereigns ousted by the English, befell King Thebaw. He was imprisoned and brought to Madras in 1885, where he was kept under house arrest, far away from his homeland so that he could offer no resistance to British plans. Just a year later, in 1886, the king was again displaced and transported by boat, to Ratnagiri. He was incarcerated in the Outram bungalow, while his family lived in the Baker bungalow. The king was destined to spend the rest of his life in this coastal town. The Ratnagiri of a hundred years ago must have been a beautiful, serene place, where the Arabian sea touched its shores and coconut trees spread their growth as far as the eye can see. When it was quite plain that the king would be exiled for a long time, a huge mansion was commissioned and built at a princely sum (in those days), of a lakh of rupees. In 1910, the King came to stay here with his family.

Fact File

Best time- All the year

Location -- Ratnagiri city

Getting there - By ST or private buses, or by train

Where to stay -- Ratnagiri private hotels

Where to eat - Many eateries

After India attained freedom, the palace, like many other colonial relics, was converted into a residence for local civil servants. A Government technical institute was established here after some time. Now, the palace is safely in the hands of the archaeology department, and plans are afoot to turn this into a well-preserved museum. With such a large area, the palace might even have rooms for tourists to stay over and experience first hand the kind of life that the king of Burma led here. If this attempt is successful, it could reforge the links between India and Myanmar.

Aurangabad

Aurangabad is a town well-known for its heritage structures, a long and colourful history and is now struggling to be a modern city. It is often referred to as the town of 52 Peths (also called Puri). The city has had a succession of names, from the original Rajtilak, to Khiki Khadki, Fatehnagar, and currently, Sambhajinagar. Yet, for some reason, the name 'Aurangabad' has endured.

Aurangabad is unique for many reasons. Twelve great doorways, paved and ceremonially built, guard the periphery of this city.

Fact File

Best time- All the year

Location -- Aurangabad city

Getting there - By ST or tourist buses

Where to stay -- MTDC or private hotels

Where to eat - Many eateries

Industry and enterprise has made inroads into every facet of the town. The charm of the city, however, lies in the fact that it retains its romantic and secretive image. There is much to see here. One of the places that a tourist simply must visit is the Panchakki, a water wheel that is powered by water and runs perpetually. Its grinding sound has continued for 400 years, unabated.

Eight kilometres from Aurangabad, near the village of Harsul, there is a large natural source of water, with underground springs. These are known as Kadam-e-Rasoul. Water from these springs travels here. The water first enters a well, from where it is collected in a low level tank. The structure on which the Panchakki is constructed, is at the same level as the source of water, but the journey of the water takes place much below this level. To negotiate a slope along which the water will be able to reach its ultimate destination, three tower-like structures have been constructed underground. The topmost slab of these minars are at ground level. Water from its source at Kadam-e-Rasoul flows in a conduit over these structures, and inundates the towers three times before falling into the lake. For years, the natural springs have sent water which gushes with a tremendous amount of pressure.

The Panchakki is a reminder of the level of India's technology and the ingenuity of some of our engineers - to use the water of a natural spring and channelize its power to run a water mill. Above all, miraculously, the source of the water at Kadam-e-Rasool has not dried up in 400 years!

Tara Paanwala

Now a landmark, Tara Paanwala is the shop where gourmets go to soothe full stomachs with a juicy paan, the store where friends gather for a late night gupshup, where everyone gathers to enjoy what is a passion in Aurangabad—the paan (betel leaf).

Fact File

Best time- Open round-the -clock

Location -- Usmanpura, Aurangabad city

It is perhaps the only 'paan' shop that works in three shifts. The proprietor, Shafibhai, is justifiably proud of the shop's rise to fame through the 30 years of its existence.

Shafibhai, now in his sixties, recalls the early days, when his mother would teach him how to put together a good paan. She was an expert at making kaat, a pungent ingredient used in making a paan. When her son decided to put up a paan shop, he made it a point to use the kaat made by his mother. As Shafibhai's clientele grew, so did the size of his shop. From a humble kiosk, it expanded to a full fledged paan-catering unit, which employs 24 men who work round the clock to serve a hundred different palates.

As Shafibhai himself admits, being a paan shop owner is a very different cup of tea. Different men come up to you, treat you like a friend, a confidante, even a philosopher. Some of his customers have been coming to his shop for decades, some drop by once in a while, while some are never seen again. Whatever the case, a paan wala has to understand the temperament of the person he serves. In an area where a dozen different concoctions of paan are routinely favoured by knowledgeable paan connoisseurs, it takes the intuition of a superbly-tuned mind to anticipate just what kind of paan a particular person will appreciate. It has also led to his uncanny ability for judging people.

When you visit Aurangabad, do not leave without buying a paan at Tara Paanwala. There are more than two dozen varieties to choose from. As you munch on the crunchy leaf, you will realize why Shafibhai's paan never fails to satiate consumers.

Bibi Ka Maqbara

This monument, though famous for being a replica of the Taj Mahal, is a superb example of architectural skill in its own right. In 1679, Aurangzeb's son, Shahzada Azam, commissioned this

Fact File

Best time- 8am to 6 pm, all year round

Location -- Aurangabad city

work as a memorial to his late mother and Aurangzeb's wife, Raabiya Durrani. While the Taj is built entirely in marble, the more humble Bibi Ka Maqbara is made in white alabaster, marble and white plaster. Its proportions are identical to those of the Taj, and a skilful photographer could perhaps pass off the Bibi Ka Maqbara as the Taj.

Every full moon night, the splendour of the Bibi Ka Maqbara unveils the skill with which this monument was designed. It is often assumed that this tomb to Raabiya Durrani was built by her husband, Aurangzeb. This, however, seems very unlikely, for this emperor was known for his ascetic habits. Every single record in history mentions him as a man who lived very simply. He shunned extravagance of any kind. It, therefore, seems highly unlikely that he would spend lakhs of rupees in constructing a monument so lavish. It was most definitely his son who wanted to preserve the memory of his mother with this beautiful structure.

Mhaismal

This tranquil hill station is situated on the same hill range as the world famous Ellora caves. At a level of 3250 feet above sea level, it is, for some reason, relatively unknown and unexplored. I, however, make it a point to spend at least a night here.

Legend has it that once Goddess Parvati was playing a game of draughts with Lord Shiva. The Lord lost, and in a huff, came to the Maheshmal hills. These hills have been mentioned in the Navnath chronicles as Garbhagiri or Kaamyak. Devi Parvati took on the disguise of a Bhil girl, and came here to placate her lord.

The hills are made of yellow murum, as a cursory dig will reveal. Therein lies another story. According to the Navnath, Macchindranath is believed to have brought a gold block from the hills of Rajal. Gorakhnath saw it and threw it away. A furious Macchindranath made a stubborn demand for the gold. To pacify him, Gorakhnath created an entire hill of gold.

Fact File

Best time- All the year

Location -- 37 kms. from Aurangabad city

Getting there - 3 kms. before Ellora is the Khuldabad fork, Mhaismal is 3 kms. from here

Where to stay -- Rest house at Khuldabad

Where to eat - Same

There is a huge tableland on top of the Mhaismal mountains. At its edge, there are rest houses. A temple of Girijashankar and Audumbar is also seen here. A recently-constructed temple of Lord Balaji has been placed at the other end of the plateau. There is a fair at the shrine of Lord Girijashankar, on every Shudhha Poornima and on Dandi Poornima. Devotees come all the way from Aurangabad and its outskirts to visit the Lord.

The PWD and the Forest Department have built rest houses at one end of this plain. They have been constructed at a place just right for mountain gazing.

On the way back from Ellora, 3 kilometres away, is the fork of Khuldabad. Mhaismal is 10 kilometres from here. On the way, you will see the rest house of the Khuldabad PWD, also built at an extremely lovely location on the edge of a row of hills. You can book rooms here. Mhaismal is 37 kilometres from Aurangabad.

When you return from Mhaismal, you can halt at the place where Aurangzeb's tomb stands. It is 1 kilometre from the Khuldabad turning. To make reservations at the rest house in Khuldabad, you can write to

The Executive Engineer,

PWD, Padampura, Aurangabad, 431 001.

Vathar Nimbalkar

The Naik-Nimbalkar clan have a record that dates back to the sixteenth century. Malojirao, the head of this family at this time, was an eminent citizen. He had three children - Mhakoji, Arjoji, and Deepabai. Of these, Mhakoji soon became the patriarch of the Vatharkar homestead that spanned many centuries and had a large

Fact File

Best time- All the year

Location -- Vathar, 5 kilometers west of Phaltan

Getting there - By road

Where to stay -- Phaltan

Where to eat - Same

base in the entire region of Phaltan. One wing of the Naik-Nimbalkar household moved to Vathar, where they again established themselves over vast tracts.

Vathar is 5 kilometres to the west of Phaltan. Kushaji, who was the fifth direct descendant of Mhakoji, laid the real foundation to a homestead that was to hold firm for more than 200 years. Kushaji was the resident minister of Vathar. In 1801, he received this land as a gift from none other than the legendary Bajirao Peshwa I. A year before, he had already received a considerable amount of land from Pant Sachiv in return for some money which the latter had borrowed from Kushaji. The head of the Naik-Nimbalkar family now began to set up the new town of Vathar, with brand new bungalows, huge courtyards and strong walls. His foresight saw this town rise to a position of wealth and prosperity.

Kushaji used his intellect and ideas to amass great wealth. How rich he was, can be ascertained by records that show the amount of money he lent to many important personalities of that era.

After Kushaji passed away, his sons came to Vathar and settled down here. Most of these 9 sons held positions of importance in the durbars of the Shinde clan. The ceremonial thrones of Kushaji and his wife Mainabai are still preserved in Vaathar. One of the main attractions of this town is the grandeur of the 9 villas that Kushaji built for each of his sons. Though half of these have collapsed totally, whatever remains of them, are enough to tell us that they were constructed with no expense spared. Each wada is more of a castle within itself, a stronghold which could have effectively acted as a fortification in emergencies. The principal wada has walls that are 15 feet thick and more than 50 feet high, surrounding the inner structures. This villa has nine towers.

Around this wada, nine smaller residences for Kushaji's sons were built in the period from 1796 to 1805. Of these, the prominent wada was known as Samayik Wada. Some of the descendants of the Nimbalkar clan still reside in the few bungalows that are in a reasonably good condition. The truth is, these homes are so huge and built in such palatial style, that their maintenance and upkeep is impossible for any single family.

Ranjit Naik-Nimbalkar, It is one of the descendants of this family. He gave me all this information. He, however, rues the fact that unless conservation efforts are made in a systematic manner, whatever remains today of the great Naik-Nimbalkar mansions, will be reduced to dust. And a chapter of history will simply vanish.

Sitabai hill

> **Fact File**
>
> *Best time- June to March*
>
> *Location -- On the Satara-Pandharpur route*
>
> *Getting there - ST buses to Mahimangad village from Dahiwadi, Pusegaon or Koregaon*
>
> *Where to stay -- Satara*
>
> *Where to eat - Carry your own food*

This hill is where two rivers, the Banganga and the Manganga originate. There is a temple of Sita here. The peaks of Sitabai hill are known for being a major attraction for serious rock climbers and mountaineers.

Sitabai is located along the Mahadev ridge of the Sahyadris. The climb to the hill begins from the village of Mahimangad. There is a fort by the same name to the north of the village. It takes just 10 minutes to scale the summit of Mahimangad. There is a reservoir and a temple of Lord Maruti at the top. The valley chiselled out by the river Manganga is seen from here. The pathway to Sitabai starts at the northern side of the village. After 3 hours of walking, you will come to Malwadi, on the banks of the Manganga. Continue along the valley, and you will reach a plateau to the south of Varugad. The plain slopes to the north, where Varugad immediately catches your attention. Descend into the gorge and half an hour later, you are at the foothills. There is a small temple here.

A climb will once again lead you to another flat land to the south. It takes about half an hour to reach this tableland. Continue westwards, towards Palvan, Kalsakarwadi, and a trek of 2 hours will take you to the Sitabai hill. The weather is lovely and the view, superb. These are ample rewards for slogging it out on the tough climb. To get to Dahiwadi, Pusegaon, or Koregaon, there are frequent buses from all parts of Maharashtra, especially along the Satara Pandharpur route.

Shivtharghal

Shivtharghal is the place where the great Maharashtrian saint Samartha Ramdas Swami wrote the *Dasbodh*. A road at the start of the Varandha ghat, along the Bhor-Mahad road, branches off to Shivtharghal. The enthusiastic trekker can also make it on foot from the Maazeri village that is close to where this road begins. A cross-country route of approximately three hours will take you to Shivtharghal. Otherwise, the road, too, can take you right up to this place.

In the serene environs of Shivtharghal, Swami Ramdas worked on the writing of *Dasbodh*. To achieve a systematic reading and discussion of this book, Swami set up the Sundarmath, a hermitage of learning. As Ramdas Swami spoke his disciple Kalyanswami would write down all his words of wisdom in great detail.

Shivaji Maharaj, who regarded the Swami as his supreme Guru, once set out to meet him at Shivthar. His journey was interrupted by the rivulets and water canals that did not allow his retinue to proceed. He, therefore, camped at a place called Birwadi. Legend has it that the Samartha appeared before the Chhatrapati in a dream, and offered him his blessings. In 1598, Shivaji Maharaj, by a royal decree, provided for an ashram to be established at Shivthar. He came here himself and met the great man. It is said that at the time, the king received some arms from Swami Ramdas.

Around 1915, it was observed that the holy site of Shivtharghal had started filling up with loose boulders and small landslides. There was a danger of these sediments blocking up the shallow land. In 1930, the entire region was cleaned and repaired. The depression here is 20 to 22 metres in length, and 15 metres wide.

The site is divided into three distinct parts. One of these contains the statues of Samarth Ramdas, his pupil Kalyanswami, and idols of Lord Ram, Goddess Sita, and Laxman. A brook by the name of Khutyacha Vira flows very close to the ashram. It continues on to become a waterfall. The upper stream of this fall also includes 3 small ponds and a smaller waterfall which is particularly scenic during the monsoons.

Fact File

Best time- October to January

Location -- On the Bhor-Mahad route at Varanda Ghat

Getting there - By road

Where to stay -- Shri Samarth Seva Mnadal, Sajjangad and Shri Sundarmath Seva Samiti at Shivtharghal

Where to eat - Same

At the top of the hill adjoining Shivtharghal, one can see ruins of 2 huge ancestral wadas belonging to Chandrarao More. There is a tank with clean, cool water close to this. This is a very good place to pause and take in the sights. The Waghjai temple, Kavlya Killa, and the entire verdant stretch of the lovely Varandha ghat make for a great picture. A path goes down all the way from Kavlya Killa to the base of Shivtharghal, via Parmachi. From the Varandha ghat too, a narrow route takes you there amidst the thick foliage.

The ideal time to visit Shivtharghal is from October to January. There are 2 temples here that you must visit. One is the shrine of Lord Maruti set up by Swami Ramdas himself. The other is the Samartha Mandir, near the village of Sonubhau. This temple is situated on the Samartha plateau. Three kilometres from Shivtharghal, there is another flat plain - the Nalawade plateau, where Kalyanswami had a hermitage. This plateau is now called the Ramdas plateau.

In 1960, the tricentennial anniversary of the *Dasbodh* was observed here with great enthusiasm and piety. Since then, a number of improvements have added to the beauty of Shivtharghal. Today, the Shri Samartha Seva Mandal, Sajjangad, and the Shri Sundarmath Seva Samiti at Shivtharghal provide food and shelter for travellers who stop for darshan at the hermitage of the 'Samartha'.

The best time to feast your eyes on nature's bounty is during the monsoons, when this place blooms magically.

The Rock Bridge of Gulanchwadi

Fact File

Best time- June to March

Location -- 47 kms. from Junnar

Getting there - ST buses via Narayangaon, Alephata, Velhe and to Gulanchwadi

Where to stay - Hotel Poonam in Narayangaon

Where to eat - Same

Gulanchwadi is 47 kilometres from Junnar. There are 4 halts on the way - Junnar-Narayangaon, at 16 kilometres, then Alephata a further 15 kilometres, and from here, to Velhe, another 12 kilometres. From Velhe, Gulanchwadi is just 4 kilometres.

Gulanchwadi has been endowed with a unique gift from Mother Nature. There is a rock bridge here, spanning a distance of about 50 metres. It is located near the Mathabai dam. You will have to take the Aney ghat route to get there. About 3 kilometres short of the village of Aney, to the left is the Darshan bridge. It is a comfortable descent from here, that is completed in under 15 minutes. A waterfall gushes below the bridge. There was a tunnel to the left of this natural span. The local villagers blocked the mouth of the hollow some time ago. The bridge is a site for a congregation of devotees who come here every year in the month of Shravan, on the fourth Tuesday, to be precise. The temple of Mathabai takes on a very festive look then.

The Salt Pillar of Vadgaon Darya

The valley of Vadgaon is pleasing to the eye and lies in the lap of nature. There are temples of Velhabai and Daryabai here. One has to climb down a long series of steps to reach the temples. There is a very thick foliage of old, gnarled trees that surrounds the shrines.

Fact File

Best time -- June to March

Location -- Off Ale Phata on the Pune -Junnar - Narayangaon route

Getting there - By road via Velhe, Parnar Alkuti to Vadgaon Darya

Where to stay - A day's trip from Pune or Narayangaon

Where to eat - Same

To come to the Vadgaon Darya, you will have to reach Alephata via the Pune-Junnar-Narayangaon route. Come to Parner from Velhe, and then onwards, to Alkuti. The road now branches off to the left and continues to Vadgaon Darya. From Alephata, Parner is 40 kilometres At the fork, Kanhur is 12 kilometres away, and from here, a six kilometre drive or trek will take you to Vadgaon Darya.

The interiors of the temples are constructed of layers of limestone and sediment. The saline pillar, however, is not clearly visible. To combine a trip here with a visit to the nature-made bridge at Gulanchwadi, it is necessary to leave from Pune early in the morning.

Ramtek and Khindsay Lake

Fact File

Best time -- June to March

Location -- 47 kms. from Nagpur on the Nagpur-Jabalpur highway

Getting there - Frequent ST and tourist buses

Where to stay - MTDC guest houses

Where to eat - Same

Ramtek has an awesome claim to fame. It was the site where the great poet, Mahakavi Kalidas, wrote the immortal Meghdoot. The hill lies on the Nagpur-Jabalpur highway, 47 kilometres from Nagpur. There is a memorial to Kalidas on Ramtek. This place also has a sacred association. It is said that Lord Rama, on his way to exile in the Dandakaranya, stopped here to rest. There are temples of Lord Rama, Lakshman, and Lord Hanuman at the summit. The temples of Hanuman and Lakshman are relics of the fourteenth century.

Nagpur has buses that travel frequently to Ramtek. MTDC manages a guest house here where you can book rooms. Eight kilometres from Ramtek is an extremely lovely lake, the Khindsay Talav. The slope leading from road level to the lake is negotiated by several steps. The area is dotted with trees. Water sports are a major attraction for tourists here. The equipment is well-maintained and the facility supervised by Vir Rajkamal Tourist Complex. The waters of the lake are deep blue and photographs taken here often resemble a European holiday postcard.

The MTDC has a second rest house on the banks of the lake. The room charges are Rs. 100/- per day. A visit to Ramtek and Khindsay lake will make a fitting finale to any Nagpur trip that you may make.

Parvati

Fact File

Best time -- June to March

Location -- Pune city

Getting there - City transport

Where to stay - Pune city

Where to eat - Same

Each and every time I visit Pune, I keep a special morning for a very special place. It is the favourite haunt of many Puneites who have been coming here for years together. This is the Parvati hill, located in the heart of the city and in the heart of every citizen of Pune.

Almost halfway up the ascent, which is more than 50 steps up, there is a Sati Smarak. It is an unofficial place to make a halt and catch your breath. A legend surrounds this memorial. It tells of a pious Brahmin who lived here and offered regular prayers at the temples. After his demise, his wife was inconsolable, and immolated herself on her husband's funeral pyre. A small shrine was built here in her memory.

It takes a considerable amount of energy to reach the top. It is time now to take in the many sights and sounds of Parvati. To the right, there is an underground cellar, now shut and closed off for entry. A set of steps begins from here and leads up to the temple of Devdeveshwar. The tall spire of the temple is visible even at a distance.

The patio in front of the temple gives you a wide-angle view of sprawling Pune. While the Sahyadri ranges are faintly outlined in shades of green and grey, the rapidly encroaching arms of urban Pune are a mite frightening.

Centrally located in the temple of Devdeveshwar, is the shrine of Lord Shiva. This shrine is surrounded by four temples of Suryanarayan, Gajanan, Bhavanidevi, and Vishnu. This kind of arrangement, incorporating 5 places of worship, is called the panchayatan design. The inner chamber contains a Shivalingam, as well as a silver idol of the Lord. The idols of Lord Gajanan and Goddess Parvati are made of Panch Dhatu - an alloy of five metals. The marble idol of Lord Ganapati is particularly striking. There are just a handful of temples to Lord Suryanarayan, and the one at Parvati is one of them.

The rear portion of the temple is reserved for the ancestral wada belonging to the Peshwas. The backyard of the house is called the Sahanichi Kholi. It was here that Nanasaheb Peshwa breathed his last. There is a memorial to him here. The walls display portraits of Bajirao Peshwa I, Bajirao Peshwa II, Raghunathrao Peshwa, Narayanrao Peshwa, and Madhavrao Peshwa.

To the right of the Sahanichi Kholi, there is a temple of Lord Kartikeya, the eldest son of Lord Shiva. The temple does not permit women to enter. To the left of this temple, there is a Vishnu shrine. The deity is sculpted in black stone. It is a beautiful and moving depiction of the Lord. The idol is made of the sacred Shaligram stone, a particularly auspicious and holy rock.

The Vitthal Mandir is close to this shrine. Parvati also has a museum where a number of objects, books, arms, from the Peshwa era can be seen.

It may sound strange, but there are a fair number of Puneites who have yet to visit their city's most famous site. They have certainly missed much, for Parvati is a repository of the city's history.

Manas Resorts

This is the brand new face of Pune. Even for the middle-class, a week of hard work usually ends in weekends spent with friends and family. Manas is situated near the Bhugaon lake, about 12 kilometres from Pune, along the Paud Road. The resort lies on the banks of the lake. Go-karting, parties on a floating deck, a discotheque and excellent food - Manas has everything!

Fact File

Best time - All year round

Location -- 12 kms. from Pune on the Paud road on the Bhugaon lake

Getting there - Private transport

Where to stay - Pune city

Where to eat - Same

Aahupe Ghat (Hill stations).......132
Ajanta Caves (Caves).......222
Ajinkyatara (Forts).......67
Ajoba Mountain (Hill stations).......131
Alibag (Forts).......77
Ambakhori (Jungles).......170
Ambarnath (Temples).......114
Aurangabad (Unusual places).......243
Avchitagad (Forts).......18
Bamnoli (Lakes).......203
Bedse caves (Caves).......227
Bhairavgad (Forts).......76
Bhaje Caves (Caves).......227
Bhandardara (Lakes).......195
Bhilawale Lake (Lakes).......209
Bhimashankar (Hill stations).......150
Bhoj Lake (Lakes).......201
Bhor (Temples).......116
Bibi Ka Maqbara (Unusual places).......245
Bilya Mountain (Jungles).......158
Borivali National Park (National Parks).......173
Chandan (Forts).......56
Chanderi (Forts).......74
Chandoli (Nature Parks).......177
Chaul (Temples).......100
Chikhaldara (Hill stations).......123
Dabhosa Waterfall (Waterfalls).......215
Dajipur Sanctuary (Sanctuaries).......153
Darya Ghat (Unusual places).......238
Devbandh (Hill stations).......148
Devgiri (Forts).......71
Devkop Lake (Lakes).......210
Dhakoba (Forts).......49
Dhodap (Forts).......52
Doorshet (Unusual places).......240
Dr. Ambedkar Museum (Museum).......236
Ellora Caves (Caves).......224
Gadeshwar Lake (Lakes).......192
Gambhirgad (Forts).......32
Gandhaar-Pali Caves (Caves).......227
Ganpatipule (Temples).......118
Gautala Forest Reserve (Nature Parks).......175
Ghosalgad (Forts).......20
Gorakh (Forts).......31
Hadsar (Forts).......61
Harishchandragad (Forts).......14
Igatpuri (Hill stations).......129

Jawhar (Hill Stations).......148
Jeevdhan (Forts).......58
Jyotiba (Temples).......113
Kaas Lake (Lakes).......194
Kakuli Lake (Lakes).......195
Kalote Lake (Lakes).......193
Kankeshwar (Temples).......89
Kapuskar (Museum).......235
Karla caves (Caves).......227
Karmarkar Museum (Museum).......234
Karnala Fort (Forts).......17
Kathingad or Tung (Forts).......25
Khadsamble caves (Caves).......228
Khandala (Hill stations).......144
Khanwel (Forests).......162
Khindsay Lake (Unusual places).......253
Khodala (Hill stations).......148
Kohoj (Forts).......13
Koraigad (Forts).......27
Korlai (Forts).......24
Kothligad (Forts).......73
Koyna Forest Reserve (Nature Parks).......179
Kukdeshwar (Temples).......111
Kuna Cave (Caves).......221
Kundal (Temples).......95
Kundeshwar Lake (Lakes).......201
Lenyadri (Temples).......110
Lohagad (Forts).......45
Lokmanya Tilak Museum (Museum).......233
Lonad Caves (Caves).......225
Lonavala (Hill stations).......146
Machhindragad (Forts).......31
Mahabaleshwar (Hill stations).......135
Mahad (Temples).......109
Mahuli (Forts).......54
Manas Resorts (Unusual places).......256
Mandhardevi (Hill stations).......125
Manikdoh (Lakes).......199
Manikdoha (Unusual places).......241
Manikgad (Forts).......75
Marleshwar (Temples).......107
Mastani Lake (Unusual places).......239
Matheran (Hill stations).......138
Meera Hill (Hill stations).......127
Melghat (Sanctuaries).......165
Mhaismal (Unusual places).......246
Miniature Railway Museum (Museum).......236

Mokhada (Hill stations).......148
Morgaon (Temples).......106
Mrutyunjeshwar (Temples).......105
Mulshi Lake (Lakes).......208
Murud Forests (Jungles).......167
Murud-Janjira (Forts).......22
Nadhal Lake (Lakes).......207
Nagzira (Forests).......163
Naldurg (Forts).......47
Nandur Madhyameshwar (Sanctuaries).......156
Naney Ghat (Unusual places).......237
Nannaj Bird Sanctuary (Sanctuaries).......172
Navegaon (Sanctuaries).......166
Navegaon National Park (National Parks).......186
Ozar (Temples).......103
Pal-Yaval Sanctuary (Sanctuaries).......159
Pali (Temples).......102
Pallu Waterfall (Waterfalls).......216
Pandavgad (Forts).......60
Pandavgad (Waterfalls).......217
Panhala (Forts).......29
Panshet (Lakes).......202
Parvati (Unusual places).......254
Pateshwar (Temples).......90
Pelhar Lake (Lakes).......204
Pench (National Park).......169
Phaltan (Caves).......229
Pitalkhora Caves (Caves).......225
Potholes (Caves).......231
Prabalgad (Forts).......50
Pratapgad (Forts).......43
Purandar (Forts).......63
Raigad (Forts).......41
Raja Dinkar Kelkar museum (Museum).......235
Rajgad (Forts).......34
Rajmachi (Forts).......38
Ramtek (Unusual places).......253
Ranjangaon (Temples).......101
Ratanwadi (Temples).......117
Rehkuri Kalveet Wildlife Park (Nature Parks).......181
Rock Bridge (Unusual places).......252
Sagareshwar (Forests).......154
Sajjangad (Forts).......46
Sakhare Lake (Lakes).......214
Salt Pillar (Unusual places).......252
Saptashrungi (Temples).......92
Satara Museum (Museum).......233

Sativali (Hot Springs).......205
Sav (Hot springs).......206
Savne Lake (Lakes).......212
Shegaon (Temples).......96
Shivneri (Forts).......69
Shivsagar Lake (Lakes).......203
Shivtharghal (Unusual places).......250
Shri Gondeshwar Temple (Temples).......96
Siddhatek (Temples).......104
Sindhudurg (Forts).......81
Sinhgad (Forts).......37
Sitabai hill (Unusual places).......249
Sudhagad (Forts).......40
Surya River (Lakes).......211
Suryamal (Hill stations).......148
Tadgaon (Hill stations).......147
Tadoba Sanctuary (Sanctuaries).......164
Talgad (Forts).......21
Tansa Sanctuary (Sanctuaries).......161
Tapola Lake (Lakes).......191
Tara Paanwala (Unusual places).......244
Thanale (Caves).......228
Thebaw Palace (Unusual places).......242
Theur (Temples).......98
Thoseghar (Waterfalls).......218
Tikona (Forts).......28
Tilsa (Caves).......228
Torna (Forts).......36
Trimbakeshwar (Temples).......99
Tungareshwar (Temples).......93
Uddhar (Hill stations).......147
Unhere (Hill stations).......147
Upper Vaitarna (Lakes).......198
Vandan (Forts).......56
Vandri Lake (Lakes).......205
Varandha Ghat (Hill stations).......126
Vasota (Forts).......83
Vathar Nimbalkar (Unusual places).......247
Vihigaon (Waterfalls).......216
Vikramgad (Jungles).......157
Visapur (Forts).......45
Vishalgad (Forts).......85
Wood Exhibits (Museum).......234

M A P S

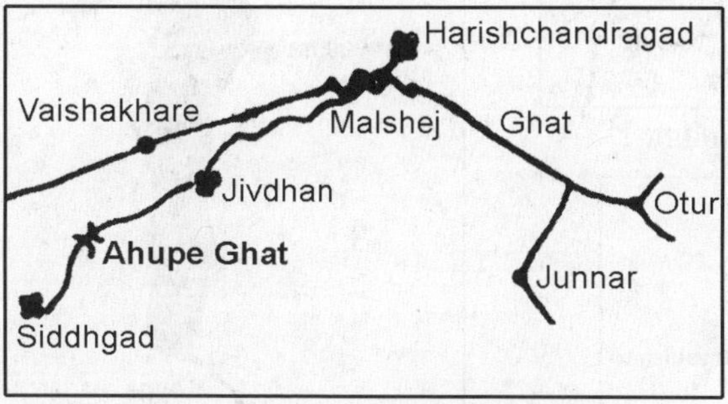

Ahupe Ghat - See page 132

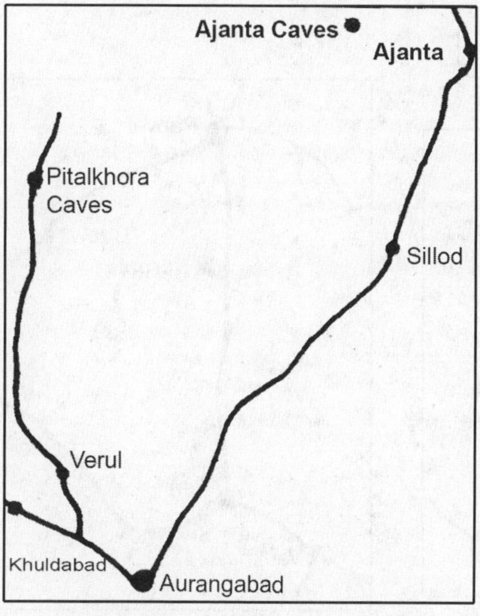

Ajanta Caves - See page 222

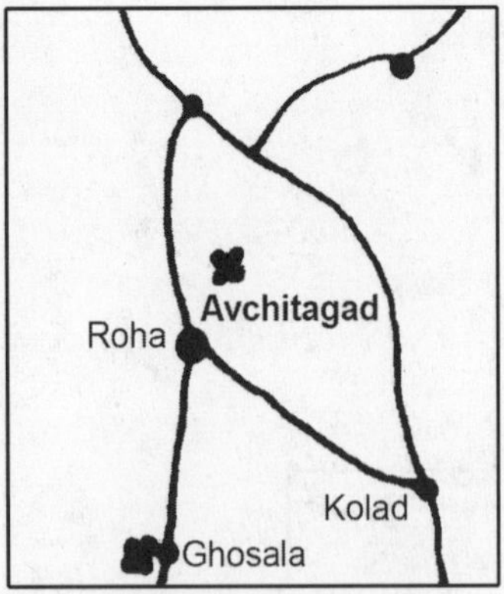

Avchitgad See page 18

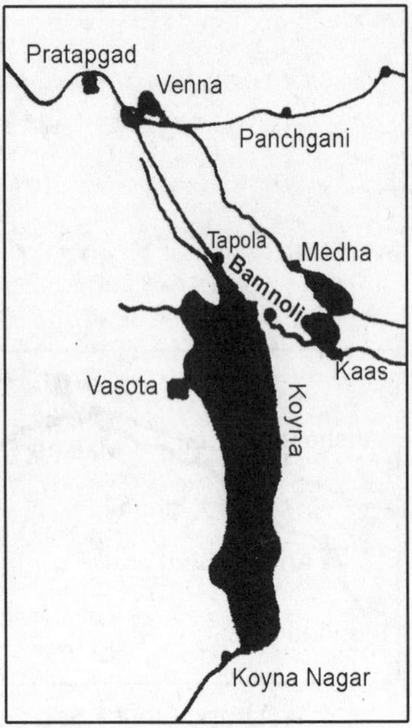

Bamnoli - See page 203

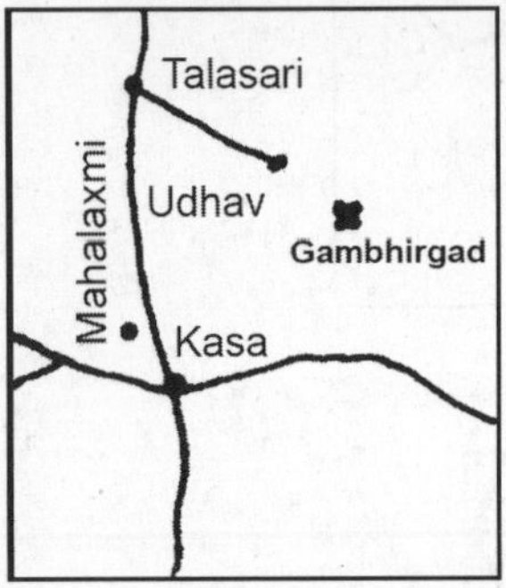

Gambhirgad See page 32

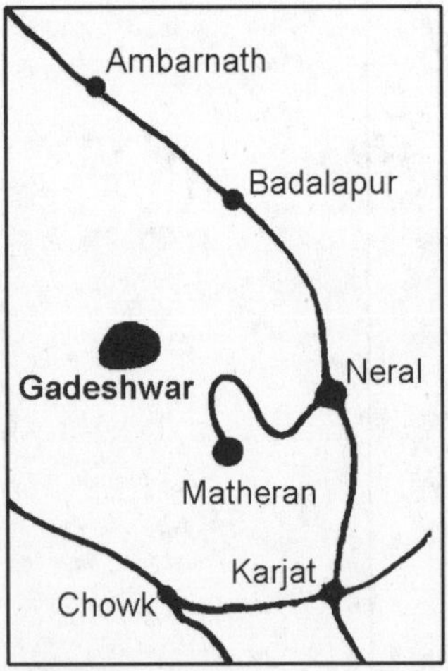

Gadeshwar Lake - See page 192

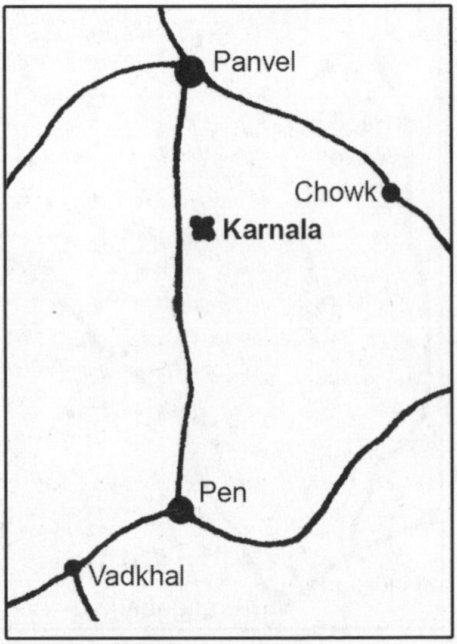

Karnala - See page 17

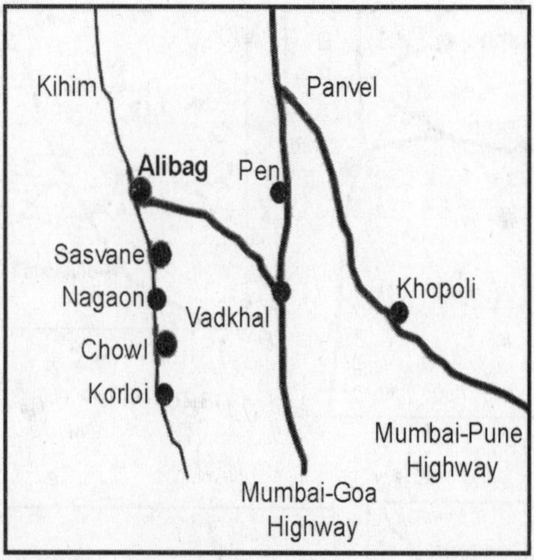

Alibag - See page 77

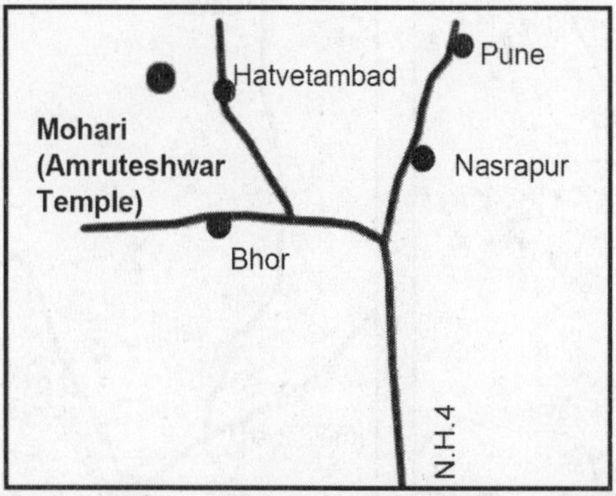

Amruteshwar Temple, Bhor - See page 116

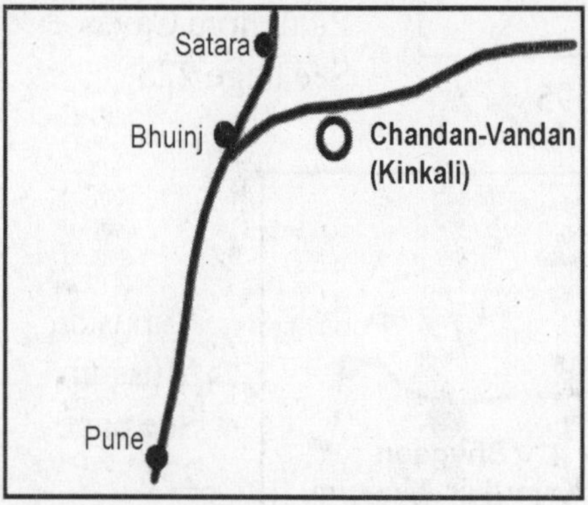

Chandan-Vadan - See page 56

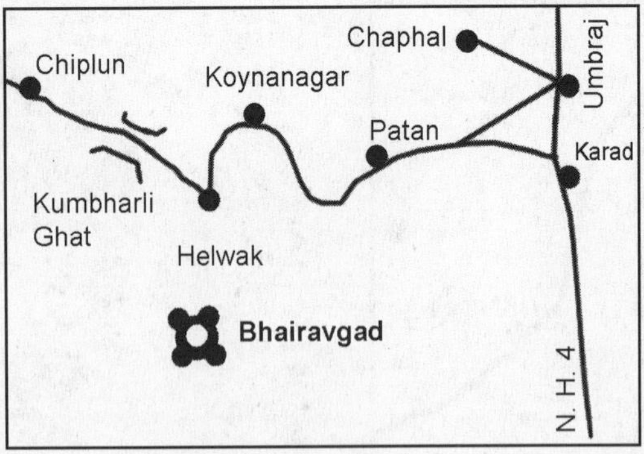

Bhairavgad - See page 76

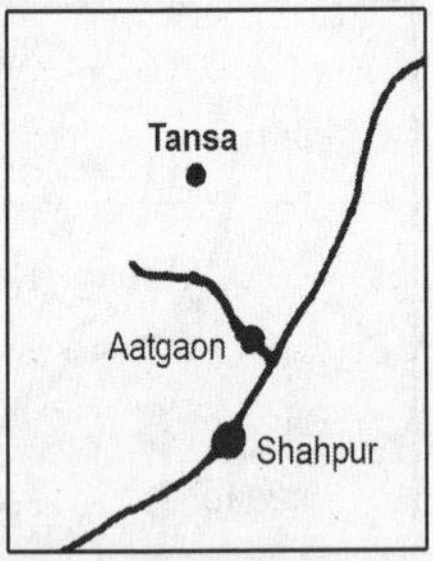

Tansa - See page 161

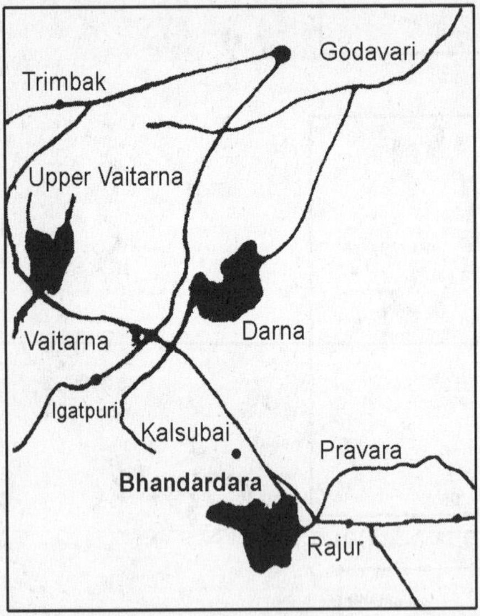

Bhandardara - See page 195

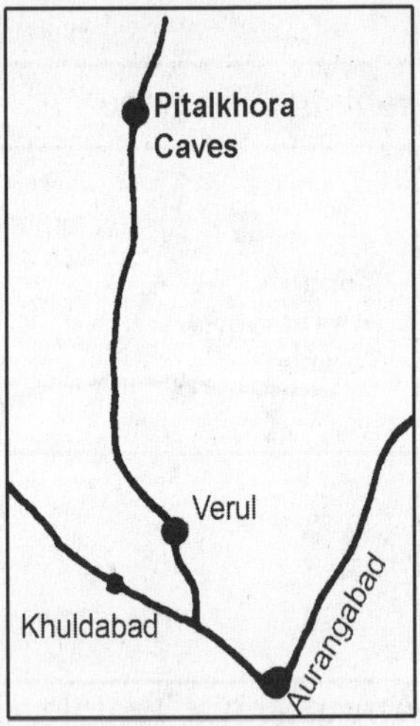

Pitalkhora Caves - See page 225

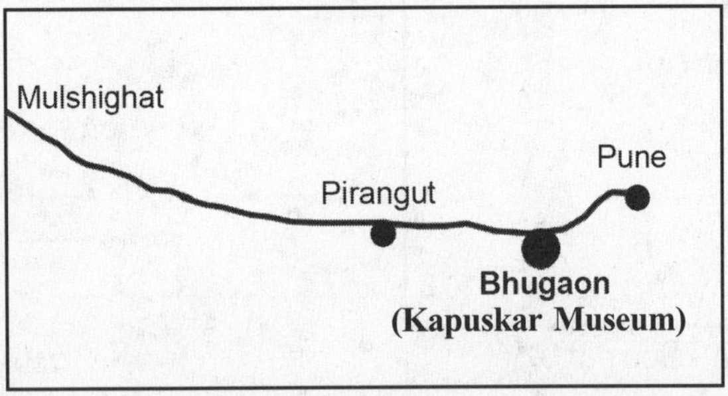

Kapuskur Museum - See page 235

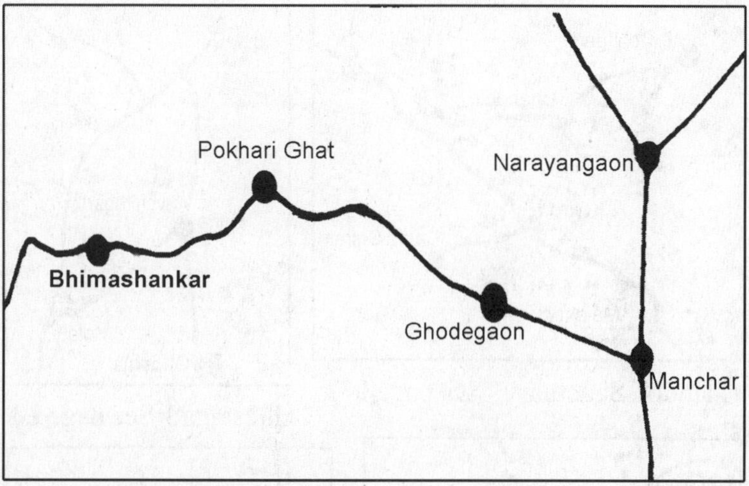

Bhimashankar - See page 150

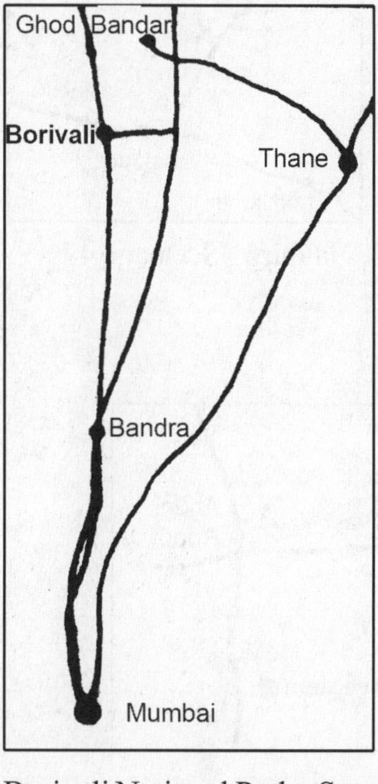

Borivali National Park - See page 173

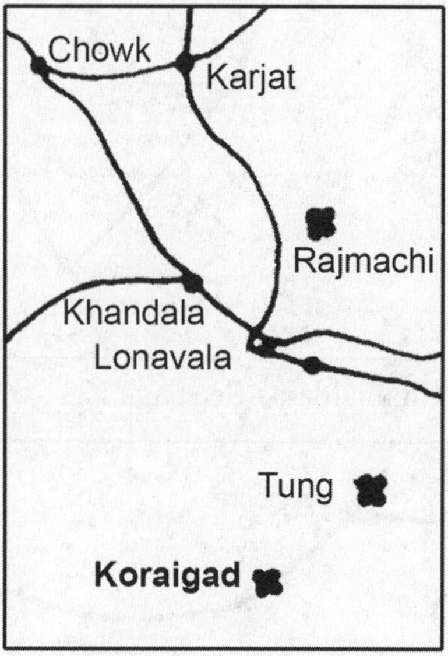

Koraigad See page 27

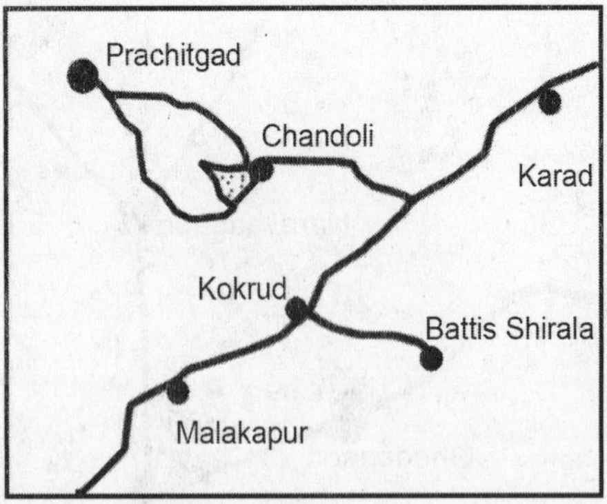

Chandoli Sanctuary - See page 177

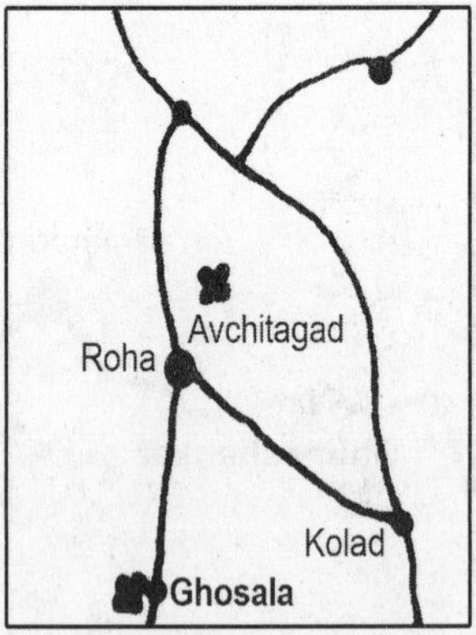

Ghosalgad See page 20

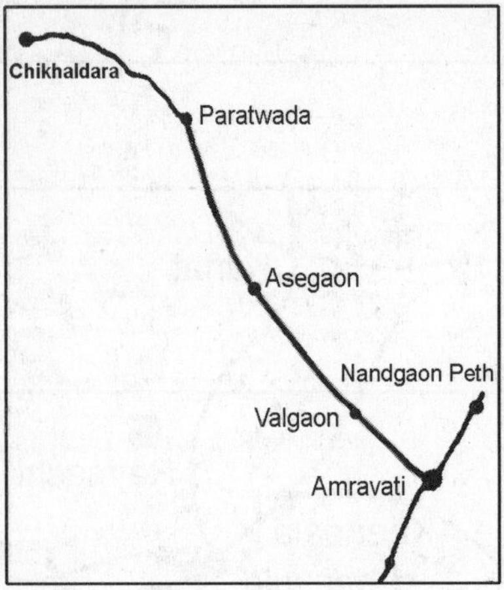

Chikhaldara - See page 123

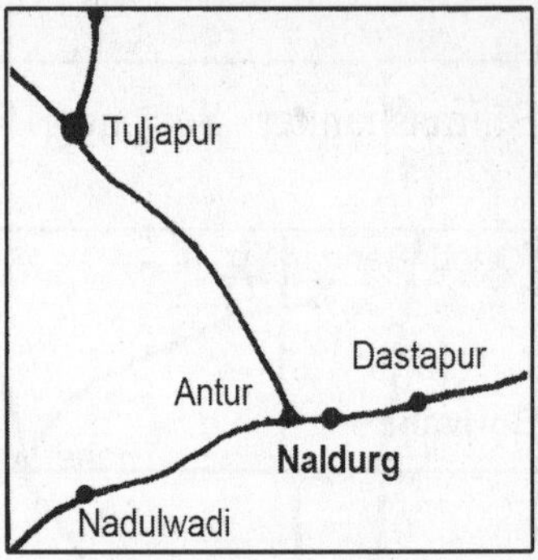

Naldurg - See page 47

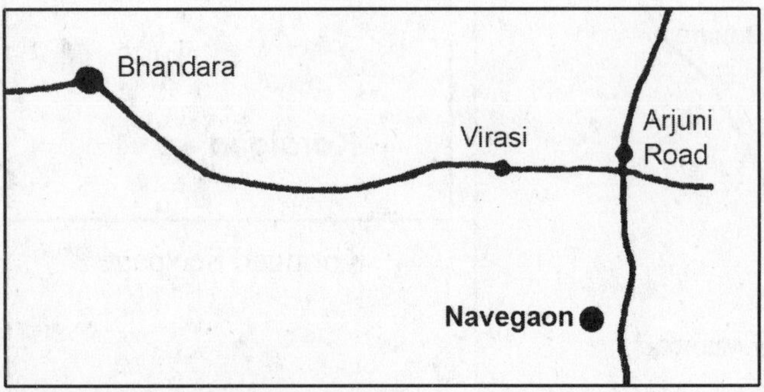

Navegaon - See page 166

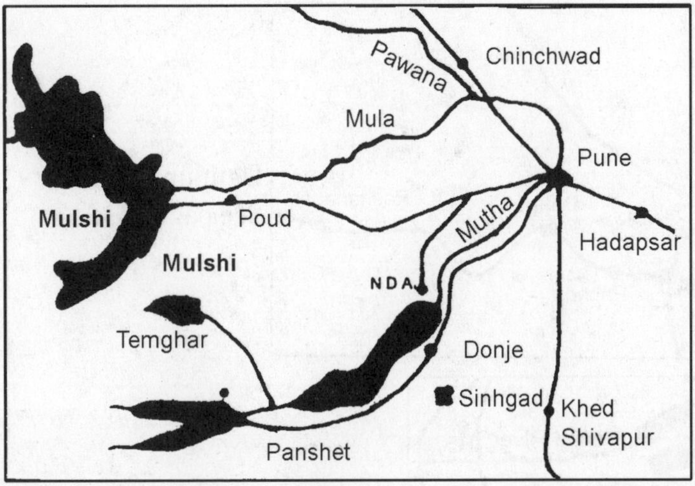

Mulshi Lake - See page 208

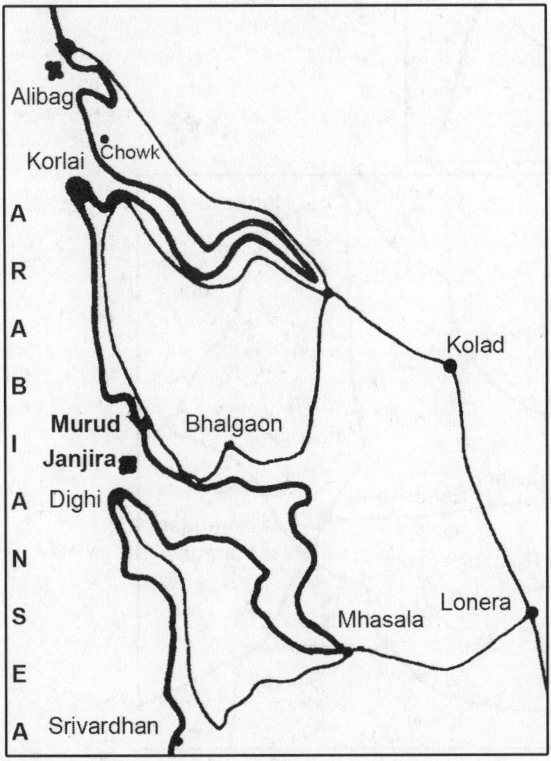

Murud Janjira See page 22

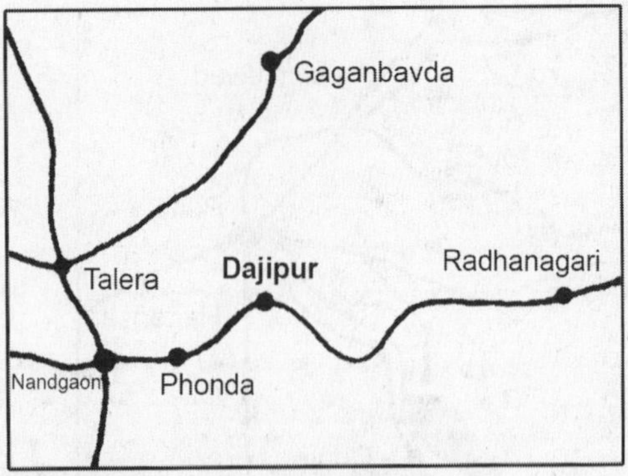

Dajipur Sanctuary - See page 153

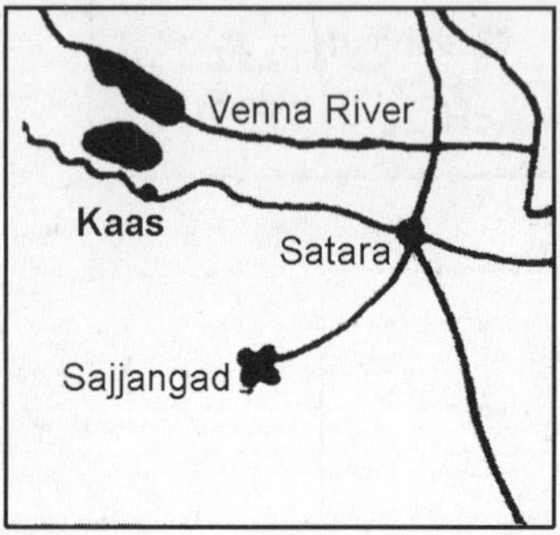

Kaas Lake - See page 194

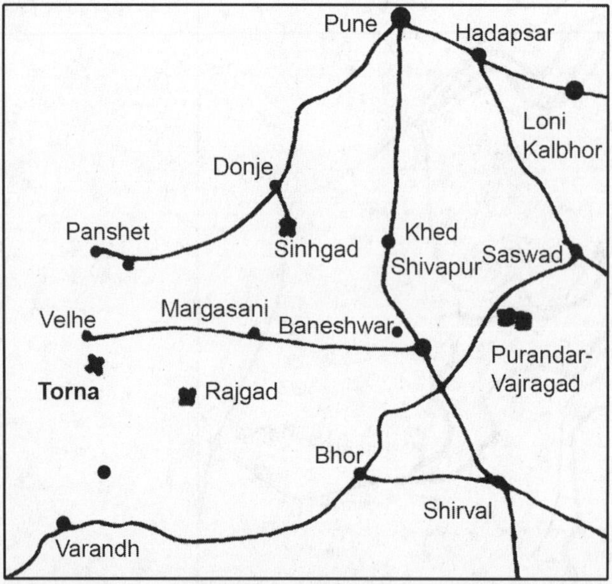

Torna - See page 36

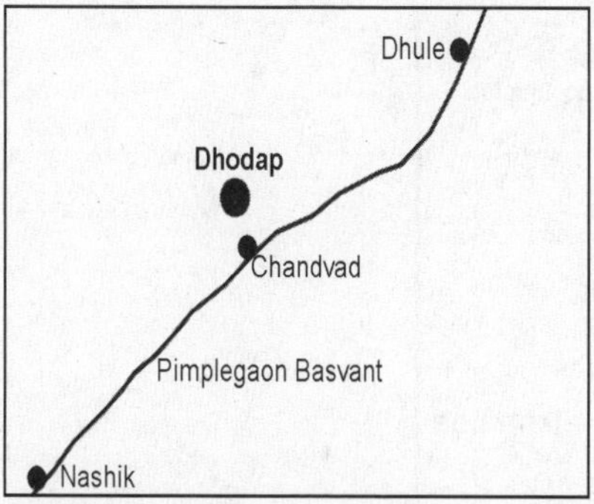

Dhodap - See page 52

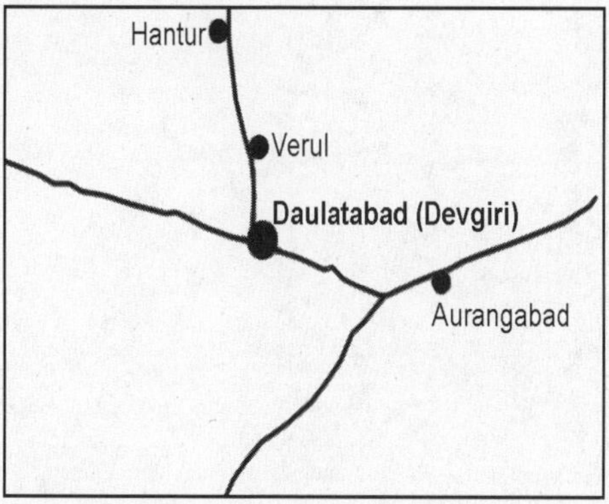

Devgiri - See page 71

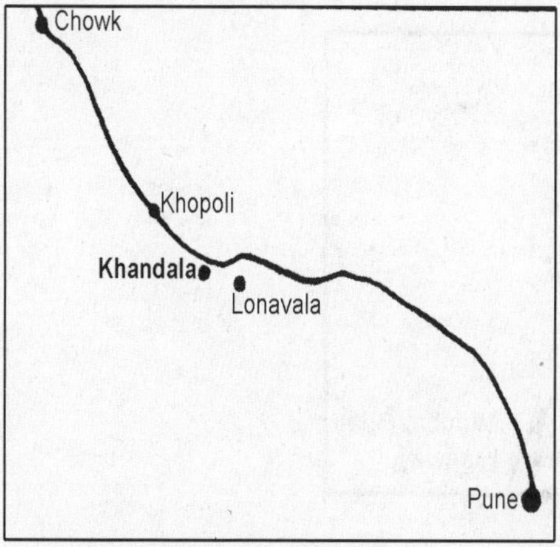

Khandala - See page 144

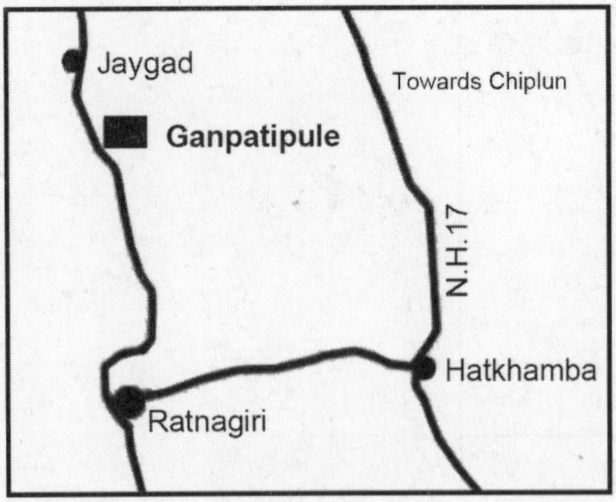

Ganpatipule- See page 118

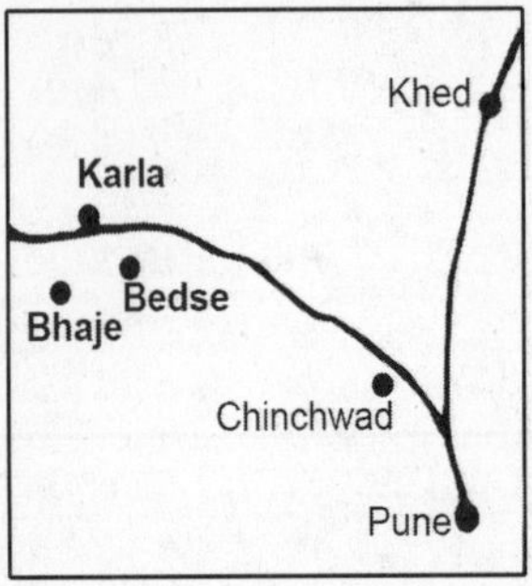

Karla Caves - See page 227

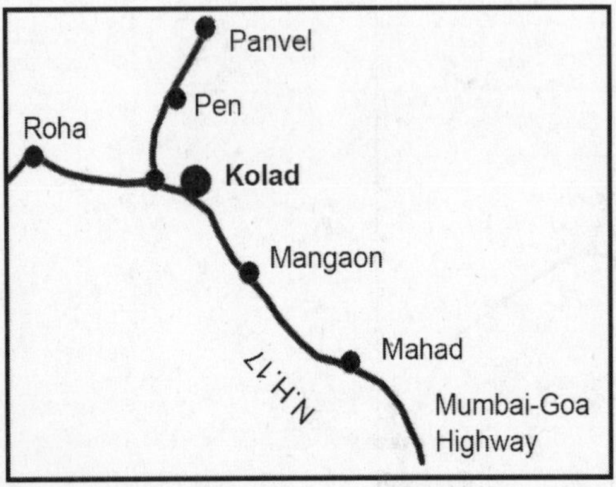

Kolad - See page 234

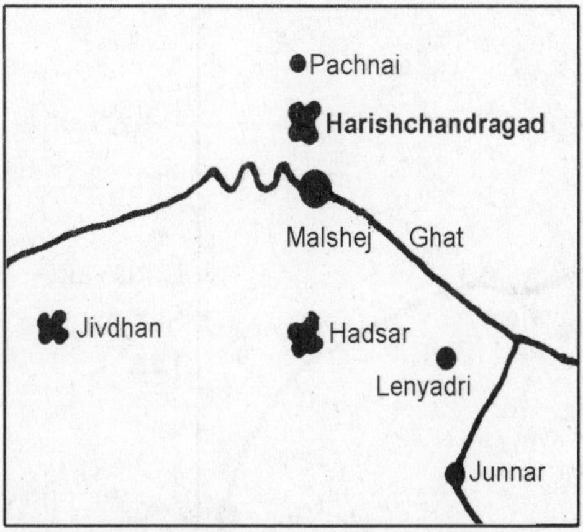

Harishchandragad - See page 14

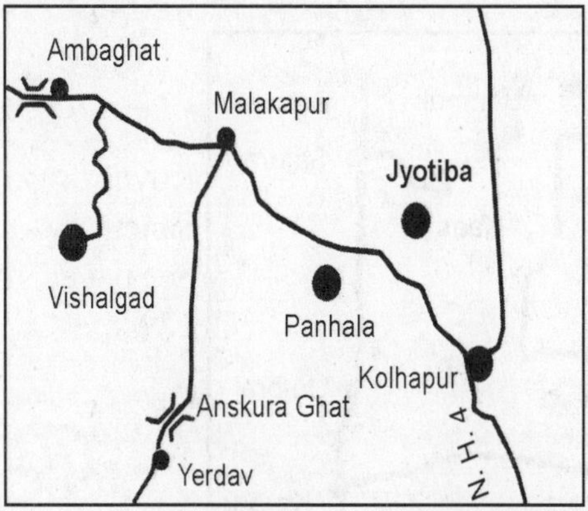

Jyotiba - See page 113

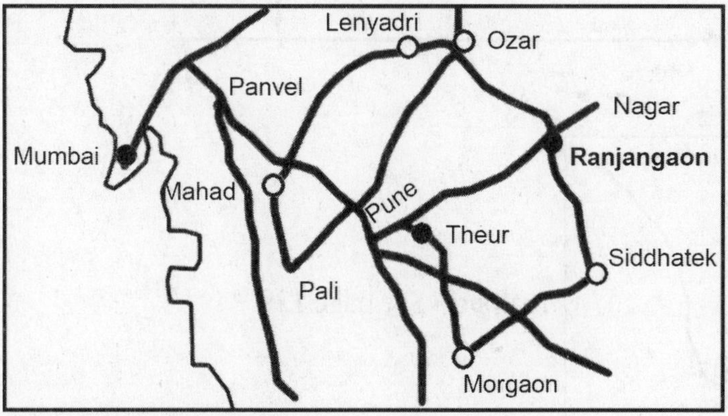

Ranjangaon - See page 101

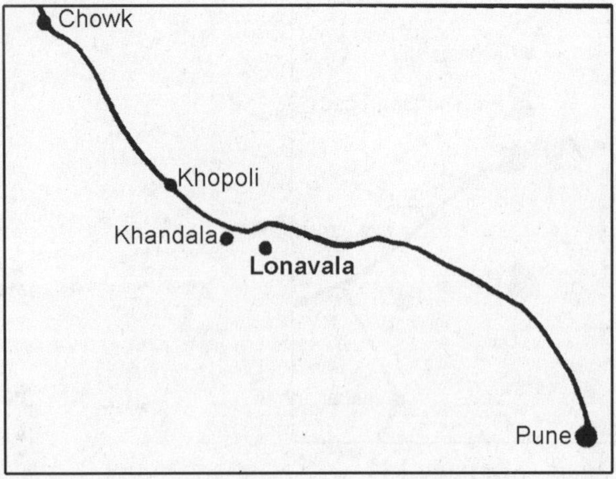

Lonavala - See page 146

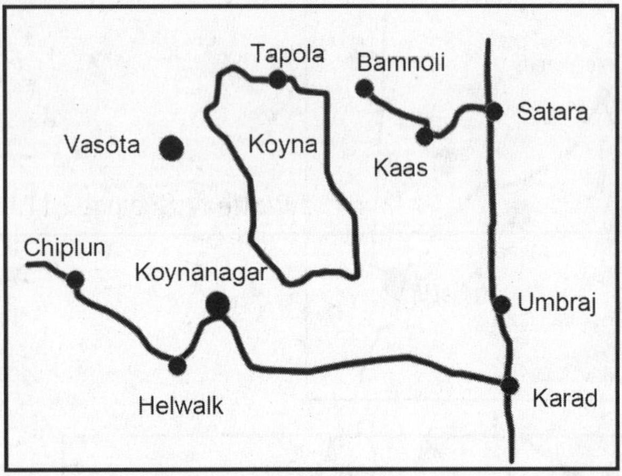

Koyna Sanctuary - See page 179

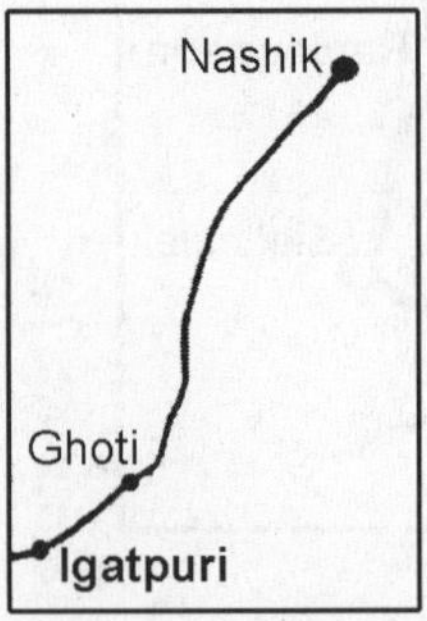

Igatpuri - See page 129

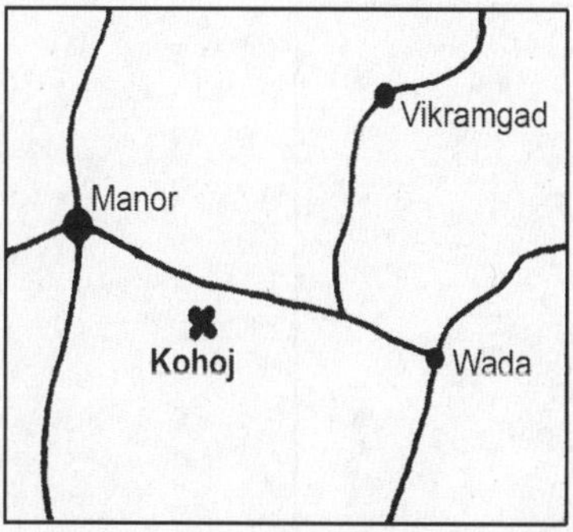

Kohoj - See page 13

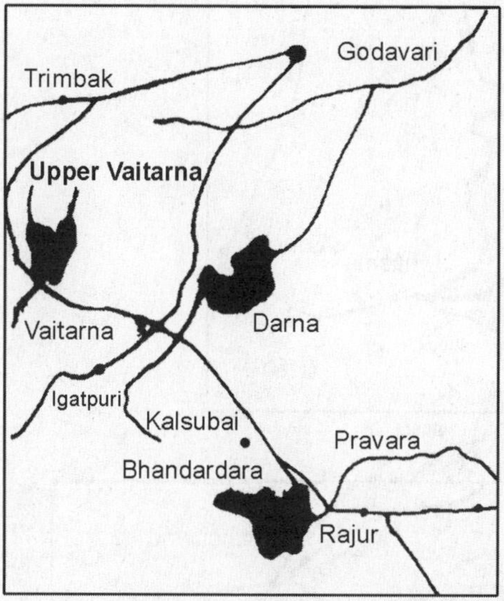

Upper Vaitarna - See page 198

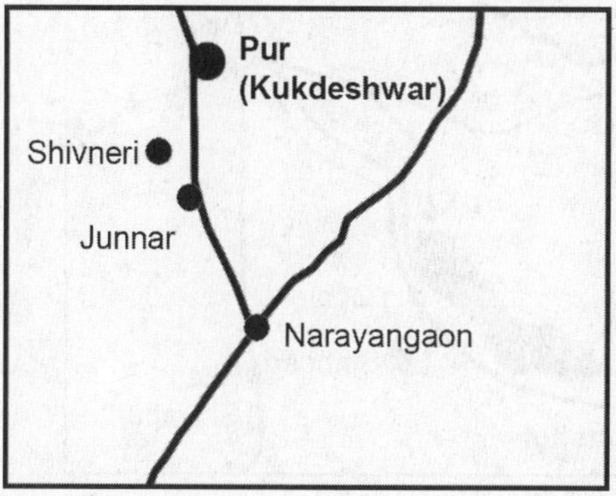

Kukadeshwar - See page 201

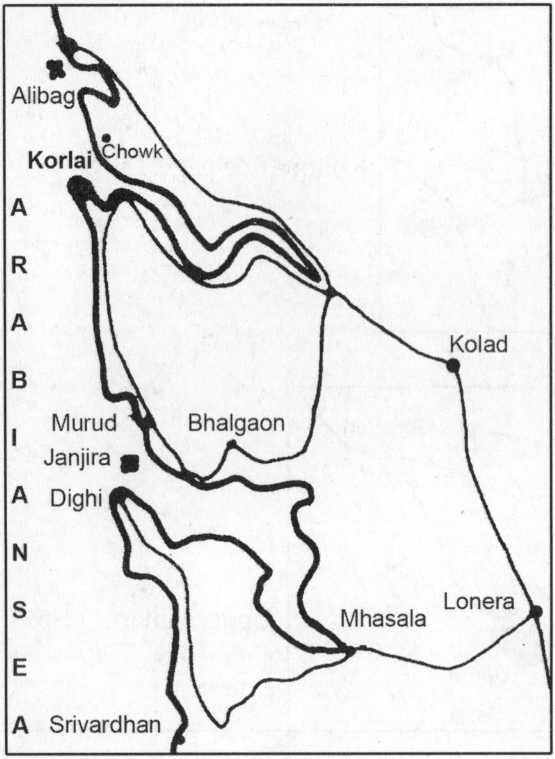

Korlai See page 24

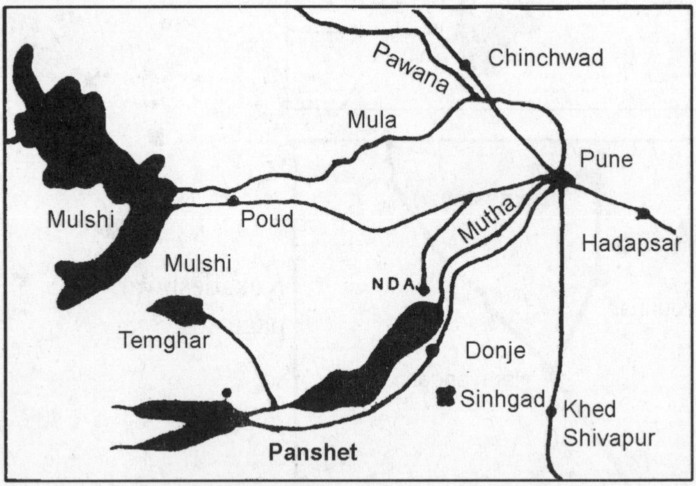

Panshet - See page 202

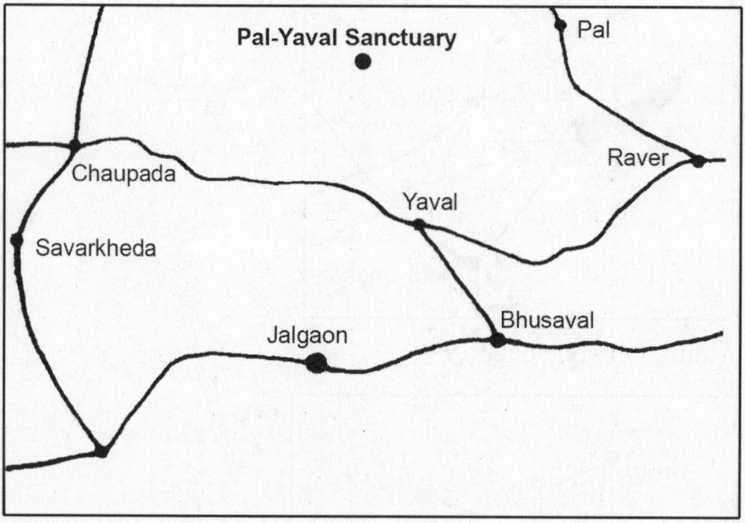

Pal-Yaval Sanctuary - See page 159

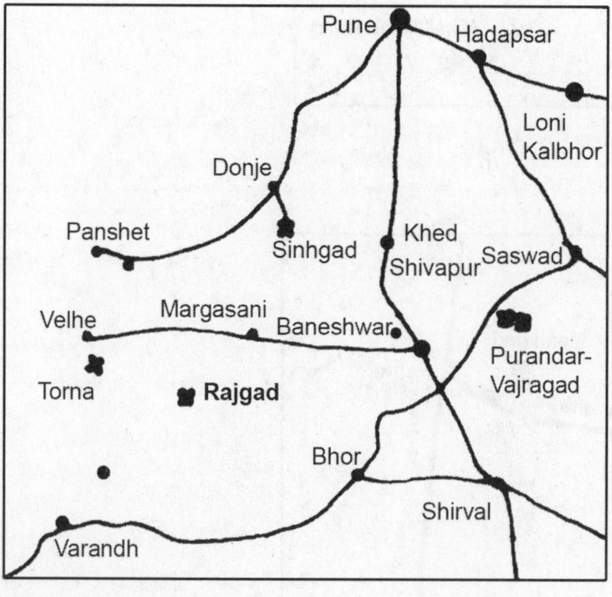

Rajgad - See page 33

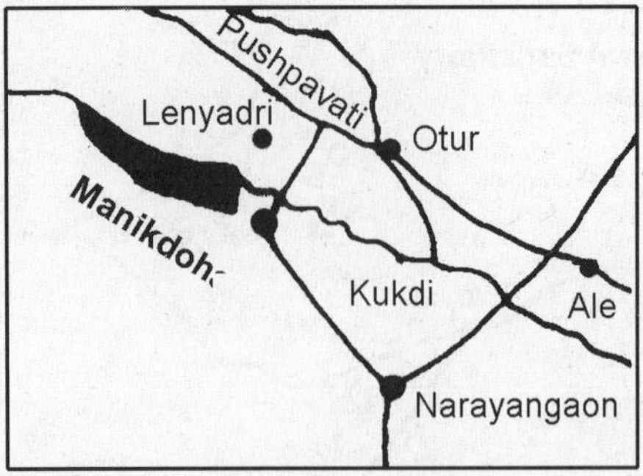

Manikdoh - See page 199

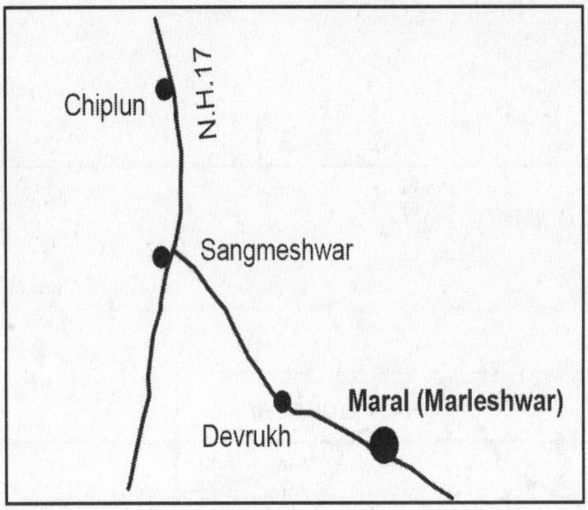

Marleshwar - See page 107

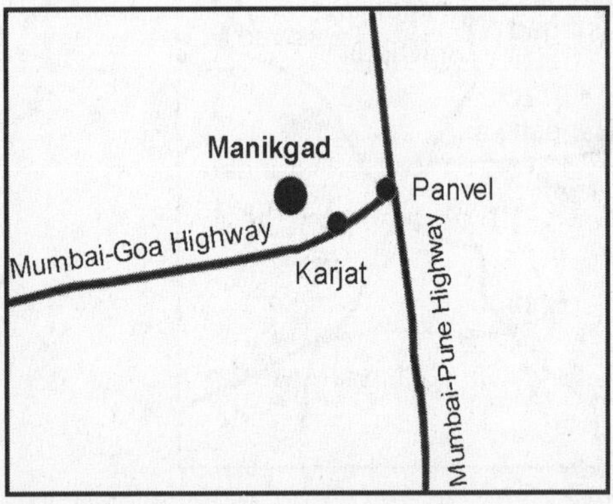

Manikgad - See page 75

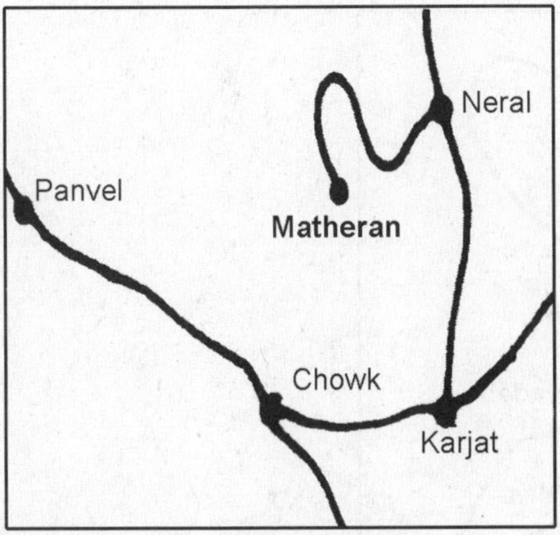

Matheran - See page 138

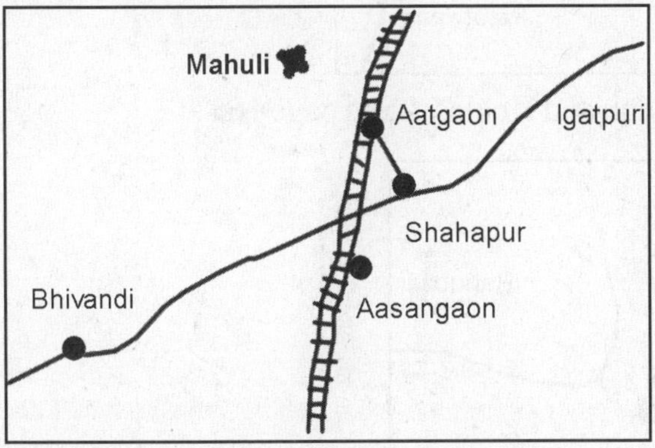

Mahuli - See page 54

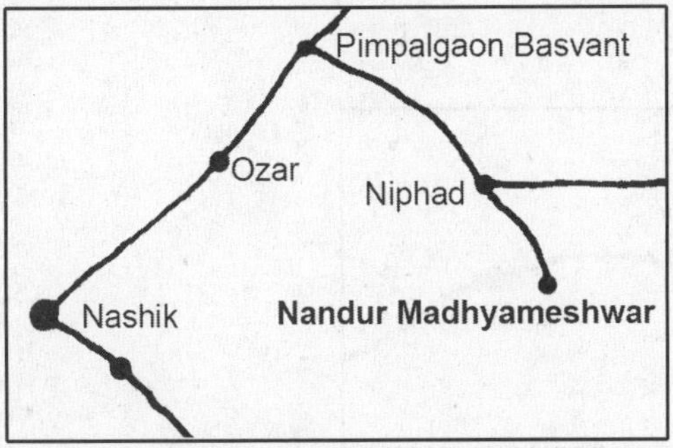

Nandur Madhyameshwar - See page 156

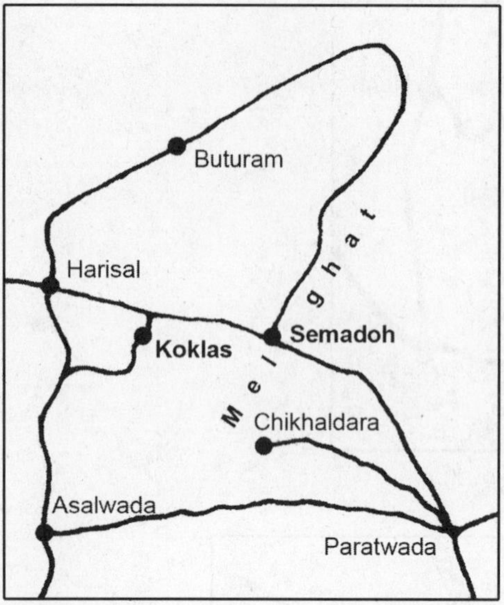

Melghat (Semadoh and Koklas) - See page 165

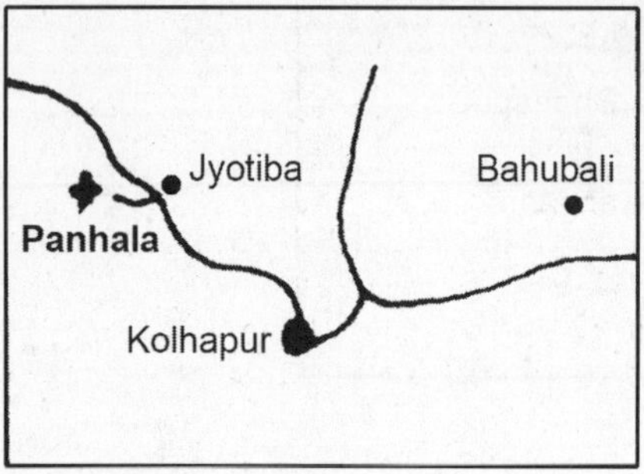

Panahala See page 29

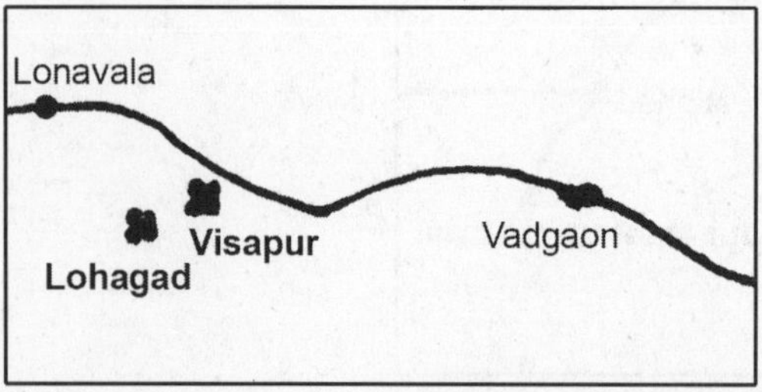

Lohagad-Visapur - See page 45

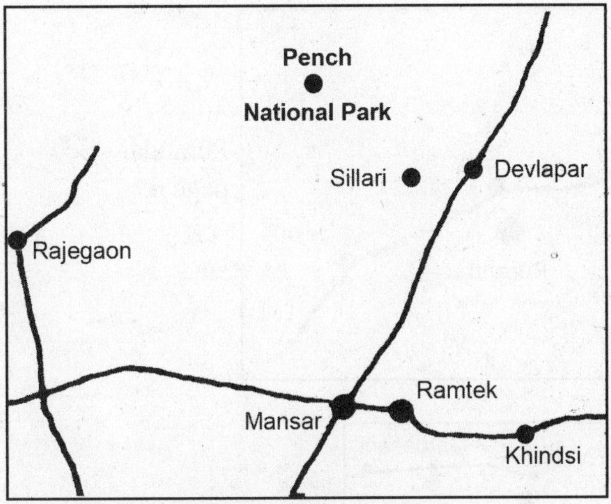

Pench National Park - See page 169

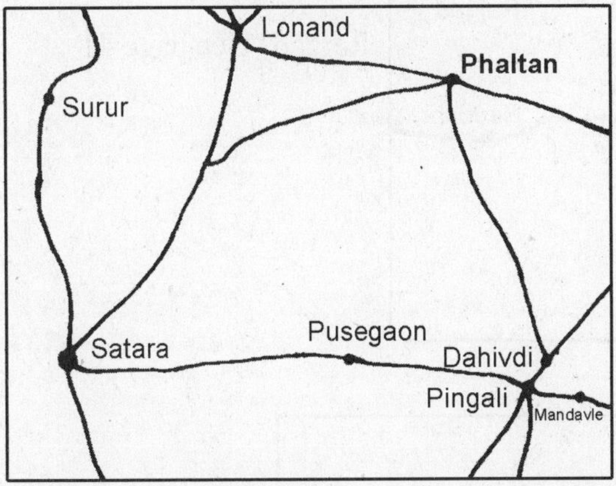

Phaltan - See page 229

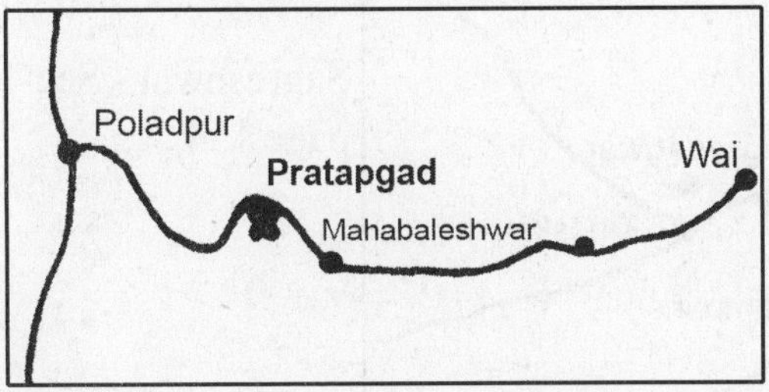

Pratapgad - See page 43

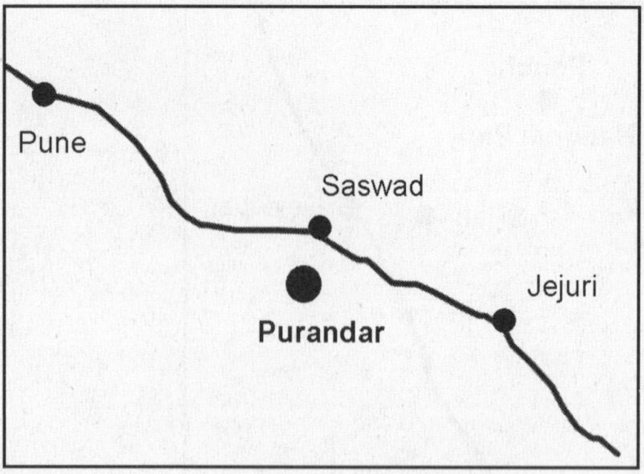

Purandar - See page 63

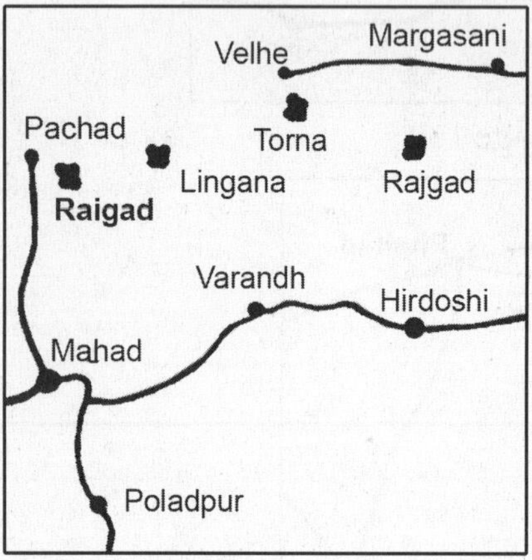

Raigad - See page 41

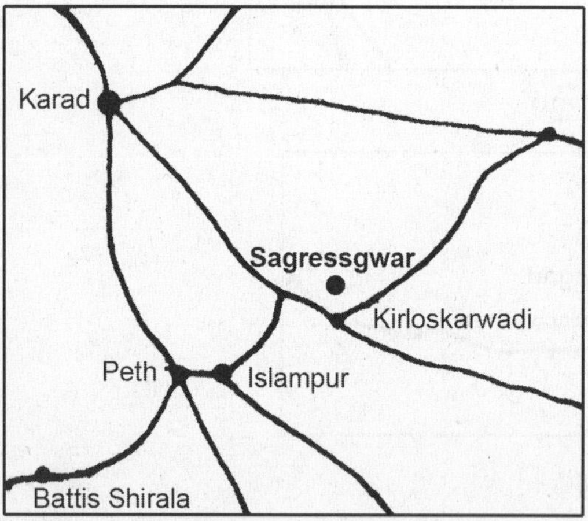

Sagreshwar - See page 154

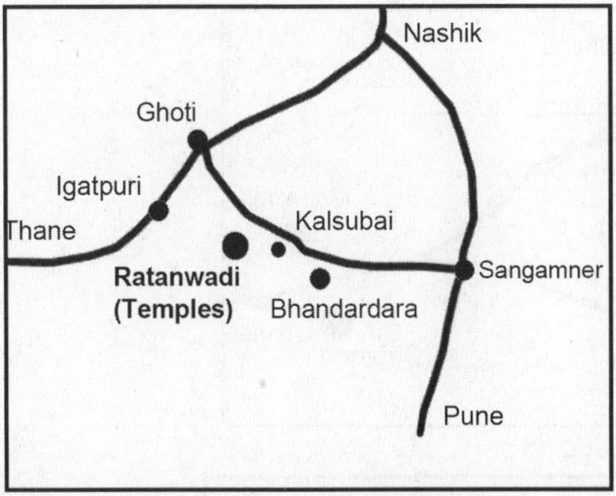

Ratanwadi (Temples) - See page 117

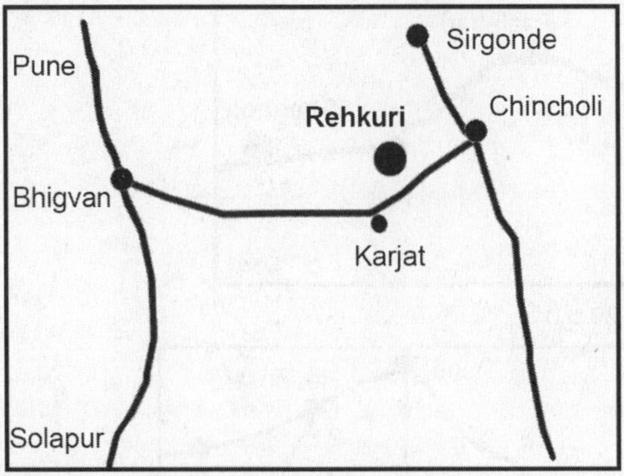

Rehkuri Sanctuary See page 181

Sakhare Lake - See page 214

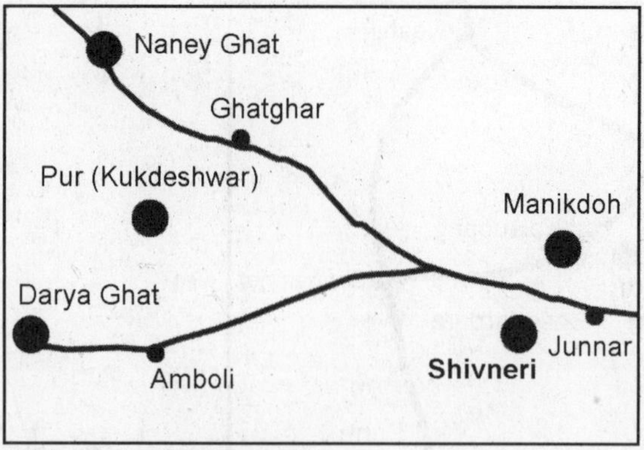

Shivneri - See page 68

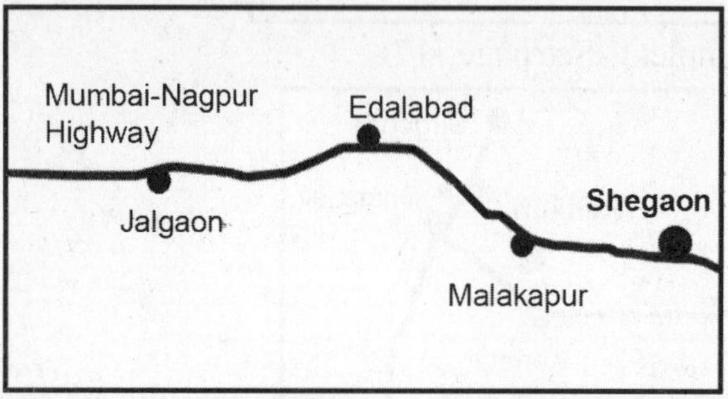

Shegaon - See page 96

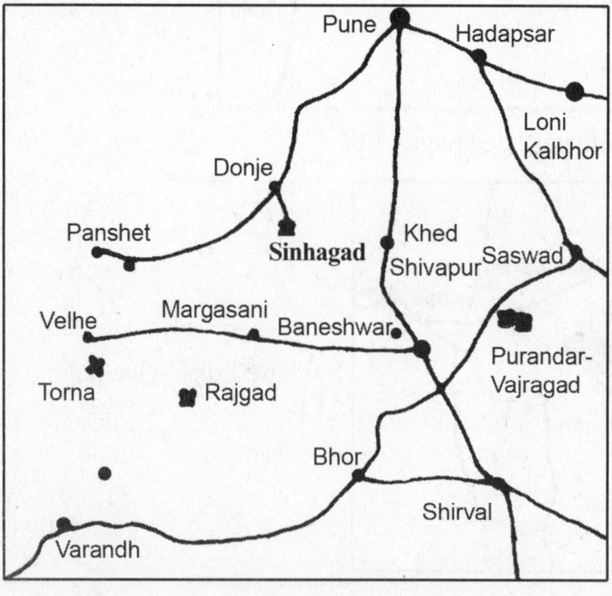

Sinhagad - See page 37

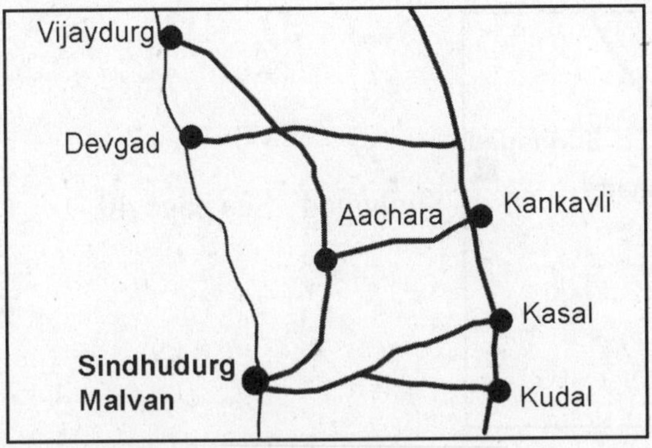

Sindhudurg - See page 81

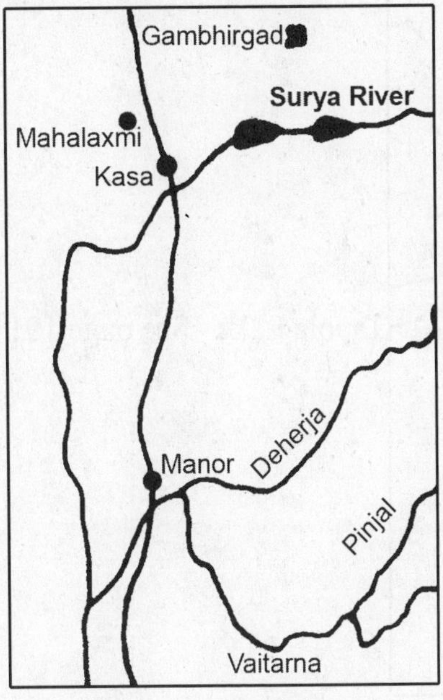

Surya River - See page 211

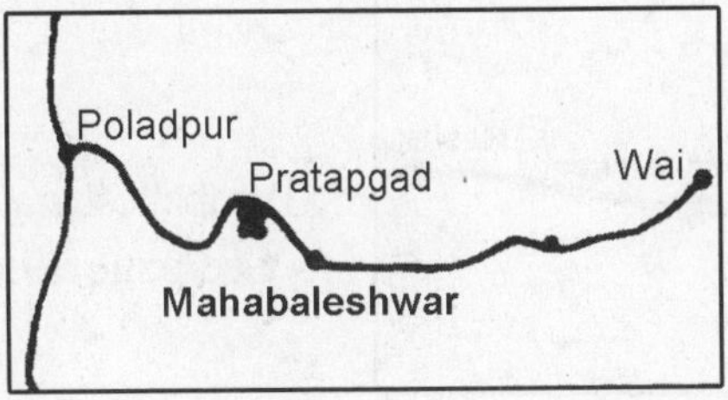

Mahabaleshwar - See page 135

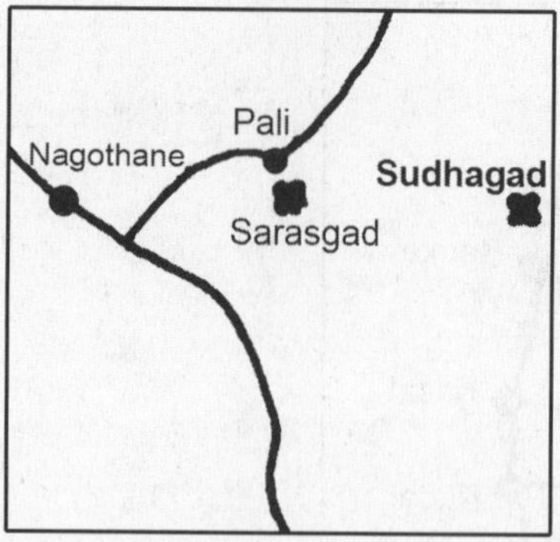

Sudhagad - See page 40

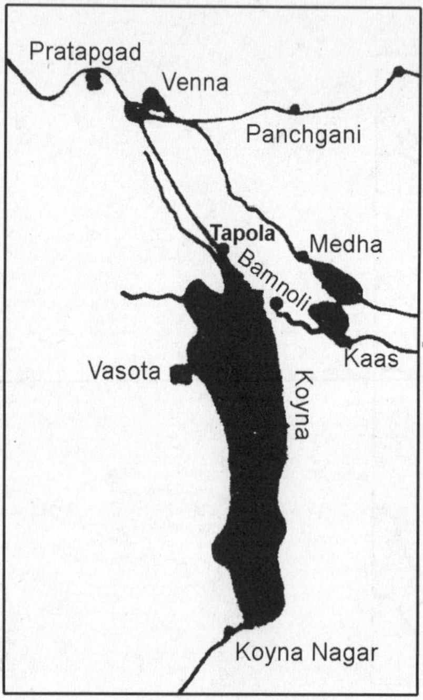

Tapola Lake - See page 191

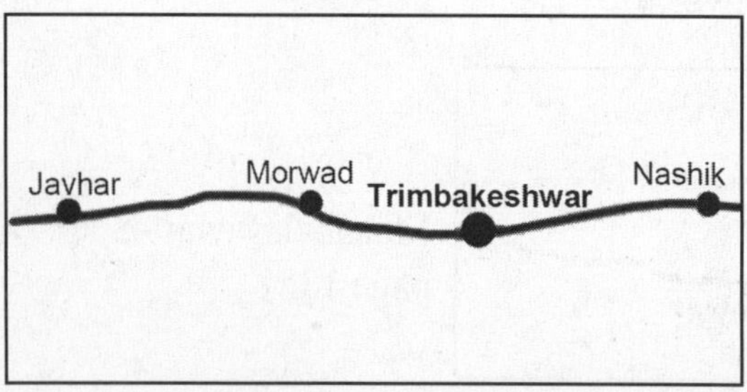

Trimbakeshwar - See page 99

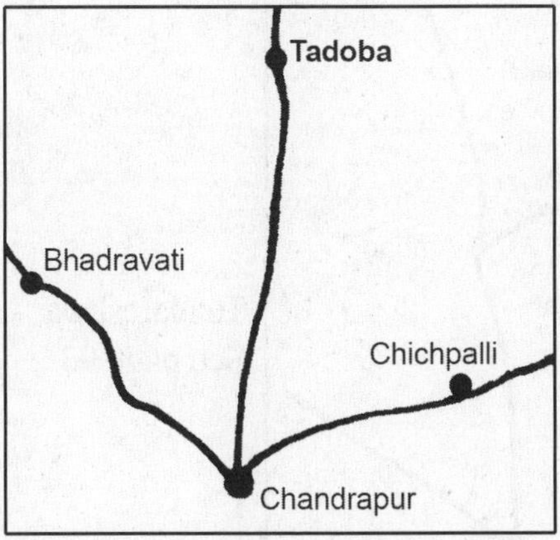

Tadoba - See page 164

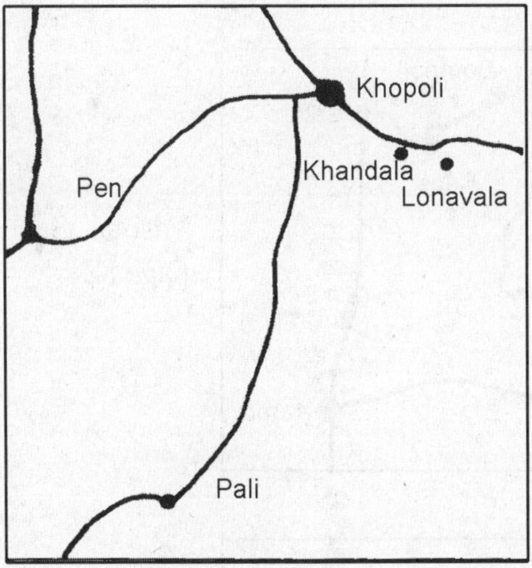

Tilsa - See page 228

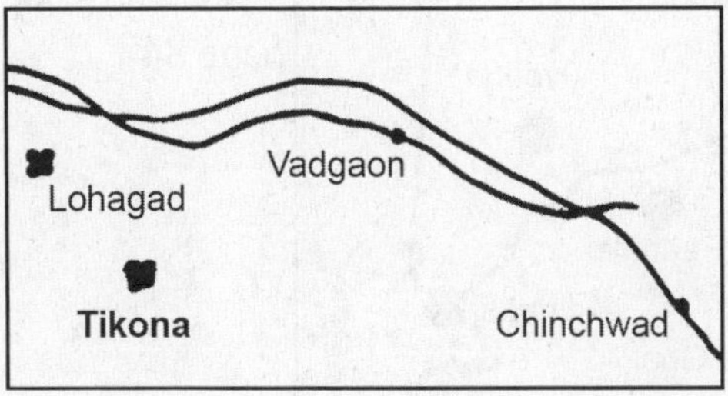

Tikona See page 28

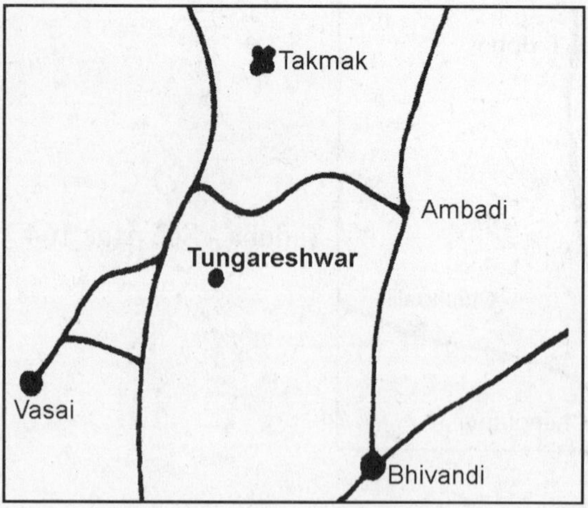

Tungareshwar - See page 93

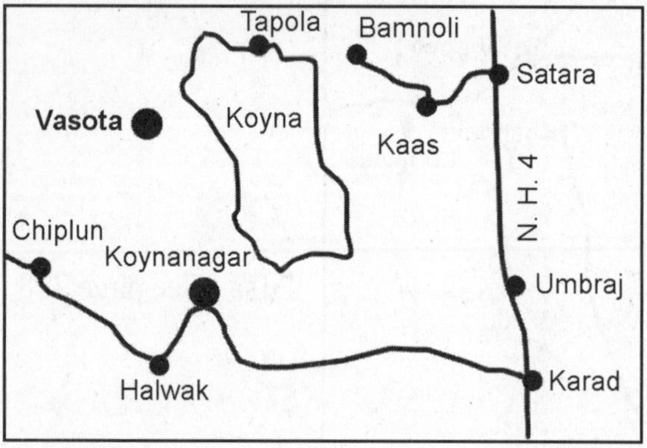

Vasota - See page 82

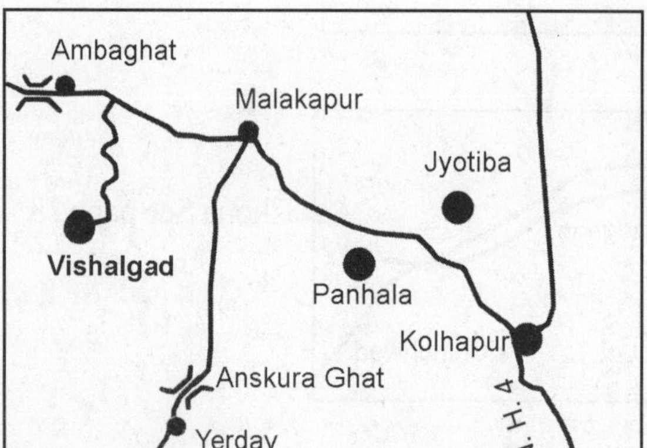

Vishalgad - See page 84

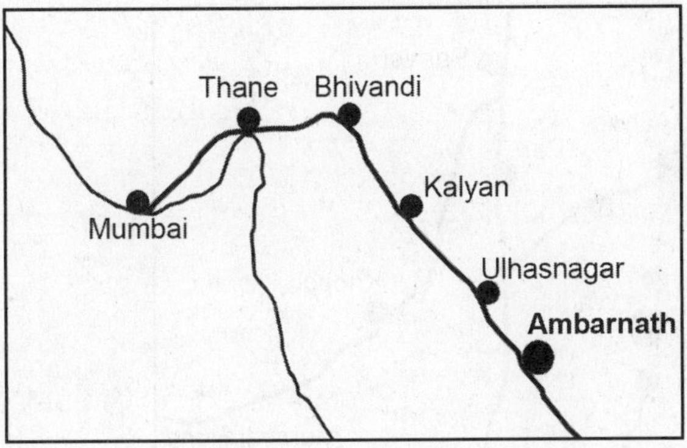

Ambarnath - See page 114

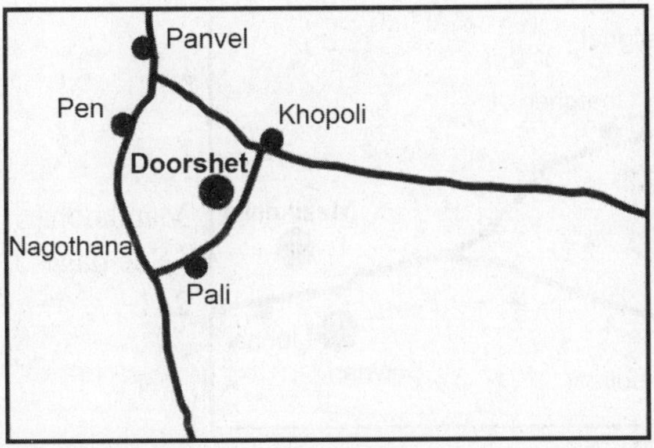

Doorshet - See page 240

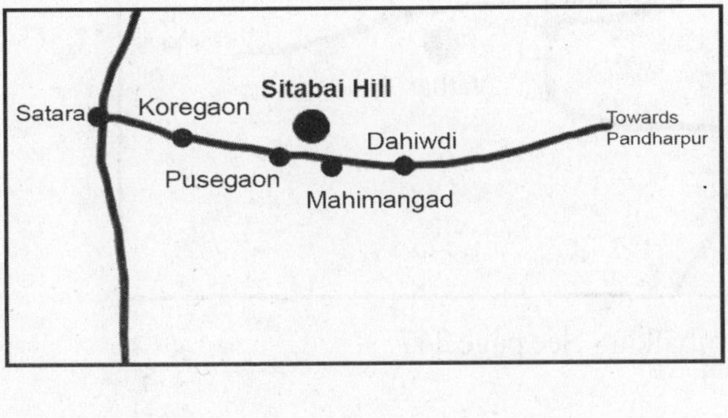

Sitabai Hill - See page 249

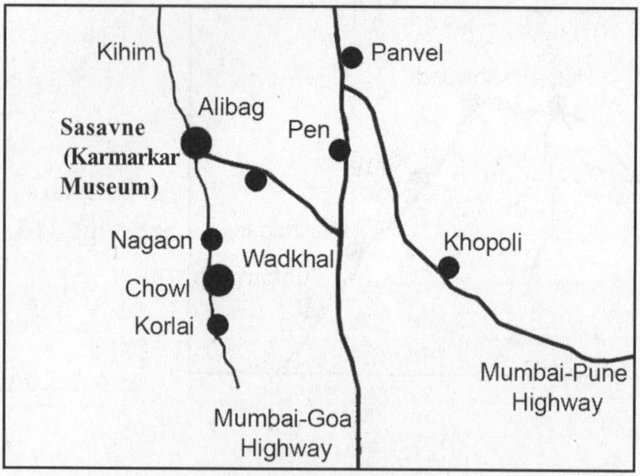

Karmarkar Museum - See page 234

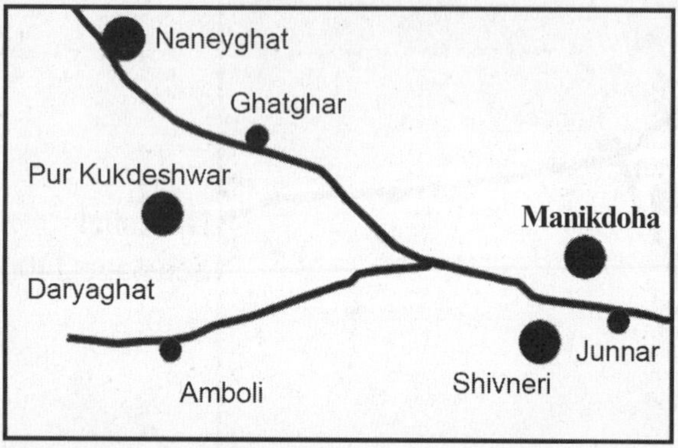

Manikdoha - See page 241

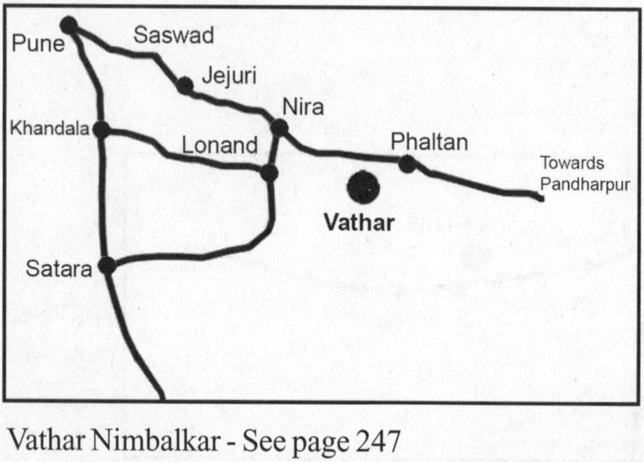

Vathar Nimbalkar - See page 247

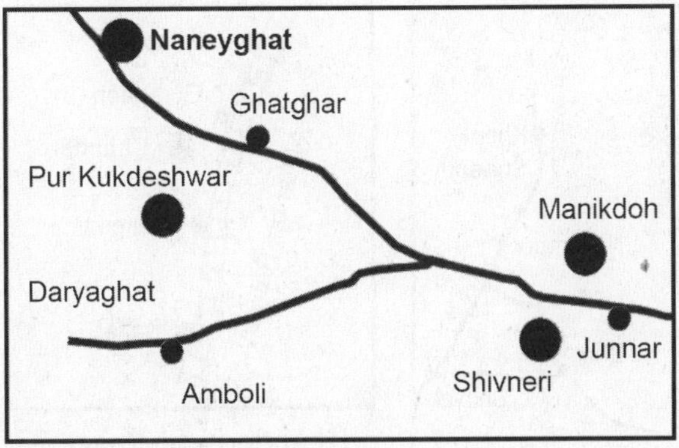

Naney Ghat - See page 237

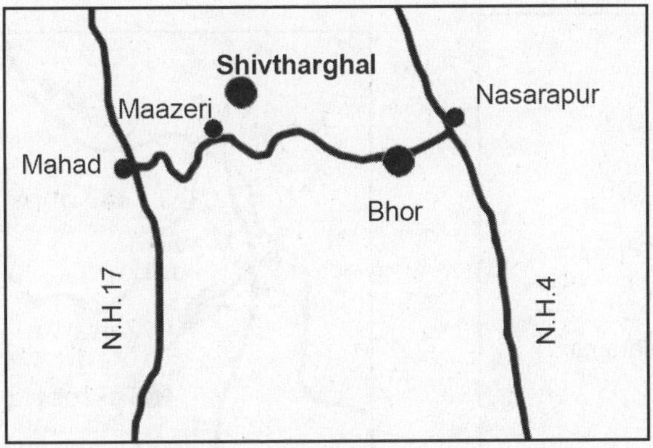

Shivtharghal - See page 250

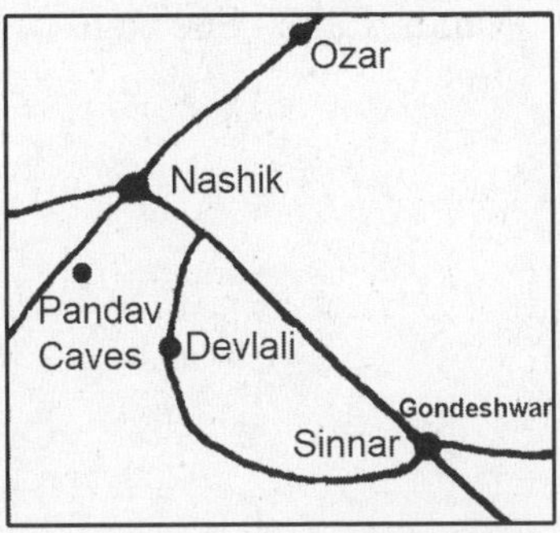

Gondeshwar temple of Sinnar - See page 96

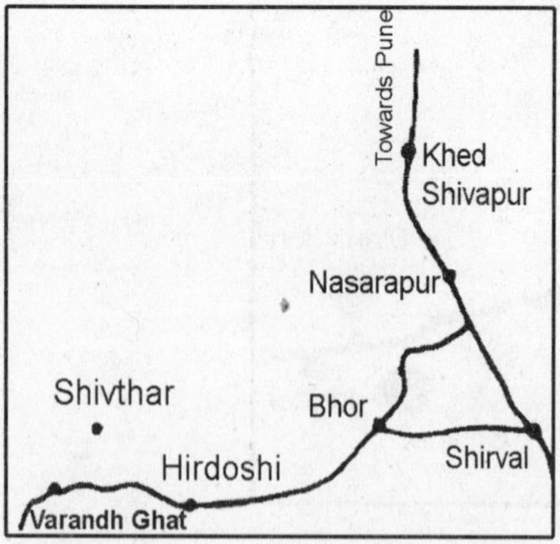

Varandha Ghat - See page 126

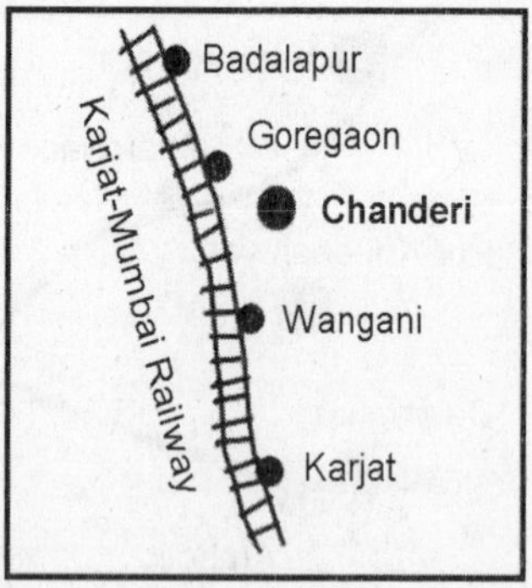

Chanderi - See page 73

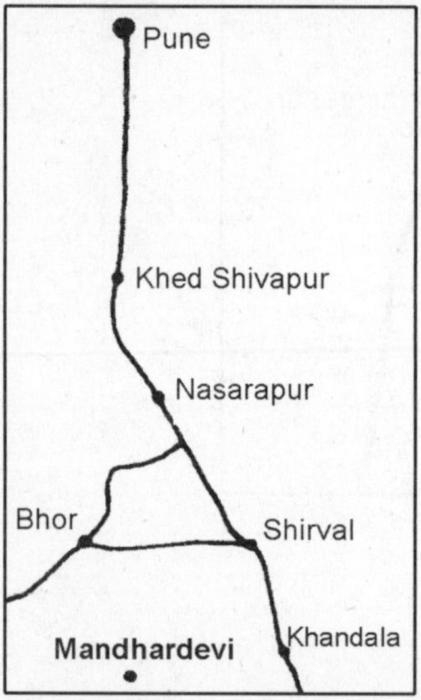

Mandhardevi - See page125

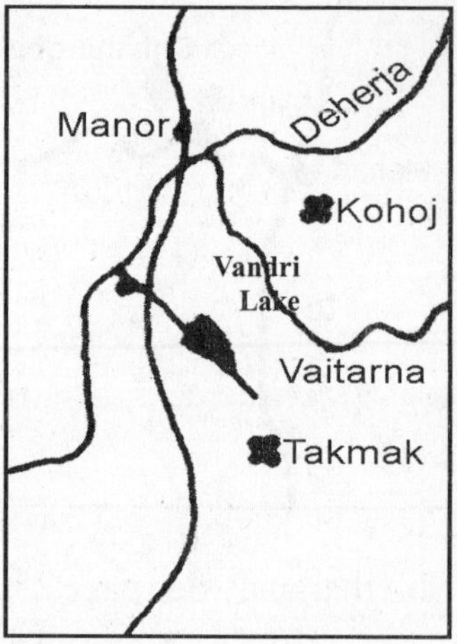

Vandri Lake - See page 205

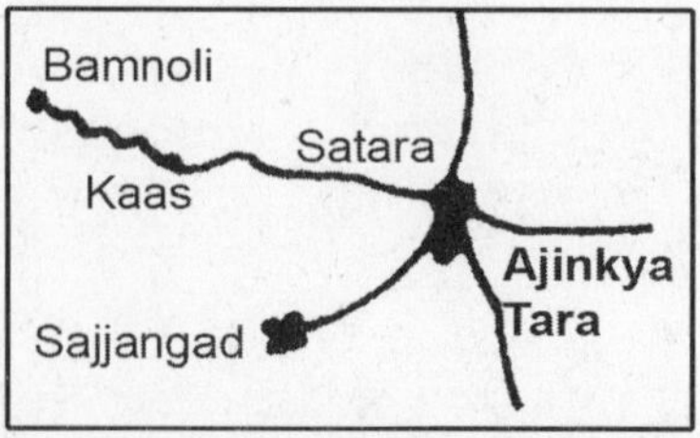

Ajinkya Tara - See page 66 & Sajjangad - See page 46

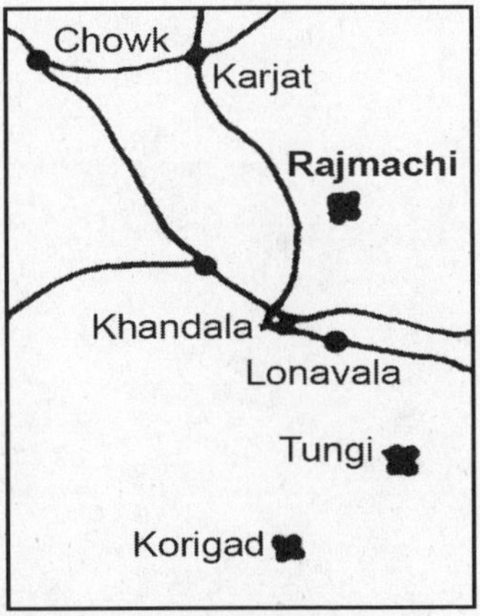

Rajmachi - See page 38

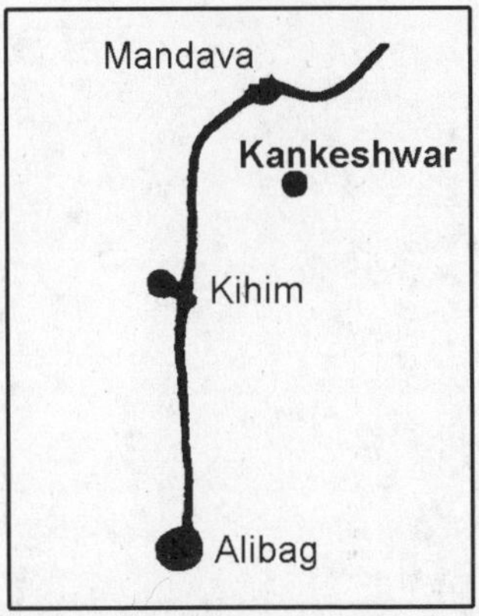

Kankeshwar - See page 89

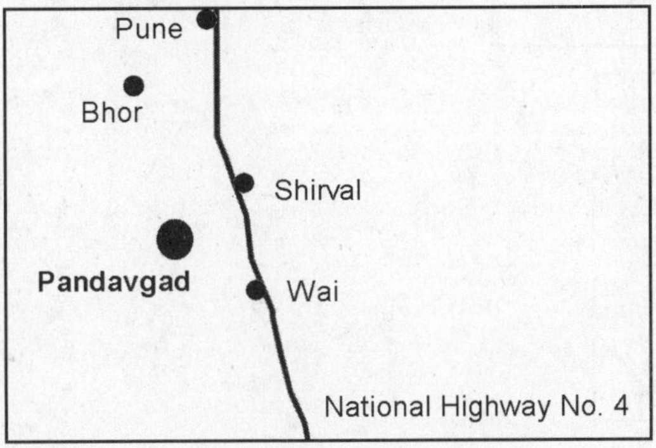

Pandavgad - See page 59

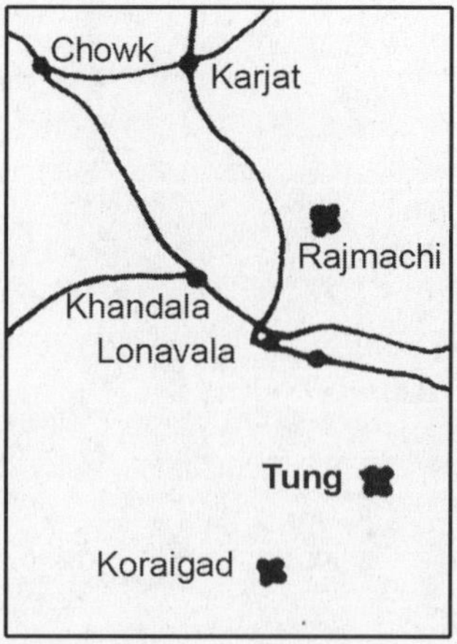

Kathingad or Tung See page 25

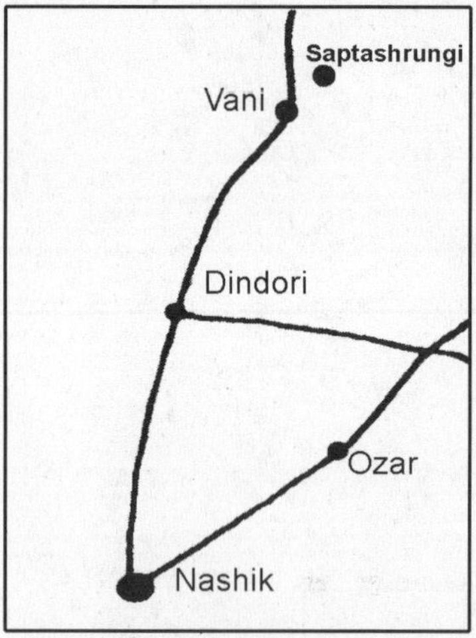

Saptashrungi - See page 92

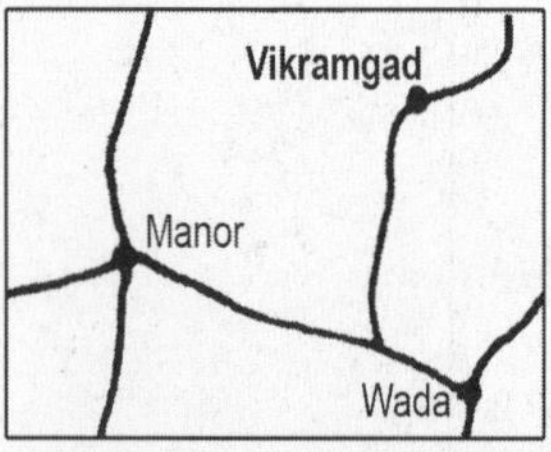

Vikramgad - See page 157